# IMMIGRANT ENTREPRENEURS AND IMMIGRANT ABSORPTION IN THE UNITED STATES AND ISRAEL

# Immigrant Entrepreneurs and Immigrant Absorption in the United States and Israel

Edited by
IVAN LIGHT
*University of California at Los Angeles*

RICHARD E. ISRALOWITZ
*Ben-Gurion University of the Negev*

Routledge
Taylor & Francis Group

LONDON AND NEW YORK

First published 1997 by Ashgate Publishing

Reissued 2018 by Routledge
2 Park Square, Milton Park, Abingdon, Oxon OX14 4RN
711 Third Avenue, New York, NY 10017, USA

*Routledge is an imprint of the Taylor & Francis Group, an informa business*

Copyright © Ivan Light and Richard E. Isralowitz 1997

All rights reserved. No part of this book may be reprinted or reproduced or utilised in any form or by any electronic, mechanical, or other means, now known or hereafter invented, including photocopying and recording, or in any information storage or retrieval system, without permission in writing from the publishers.

Notice:
Product or corporate names may be trademarks or registered trademarks, and are used only for identification and explanation without intent to infringe.

Publisher's Note
The publisher has gone to great lengths to ensure the quality of this reprint but points out that some imperfections in the original copies may be apparent.

Disclaimer
The publisher has made every effort to trace copyright holders and welcomes correspondence from those they have been unable to contact.

A Library of Congress record exists under LC control number: 97070893

Typeset by Catherine T. Logan Mabuim, No 1 DN HaNegev 85360 Israel

ISBN 13: 978-1-138-31729-1 (hbk)
ISBN 13: 978-1-138-31732-1 (pbk)
ISBN 13: 978-0-429-45186-7 (ebk)

# Contents

*Preface* vii

**Section 1 - The economics of immigration**

1   Economic saturation and immigrant entrepreneurship 1
    Ivan Light & Stavros Karageorgis

2   The four Iranian ethnic economies in Los Angeles 18
    Ivan Light, Georges Sabagh, Mehdi Bozorgmehr
    & Claudia Der-Martirosian

3   Issues in the absorption of older immigrants in employment 38
    Judah Matras

4   Social networks, local opportunities and entrepreneurship 57
    among immigrants in Israel
    Eran Razin

**Section 2 - Immigrant absorption studies**

5   Ethnic conflict and social cohesion among Israeli adolescents 82
    Richard E. Isralowitz and Ismael Abu Saad

6   Social cohesion and intergroup conflict in the Negev: 95
    Jewish and Arab attitudes toward the absorption of Russian
    immigrants
    Ismael Abu Saad and Richard E. Isralowitz

| | | |
|---|---|---|
| 7 | Immigrant women as child care providers<br>*Julia Wrigley* | 117 |
| 8 | Korean and Filipino immigrant women in the Los Angeles labor market<br>*Hye-Kyung Lee and Stavros Karageorgis* | 140 |
| 9 | We don't want no goddamn black refugees! The politics of Haitian refugees in Florida<br>*Alex Stepick and Tareena Joubert* | 167 |

**Section 3 - A visual perspective on immigration**

| | | |
|---|---|---|
| 10 | Application of photography to immigration studies: Iranians and Yemenis in California<br>*Jonathan Friedlander, Mehdi Bozorgmehr and Ron Kelley* | 185 |
| 11 | Israeli immigrants in Los Angeles<br>*Steven Gold* | 209 |

Index — 239

# Preface

Many nations invite foreigners to work within their borders, but few welcome them. When nations welcome foreigners, they offer them the same political rights that their own citizens already enjoy. Citizenship is the most basic right, but social and economic rights are important too. Of the many nations that accept or tolerate foreigner workers, only five now encourage foreigners to migrate, to settle permanently, and then to obtain citizenship and naturalization. These are Australia, Canada, Israel, New Zealand, and the United States.

The four English-speaking countries on this list have become pluralist democracies whose national self-conception now includes immigrants outside what Canadians call the 'charter groups'. Charter groups are those immigrant groups that were present when the modern state and society first came into existence. Admittedly, the history and culture of the charter groups dominate these four societies to this day, and foreigners entering them still feel social pressure for acculturation to their Anglophone standard or, in the case of Canada, their Anglophone or Francophone standard. Possibly these societies once differed in the extent to which they exposed immigrants to assimilation pressure, with Canada the most tolerant of the four. However, whatever international differences in assimilation pressure once existed, Reitz and Breton (1994, p. 29) have shown that Canada and the United States do not differ any more in this respect. Indeed, with the exception of Canada's Quebec Province, all four societies have abandoned acculturation and assimilation as official policy goals. Their publics have importantly, if incompletely, renounced the ideological demand as well, leaving to immigrants the decision of whether, how much, and how soon they should acculturate and assimilate. This policy they call multiculturalism. Multiculturalism dominates the social agenda of all four of these immigrant-reception societies.

Israel resembles the other four immigrant-reception countries with respect to its ethnic pluralism, but differs from them in its assimilationist ideal. Accepting immigrants equally from all corners of the world, and without racial restrictions, Israel imposes an ethno-religious test of fitness for naturalization. Only Jews are acceptable for automatic naturalization under Israel's law of return. Yet, despite that preliminary selection, the Israeli process creates what is arguably the most ethnically diverse population of the five immigrant-reception societies, in terms of the high percentage of foreign-born residents and those who speak two languages. On the grounds of how pluralistic the recipient society is, one cannot distinguish Israel from the other immigrant-reception societies. Nor can one dismiss the comparison of Israel and the United States on the grounds that Israel is a small country, and the USA a big one. The key immigration issue is always the speed of absorption effort rather than the absolute size of the immigrant population.

Regardless of size, rapid immigration poses an absorption problem that taxes society's ability to cope. Even if immigration has long-run benefits for reception societies, as we believe it does, very rapid immigration imposes the same absorption problem on society that a person experiences who tries to swallow a grapefruit whole. A nutritious food, which supports one's health if eaten section by section, grapefruit swallowed whole will harm one's health, not improve it. Immigration is very rapid in the USA now, but it is even more rapid in Israel. Between 1970 and 1990, the United States received 14 million immigrants, who increased its population by 6%. Between 1989 and 1992, Israel received 300,000 immigrants, who increased its population by 6% as well. In other words, in only four years, Israel added proportionately as many immigrants to its population as did the United States in twenty years.[1] Obviously, one cannot reject Israel's immigration experience on the grounds that the small size of the immigrant cohort renders that experience of no international interest.

The appropriate grounds for distinguishing Israel's immigration from that of the United States are ideological, not demographic. Unlike the pluralist democracies, which have embraced multiculturalism, Israel still asks both acculturation and assimilation from its immigrants.[2] Acculturation means fluency in Israeli culture and in the Hebrew language. Assimilation means ultimate absorption of ethnic groups by intermarriage, exclusive identification of immigrants with Israel, elimination of inter-group prejudice, and the internal absence of ethnic conflict. Immigrants to Israel confront a state and a civil society that demand Hebraization as promptly as realistically possible. Hebraization is the process whereby Jewish immigrants to Israel shed their diaspora-derived ethnic cultures, including their foreign names, and acculturate fully to Israeli society. As a state, Israel formally retains the Zionist goal of forging a homogeneous nation out of the ethnically pluralist Jews of the in-gathered diaspora. Israel's civil society supports and endorses this Zionist goal; and those who emigrate to Israel have implicitly accepted it as well. On the side of the immigrants and on the side of the recipient society, foreign and native-born Israelis agree that acculturation and assimilation are desirable long-term goals.

Public response to incapacity in the host society's language illustrates the difference this value consensus makes in daily life. When Israelis quarrel, they often belittle each others' competence in Hebrew, offering to explain the subject in some foreign language. This offer conveys an insult, because Israeli society expects competence in Hebrew. Hebrew language competence is a badge of successful acculturation. Therefore, an immigrant's incompetence in Hebrew reflects a shameful slowness of acculturation, born possibly of insufficient Zionist fervor.

Of course, American society is intolerant of non-English speakers, too. One proof is the Americans' notorious lack of interest in foreign languages, and the absence of foreign-language help in public places. On the other hand, American etiquette is different from Israeli etiquette. To ridicule an immigrant's incompetence in English would reflect badly on the American who did it. Inability to speak English is inconvenient, but not shameful.

In fairness, this observation requires some reference to the 'US English' movement in the United States. This contemporary social movement seeks legal protection of English as the official language of the United States and the prevention of states from printing public documents in other languages. 'US English' is acculturationist in inspiration and frankly critical of current Hispanic immigrants, whom adherents declare insufficiently interested in learning English (Portes and Rumbaut, 1989, p. 140). The US English movement commands a majority of voter support, and has several referenda on 19 states, thus far without serious legal impact.[3] Since US English opposes official multiculturalism, the movement's popularity suggests that assimilationism is alive and well in the United States.

Without wishing to exaggerate the current openness of American society to immigrants, we observe only that, in the past, popular assimilationism did not encounter official multiculturalism as it does today. Assimilationism was the both official policy and the popular policy. The contrast implies that American society has moved strongly in the direction of multiculturalism without, admittedly, achieving unanimity around that goal. Second, even US English does not question the right of immigrants to retain their native languages. It only questions the *expediency* of that choice, observing erroneously that socio-economic success requires English competence.[4] Therefore, adherents claim, official tolerance of foreign languages just creates a long-term mobility trap for immigrants. Third, US English endorses acculturation without endorsing intermarriage or deprecating ethnic identities. Therefore, it is not, strictly speaking, an assimilationist movement. Finally, the institutional assimilationism of US English does not support a climate of American opinion that justifies ridicule of an individual immigrant's lack of competence in English. Pity is closer to the mark.

Although the contrast is imperfect, these differences justify the claim that Israel and the United States differ with respect to official and unofficial commitment to assimilationism. In Israel, immigrants do not have a right to cling to their foreign ways. In the United States, they do have that right, inconvenient though it often is to exercise it. In both countries, public attitudes toward language incompetence reflect the society's underlying ideological consensus about acculturation and assimilation. The similarity between the countries is the existence of a public opinion that enforces the ideological consensus on these issues right down to the microsociety. The difference is the consensus, or lack of it, about ultimate acculturation and assimilation as societal goals.

In preparing this volume, we have felt that the Israel/USA comparison was of unusual value for immigration studies precisely because of this inter-societal difference in underlying public consensus on acculturation and assimilation. Useful as they might otherwise be, comparisons of the USA and Canada, New Zealand, or Australia would not encounter so striking a divergence in public consensus on assimilationism as does the comparison of the USA and Israel. Moreover, this consensus is a terribly important issue in immigration studies everywhere, but one-country case studies obscure it. That is, studying one country only, we lose sight of taken-for-granted basics such as societal consensus on the desirability of acculturation and assimilation. Instead, we see these basics as individual attitudinal differences, characterizing respondents as individually high or low in tolerance for foreigners, which is a psychological variable. Pressing outward from one's knowledge base toward the unknown, studies conducted in the USA would characterize Israelis as intolerant of foreigners' language incompetence, whereas, seen in context, the inter-societal difference emerges most directly from the basic social contract. Demanding acculturation, Israelis live up to their social contract just as, permissive of foreignness, Americans live up to theirs.[5] No doubt one can characterize individuals within each society as more or less tolerant, but the inter-societal comparison permits us to see that social context determines the norm.

**About this volume**

The authors in this collection wrote what they knew about, Israel or the USA. We made no effort to impose comparative perspectives upon contributors, whose research situation did not permit explicitly comparative work. Rather, we propose that the juxtaposition of Israeli and American contributors will generate comparative insights that exclusive volumes on Israel or on the USA would not achieve. For the reasons explained above, we deem this comparison a fruitful and productive one for both countries. We know of no Israel/USA comparison in the existing and voluminous immigration literature, and hope that this volume will spark interest in exactly that comparison. Nonetheless, there is no harm in pointing out comparative implications in introducing the individual papers. Indeed, in doing so, we are simply taking advantage of all the possibilities our format made possible.

*Economics of immigration*

Current immigration literature stresses economic integration for several reasons. First, economic issues are the most urgent and immediate ones that immigrants must meet. Food, clothing, education, housing, and medical care cannot wait for acculturation and assimilation. Second, how immigrants meet those initial economic challenges has long-range implications for the speed and extensiveness of their ultimate assimilation and acculturation. In a nutshell, participation in the general labor force speeds immigrant acculturation; participation in the ethnic economy slows it (Bonacich and Modell, 1981; Fugita and O'Brien, 1993). This result occurs because participation in the general labor force compels immigrants to learn the host language on the job, and that language skill opens them to other acculturating influences. Conversely, working in an ethnic economy, whether as self-employed or an employee, permits immigrants to make a living without learning very much or, possibly, any of the host society's language, the most basic step of acculturation. They work in the foreign language and associate with fellow immigrants. This semi-independence reduces the speed of acculturation, and possibly stalls it altogether in extreme cases.

Ivan Light and Stavros Karageorgis return to immigration networks and entrepreneurship, an earlier concern, attempting to apply the model to the Israeli case. Their general point is that when immigration is rapid, immigrants outstrip the host society's ability to provide jobs, and so turn to entrepreneurship for a livelihood. This course generates a large ethnic economy whose long-term effect is to delay immigrant acculturation in Israel just as in California. To avoid this outcome, Israel could reduce the volume of immigration, thus making wage and salaried jobs available to all immigrants. Unfortunately, that decision violates Israel's ideological commitment to maximize immigration from the Diaspora. In this sense, Israel's ideological commitment to maximize immigration contradicts its ideological commitment to speedy acculturation and assimilation of immigrants. The more immigrants there are, the longer the time necessary to accomplish their acculturation and assimilation. Since the United States does not insist upon maximizing immigration and rapidly acculturating those who immigrate, ethnic economies do not pose the same thorny ideological issue there that they do in Israel.

'Four Iranian Ethnic Economies in Los Angeles' broaches another absorption problem of an ethnic economy. Examining the 68,000 foreign-born Iranians in Los Angeles, Light, Sabagh, Bozorgmehr and Der-Martirosian find that the 'Iranian ethnic economy' is largely a fiction. A huge proportion of Iranians are self-employed, and these Iranians form an Iranian ethnic economy in a technical sense. In reality, however, Iranian entrepreneurs collaborate in business with Iranian co-religionists (Armenian, Baha'i, Jewish, or Moslem) rather than with just anyone who speaks Persian — much less with non-Iranians. Therefore, the Iranian ethnic economy of Los Angeles is really four separate ethnic economies: one Armenian, one Baha'i, one Jewish, and one Moslem. The paper opens up the possibility that immigrant groups fragment into sub-ethnic groups when ethnic economies are the vehicle of initial economic absorption.

Judah Matras discusses the plight of older immigrants in Israel. Having immigrated late in life, they speak Hebrew badly, and they never lose their foreign accents. Lack of skill in the host language poses a major economic problem for immigrants in the United States too, but in Israel, one supposes, the problem is more severe because of the ideological premium Israel places upon prompt acculturation. Moreover, when excluded from the labor force because of language inadequacy, older immigrants lose their main access to acculturation as well as to a livelihood. These undesirable results slow acculturation, but they emerge from the very premium Israeli society places upon prompt acculturation. Matras recommends public job creation to deal with the employment problems of older immigrants. Entrepreneurship could modestly supplement this solution by reducing the number of older job-seekers and by creating additional jobs in small firms.

Eran Razin has studied immigrant entrepreneurship in Europe and North America. His paper finds that the same ethnic networks that promote immigrant entrepreneurship abroad promote it as well in Israel. Distinguishing class and ethnic resources of entrepreneurship, Razin also finds that social capital permits Eastern-origin immigrants to Israel to partially compensate for deficiencies. These results would be unsurprising but for the reluctance of Israeli society to acknowledge entrepreneurship's economic role in the Zionist homeland. As a matter of Zionist ideology, Jews are supposed to give up entrepreneurship when they leave the Diaspora. Immigrant entrepreneurship implies a free market capitalism incompatible with Israel's socialist tradition. Further, it leans upon social capital best utilized in ethnic enclaves. Locational clustering of immigrants contradicts Israel's long-standing policy of dispersing immigrants among towns and cities. Finally, immigrant entrepreneurs utilize something foreign they brought with them from the Diaspora (their social networks) to make a living in Israel. This utilization builds upon and perpetuates ethnic distinctiveness that Israel would like to extinguish.

*Immigrant absorption studies*

For many, social cohesion is a commonsense term; yet, there is little agreement about what it really means and how it is to be achieved in practice. From a research perspective, social scientists have not been able to agree on a definition of social cohesion, nor its application as a analytical or descriptive term. It is not a discrete phenomenon, but rather a constellation of social relationships that are connected to economic and political structures which lead to inequality, competition and conflict (Cope, Castles and Kalantzis, 1991).

Ismael Abu Saad and Richard Isralowitz examine factors of ethnicity and socio-economic status among Jewish and Arab citizen of Israel as determinants of social cohesion and conflict with Russian immigrants. Israel, as a modern state, has reflected a tripartite ethnic order consisting of European-American Jews, Asian-African Jews, and Arabs. This pattern, however, has been altered by the large numbers of Russian immigrants who have entered the country during the 1990s. The authors point out that the recent immigration has, expectedly so, most affected the attitudes of low income Jews and Arabs in terms of their socio-economic status and quality of life. The influx of Russians to Israel is viewed by these people as a dysfunctional and negative condition precipitating conflict and disrupting the social order that has evolved, including the incremental improvements on quality of life already achieved. While Israel maintains a fundamental position of absorbing Jewish immigrants, improvement of social cohesion and amelioration of social conflict among veteran Israeli citizens and new immigrants cannot be expected unless policies and programs are put into practice to address the needs of the underclasses — Jews and Arabs alike — in areas such as employment, housing, education, and health services.

From another perspective of Israeli society, Isralowitz and Abu Saad study Israeli youth to determine whether educational status (i.e., general or vocational) affects ethnic conflict and social cohesion in terms of Russian immigrants. The attitudes of more than 200 male youths from an Israeli 'development' town — typified by high unemployment, semi-skilled to unskilled labor, and a predominately Sephardi population (i.e., Jews whose origin was North-African or Middle-Eastern countries) — were examined. Findings show that vocational education students, those who tend to be less scholastically oriented and more inclined to under-achievement, problem behavior, and those who have lower self-concept, are more negative toward Russian immigrants. While religious and educational institutions appear to have an important role in shaping the attitudes and values of Israeli-born and immigrant youth toward each other, few constructive in-roads for improving social cohesion and social conflict appear possible unless young people are to be given improved opportunities such as education and employment.

Julia Wrigley examines the role of immigrant women as childcare workers in the United States and how they are affected by the internal stratification of the market for children's care givers. The author points out that the increasing number of households where both parents work, or where a single parent works, has led to a resurgent demand for in-home child care workers. This situation, the employment of a full-time adult worker, is only possible where there is substantial economic inequality. The pool of parents able to afford in-home care grows when there is a large supply of low-wage workers available. In the United States, these conditions are most prevalent in cities that serve as ports-of-entry for immigrants. Wrigley points out that the wide-ranging expectations of parents set the stage for conflicts between what care givers can provide and what parents expect. These conflicts are particularly acute for immigrant women of Third World countries (e.g., Central or South American), because they lack power and other personal and organizational resources to protect themselves from exploitive conditions related to child care and housekeeping work.

Lee and Karageorgis compare immigrant Korean and Filipino women in the Los Angeles labor market. In general, the Filipino women speak English fluently upon arrival in the United States; the Korean women do not. English is the chief language of primary and secondary education in the Philippines, and this skill gives Filipino women many employment opportunities in the general labor market. Lacking skill in English, the Korean women must turn for employment to the Korean ethnic economy. Sometimes they work as seamstresses in garment factories. In many cases, Korean wives become unpaid family workers in businesses owned by their husbands. Although the Koreans earn as much money as the Filipinos, their ethnic economies emerge from, as well as reproduce, their non-acculturation, even propping up family role systems imported from Korea. Were it not for the ethnic economy, the Koreans would face an economic crisis, and many would be compelled to return to Korea. In Israel, this 'failed' migration would be scandalous; conversely, Israel would be uncomfortable with the retardation of acculturation that the Korean ethnic economy imposed.

Probably no immigration issue in recent years has drawn more attention in the United States than that regarding Haitian refugees. In their paper, Alex Stepick and Tareena Joubert examine the history of U.S. policy toward Haitians fleeing repression and corruption — ranging from encouragement by the Kennedy administration to restrictions imposed by Presidents Reagan, Bush, and Clinton. The authors point to the issue of racism, principally generated by public officials in Florida, as the reason why Haitians, fleeing repression, were denied asylum. They also argue that the structure of local economies in the United States has much to do with the nature of policies that either enable or limit the flow of immigrants. For example, agricultural interests in California and neighboring states have played a significant role in undermining efforts to restrict Mexican workers to the United States. Haitians, on the other hand, have been negatively stereotyped, particularly among public officials in Florida, as being uneducated, unskilled, rural peasants with little political influence or economic value to the American economy. These attitudes have fundamentally shaped general public opinion and policy toward Haitian refugees.

## Visual perspectives of immigration

Photography has long been used to document the process of immigration. In the United States, perhaps the best-known photographer is Lewis Hume, a self-proclaimed sociologist, who photographed immigrants on Ellis Island in New York at the turn of the 20th Century. Following in his path, Jacob Riis documented the tenements of New York inhabited by immigrants and depicted a wide range of social problems, including poverty and squalid living conditions.

In their article, Jonathan Friedlander, Mehdi Bozorgmehr and Ron Kelley provide the important theoretical context for understanding the relationship between social science research and photography. They point out that 'like a good scientist, the function of a good photographer is not to just record data, but, rather, to actively synthesize, structure, interpret, and attempt to understand what is being witnessed'. This approach, of course, centers on the photographer's world view or paradigm. The photography for their article of Iranians and Yemenis in California is drawn from the work of Ron Kelley, who reflects the influence of Robert Frank and Gary Winogrand — two photographers well-known for capturing the tension and alienation that prevailed in America from the 1950s through the 1970s. The photographs and analysis of Friedlander, Bozorgmehr and Kelley show Yemeni farm workers as part of a largely low-skilled agricultural and service-oriented labor force, disenfranchised and on the fringes of the host society. On the other hand, Iranians are shown to be an entrepreneurial and professional immigrant group preoccupied with class and status in one of America's richest cities. The authors point out that the overriding theme of displacement conceptually joins the two very different study groups in a comparative framework.

In his article on Israeli immigrants in Los Angeles, Steven Gold uses interviews, participant observation, and photography to understand how the social, economic, and legal context of American society interacts with immigrants and the absorption process. The immigration literature suggests the possibility of including Israeli immigrants into each of three categories — professionals, entrepreneurs, and unorganized marginals. Gold concludes from his findings that, while a number of Israelis embody the characteristics associated with professional immigrants, many remain strongly associated within the ethnic community. Little evidence was found to support the notion that Israeli immigrants are unorganized marginals. In fact, many Israelis who are professionally employed and long-time residents of the United States continue to have strong attachments to their ethnic community.

This volume emerged from a joint conference held in 1992 at Beer-Sheva under the auspices of the University of California at Los Angeles and Ben-Gurion University of the Negev. This tenth annual UCLA/BGU conference was the first on a social science theme. The editors express their appreciation to the organizers of this conference, especially to Professor Fred Lazin of BGU and Professor Samuel Aroni of UCLA. The conference organizers gave complete latitude to researchers to express their real opinions. As editors, we have supported that policy, only assisting contributors to clarify their thoughts. Therefore, in a way, the editors share the contributors' responsibility for errors of fact, method, and interpretation, but the sponsors of the UCLA/BGU conference series, whom we thank, have no responsibility in this regard.

*Ivan Light*  *Richard E. Isralowitz*
*Los Angeles, California, U.S.A.*  *Beer-Sheva, Israel*

*November 1996*

**Notes**

1. On New Zealand's immigration policies, see Wearing (1993).
2. On the distinction between assimilation and acculturation, see Gordon (1964, pp. 70-71).
3. For information, write to U.S. English, 818 Connecticut Avenue NW, Suite 200, Washington, DC 20006, USA.
4. The claim is erroneous, because, as we note below, recent literature has found that ethnic enclave economies permit immigrants a rapid economic advance within a foreign-language context virtually imper-vious to Americanization.
5. Conversely, viewed from the Israeli perspective, Americans' tolerance of immigrant incompetence in English would reflect confusion and stupidity. That is, if Americans do not know what their culture is, they are confused. If they know, but do not require conformity, they are stupid. This view is also a cultural misreading.

# References

Bonacich, E. and Modell, J. (1981), *The Economic Basis of Ethnic Solidarity: A Study of Japanese Americans*, University of California Press: Berkeley and Los Angeles.

Fugita, S.S. and O'Brien, D.J. (1991), *Japanese American Ethnicity*, University of Washington Press: Seattle, WA.

Gordon, M. (1964), *Assimilation in American Life*, Oxford University Press: New York.

Light, I. and Bhachu, P. (1993), 'Introduction: California Immigrants in World Perspective', in Light, I. and Bhachu, P. (eds.), *Immigration and Entrepreneurship*, Transaction: New Brunswick, NJ, Ch. 1.

Portes, A. and Rumbaut, R.G. (1989), *Immigrant America*, University of California Press: Berkeley and Los Angeles.

Reitz, J. and Breton, R. (1994), *The Illusion of Difference: Realities of Ethnicity in Canada and the United States*, Howe Institute: Toronto.

Wearing, B. (1993), 'New Zealand's immigration policies and Immigration Act (1987): Comparison with the United States of America', in Light, I. and Bhachu, P. (eds.), *Immigration and Entrepreneurship*, Transaction: New Brunswick, NJ, Ch. 14.

# 1 Economic saturation and immigrant entrepreneurship

*Ivan Light and Stavros Karageorgis*

In the last decade, immigration research has refocused on the issue of migrant networks in both contemporary and historical migrations (Bozorgmehr, 1992; Fawcett, 1989; Boyd, 1989; Morawska, 1989, p. 260; Wilpert and Gitmez, 1987). Although based on familiar ideas (Tilly, 1978; Light, 1972), Massey's formula of 'cumulatively caused' migration usefully focused current thinking about this subject. Migrations, according to Massey, forge networks which then feed the very migrations that produced them (Massey, Alarcon, Durand and Gonzalez, 1987; Massey and Espana, 1987; Massey, 1988; 1990). Therefore, whatever macro-societal political/economic conditions may initially have caused emigration, the originating pushes and pulls, the expanding migratory process becomes progressively independent of the original causal conditions. Migrations in process self-levitate above the conditions that caused them to begin, leading thereafter a semi-independent existence. Network formation is the reason. Massey (1988, p. 396) defines migration networks as 'sets of interpersonal ties that link migrants, former migrants, and nonmigrants in origin and destination areas through the bonds of kinship, friendship, and shared community origin'.

Networks promote the independence of migratory flows for two reasons. First, once network connections reach some threshold level, they amount to an autonomous social structure that supports immigration. This support arises from the reduced social, economic, and emotional costs of immigration that networks permit; that is, network-supported migrants receive important help in arranging transportation, finding housing and jobs in their place of destination, and in effecting a satisfactory personal and emotional adjustment to what is often a difficult situation of cultural marginality. These benefits make migration easier, thus encouraging people to migrate who would otherwise have stayed at home. Unless migrants are refugees, for whom only immigration affords any hope of survival (Bozorgmehr and Sabagh, 1991; Pedraza-Bailey, 1985), potential migrants always have the option of staying home. Given that choice, the reduced cost of migration increases the volume of migration.

Second, Massey (1990, p. 8) made the same case for networks under the assumptions of a risk-diversification model. According to this model, families allocate member labor within the constraints of their own needs and aspirations in a cost-efficient and risk-minimizing way. Many Third World households are economically precarious. Such households face high risks to their well-being if they select non-migration. Moreover, modernization and development create social and economic dislocations that intensify the unstable and unpredictable economic environment created by the usual risks of drought, crop failure, and natural disasters, for rural as well as urban areas. In the absence of other ways to insure against such risks, diversification of family members' location minimizes overall family income risk (Massey, 1988, p. 398; 1990, p. 9-11).

Migration is sometimes a risk-diversification strategy for households. International migration is especially effective because international borders create discontinuities that promote independence of earnings at home and abroad: good times abroad can compensate for bad ones at home, or vice-versa. But even in the absence of earning differentials, international migration offers an effective risk-diversification strategy; especially when migrant networks already exist. Migration networks reduce the economic risks of immigration, thus rendering the strategy more attractive from a risk-diversification perspective (Massey and Espana, 1987, p. 734; Massey, 1988, p. 398). Expanding networks 'put a destination job within easy reach of most community members' (Massey, 1988, p. 398) and make migration a virtually risk-less and cost-less alternative labor power investment in the household's 'portfolio' (Massey et al., 1987, Ch. 11).

**Critique of network theory**

Although a serious improvement over the individualistic and economistic approaches (including world systems theory) that preceded it, network theory suffers some self-imposed limitations of its own.[1] Most notably, it concentrates upon facilitation and efficiency, ignoring structural changes caused by immigration networks in the destination economy; that is, in existing network theory, networks make it easier for immigrants to find housing, jobs, protection, and companionship. As they grow, networks increase their efficiency. Efficient networks expose every job and apartment in an immigrant-receiving locality or region, thus facilitating the newcomers' integration. In sum, networks are facilitators: without increasing the supply of resources, networks facilitate immigrants' access to the existing supply.

Economic saturation arises when localities have no more work or housing vacancies to offer immigrants. In this condition, a newcomer can only obtain a job or residence when an incumbent vacates it, just as someone can only get aboard a crowded elevator when someone else gets off. Economic saturation poses the obvious limit to existing network theory. As Gregory (1989, p. 17) has noted, job opportunities exercise a 'restraint on the volume of migration' in that people cannot go where no employment exists. Even hyper-efficient networks cannot find jobs or housing if none exist. Naturally, full saturation is neither inevitable nor normal, but, particularly when a migratory influx is rapid, the local supply of jobs and housing tightens in response. As saturation approaches, networks have to work harder to locate scarcer resources for participants. Immigrants have to wait longer before the network can find them anything; some become discouraged and repatriate. At the point of economic saturation, the migration network cannot locate any free resources, and some immigrants never find jobs. Repatriations and immigrant unemployment then increase, and new migration has to wait upon economic growth.

**Networks: Scope and utility**

This doomsday scenario unfolds whenever immigration reaches economic saturation. To the extent that they facilitate job searches, migrant networks bring the moment of saturation closer. However, to the extent that migrant networks also expand the supply of work, they defer that moment, possibly avoiding it altogether, and thus permit many more immigrants to be absorbed. Networks increase the job supply by improving the efficiency of searches, by increasing the actual supply of opportunities, or both. Improving searches enables migrants to find jobs and housing faster, more reliably, and with less effort, and either brings immigrants into unfilled vacancies in the job market or causes jobs to be transferred from natives to immigrants. Thus, if a network directs immigrants to housing or jobs that native workers did not want, it improves the immigrants' search without adverse economic effect upon non-immigrants; if, however, it helps immigrants obtain jobs that non-immigrants wanted and would have accepted, then the networks lock non-immigrants out of desirable niches in their own economy, transferring their jobs to immigrants. Although immigrant networks start by guiding participants to unfilled jobs, as saturation approaches, they begin to guide migrants into jobs that non-immigrants want (Grieco, 1987).

But immigrant networks also increase the aggregate supply of local opportunities, a function Massey and others have ignored. By adding new opportunities, the migrant network strengthens the economy in the destination locality, thus postponing or possibly even avoiding economic saturation altogether. Two methods encourage this result. First, reliable networks encourage non-immigrant entrepreneurs to shift capital into the immigrant-receiving locality — a shift which enhances the supply of jobs available to immigrants. An example is the numerous immigrant-staffed factories that now exist on both the Mexican and American sides of the US/Mexico border (Davila and Saenz, 1990). These factories have grown up with immigration; they did not precede it. Because the labor was there, capitalists located factories in the neighborhood.

Second, immigrant entrepreneurs apply their own capital to the employment of themselves and immigrant coethnics in the locations of destination: immigrant entrepreneurs open new immigrant-owned firms in destination economies, and immigrant-owned firms create employment for their owners and for coethnic employees. The immigrant economy consists of self-employed immigrants and their coethnic employees,[2] and supplements the earnings opportunities available in the general labor market.

If we represent the general labor market as J, the immigrant economy as I, and economic carrying capacity as S, then the earnings opportunities[3] available to immigrants are:

$$S = f(J+I) \qquad (1)$$

The carrying capacity is the sum of the jobs in the general labor market plus those in the immigrant economy. Saturation exists whenever work-seekers exceed carrying capacity. Unless I is zero, J+I must always exceed J. J is the unsupplemented job supply available to immigrants in the general labor market. In the limiting case, J is 100% of jobs, but, in reality,

J is usually a large fraction of the employed labor force. Therefore, 'the assessment of the labor market effects of immigration is not complete without mention of the jobs immigrants create' (Papademetriou, Bach, Johnson et al., 1989, p. 197), J+I is the general labor market plus employment opportunities created by immigrant entrepreneurs. Since J+I normally exceeds J, saturation of a locality's or region's economy requires saturation of both J and I. If J is saturated, but I is not, or vice-versa, then the local economy is not saturated. Under that circumstance, we normally expect growth in the unsaturated component until that component also attains saturation. Conversely, if an immigrant population depends upon some balance of J and I to support it, but political or economic changes reduce the capacity of one or the other component to carry its normal load, enhancement of the other component represents a possible alternative to the return of immigrants to their countries of origin (return migration).[4]

A treatment of immigrant networks that ignores the immigrant economy, while concentrating upon the general economy alone, underestimates the carrying capacity of destination economies. Existing network theory generally makes this error, and Massey's synthesis reflects it. One finds no reference to the immigrant economy or immigrant entrepreneurs in the index offered by Massey et al. (1987), nor any appreciation in his text of their implication for job creation. Massey (1990, p. 10) writes that migrant networks 'put a destination job within easy reach of most community member', but he neglects the enhanced access to business ownership which this same migration network affords; and while he acknowledges the role of non-immigrant entrepreneurs, he overlooks the contribution of immigrant entrepreneurs. For him, migrating causes economic expansion in the target economy only because non-immigrant entrepreneurs move capital from high-wage areas to low-wage areas. Massey suggests that this capital flow reinforces downward wage pressures of labor migration in high-wage areas and upward pressures in low-wage areas. He has also shown that, on balance, migration creates employment more than employment creates migration.

Massey argues that employment growth stimulates migration, which stimulates employment growth, which stimulates further migration. Therefore, he discerns a process of cumulative causation at work. Massey (Ibid., p. 15) claims that 'a variety of factors underlie the reciprocal causal relationship', but describes only the one which he deems the most important. This underpinning is the selectivity of international migration. Migrations select 'the younger, better-educated, and more highly productive workers — those with the greatest endowment of human capital'. He argues that this selectivity leads to higher economic growth and labor demand in receiving areas, but decreases growth and demand in sending areas, leading to additional migration, and thus creating circular and cumulative causation (Massey, 1988).

In this discussion, Massey acknowledges only the response of the host economy to immigrant labor. The more efficient the immigrant networks, the more efficiently host capital responds, because migrant networks reduce employers' recruitment costs. This response does, indeed, augment the job supply in the general labor market, thus delaying economic saturation and promoting cumulatively-caused migration, just as Massey claims. But, these economic commonplaces overlook the immigrant economy. In effect, Massey operates from a model in which J=S, but in which J expands in response to labor influx. Even if J's expansion could proceed infinitely, Massey's treatment of the general labor market quite overlooks the immigrant economy.

**Haitians and Cubans in Miami**

To illustrate this claim, Table 1 shows the sectoral representation in 1980 of Cuban Mariel refugees and Haitian refugees in Miami. Derived from the work of Alex Stepick, this table is based ultimately upon official statistics. The three sectors are: unemployment, the immigrant economy, and the general labor market of Miami. Cuban Mariel refugees are working-class Cubans, expelled from their homeland, who arrived in a massive exodus in 1979. A significant proportion of these Cuban refugees were black. Haitians are impoverished blacks who claimed political refugee status in the United States, but whom the US government defined as economic refugees.

The sectoral representation of Haitians and Cubans was drastically different. Haitian refugees had 58.5% unemployed, 0.7% working in the immigrant economy, and 40.8% employed for wages or salaries in the general economy. In contrast, Cuban Mariel refugees had 26.8% unemployed, 46.1% employed in the immigrant economy, and 27.1% employed in the general economy. In effect, the Haitian economy lacked an immigrant economy and so approximated the one-sector economy Massey's network theory assumes across the board. Haitian employment in the general economy was 13.7% higher than Cuban employment in that sector, but Haitian unemployment was 31.7% higher than Cuban unemployment. This discrepancy implies that 18% of Cubans who were employed in the Cuban immigrant economy would, in fact, have been unemployed if no immigrant economy had existed to employ them. Discharged from the immigrant sector, the remaining 13.7% of Cubans would have found wage-earning jobs in the general economy.

Table 1.
Cuban and Haitian refugee employment in Miami, 1980 (in percentages)

|  | Cuban Mariel Refugees | Haitian Refugees |
|---|---|---|
| *Immigrant Economy* | | |
| Self-Employed | 15.2 | 0.5 |
| Working in Coethnic Firms | 30.9 | 0.2 |
| *General Labor Market* | | |
| Unemployed | 26.8 | 58.5 |
| Employed | 27.1 | 40.8 |
| Total in Percentages | 100.0 | 100.0 |

Source: Alex Stepick (1989, Ch. 6). Reproduced by permission.

If immigrant economies are defined strictly in terms of the general labor market, overlooking the immigrant economy, the oversight would seemingly matter little for Haitians. However, as Stepick (1989, pp. 116-25) shows, the impression is misleading. Haitians in Miami operated a very extensive informal economy that was not and could not be measured or acknowledged in these official statistics.[5] Although operated for cash only and without the knowledge of tax collectors, the Haitians' informal economy amounted to 'informal self-employment' (Stepick, 1989, p. 122). Haitian entrepreneurs created jobs for themselves and for other Haitians. Their informal firms were chiefly in dressmaking, tailoring, food preparation, child care, transport, construction, automobile repair, and electronic repair (idem). In point of fact, then, a significant immigrant economy existed among the Miami Haitians as well as among the more affluent Cubans, but the Haitian economy was too marginal to measure. Hard to measure does not mean non-existent (Castells and Portes, 1989, pp. 20-1).

Thanks to the official statistics, our point is easier to make for the Cubans, among whom the immigrant economy was sufficiently large to permit its measurement. To overlook the Cuban immigrant economy would be to fall into two serious errors. First, this oversight would exclude 45.4% of Cuban workers from observation. Examining only 54.6% of workers, we would imagine we examined all. Second, we would overlook the choice context in which Cuban workers operated. In the general labor market, workers chose between a wage job and unemployment, making only two choices. In fact, Cuban immigrants had four choices: a wage job in the general economy, unemployment, self-employment, or employment in the immigrant economy.

This enhanced range of options creates a new choice context. As Fernandez-Kelly and Garcia (1989, p. 248) have put it, the existence of an immigrant economy 'shields' immigrant workers 'from the mainstream labor market'. This sectoral shield permits immigrant workers to exert some upward pressure upon the general labor market which, if it wants their services, must make offers that are not only superior to unemployment, but are also superior to what they could otherwise obtain in the immigrant economy, whether as employees or as self-employed. The mere fact that a substantial percentage of immigrant workers select the immigrant economy reduces the supply of immigrant labor in the general wage economy, thus exerting upward pressure on wage rates and working conditions for those in the general labor market.

In the case of immigrant women, who are frequent employees in the immigrant economy, the scholarly controversy about relative wages in the immigrant economy and general labor market (Phizacklea, 1988, p. 21; Zhou and Logan, 1989) overlooks 'ideological and subjective' influences upon women's work decisions (Schmink, 1984, p. 93).[6] Flexible hours, part-time work, and liberal child care policy are non-wage attractions that cause immigrant women to prefer the immigrant economy to the general labor market (Dallalfar, 1989, pp. 161-84). Precisely insofar as women workers have the option of an immigrant economy, the general labor market experiences pressure to modify its unyielding job requirements in order to lure women employees away from sweatshops, where, although they are underpaid, their children are flexibly accommodated (Portes and Jensen, 1989, p. 941; Zhou and Logan, 1989). Moreover, many immigrant women can only work when child care policies are liberal and hours flexible. Otherwise they must be full-time homemakers and baby sitters. For such women, the general labor market offers no satisfactory alternative to unemployment. Only the immigrant economy permits them to work at all. In this sense, the immigrant economy's flexibility increases the percentage of immigrant women who can *work for wages at all*, thus bolstering the gross income of their households.

**Networks and entrepreneurship**

In addition, 'immigrant communities are active in shaping the economic destinies of their members through self-employment and the formation of enclaves' (Papademetriou, Bach, Jonson *et al.*, 1989, p. 169). Oddly, contemporary network theory overlooks this truth — an oversight that is the more remarkable in view of the stress network theorists properly lay upon the immigrant network's cost-reducing and risk-diversifying properties. In failing to take into account the entrepreneurship-enhancing effects of immigrant networks in the destination economy, network theorists have overlooked a basic function and one, moreover, that complements and expands network theory (Birley, 1985). Therefore, our objections to network theory are constructive because they expand network theory's scope and utility. Whatever other functions they also serve, *migrant networks are entrepreneurial resources that immigrants employ to expand the economic opportunities they face* in destination economies (Light, 1972, 1984; Aldrich and Zimmer, 1986).

When migrant networks support coethnic entrepreneurship, thus expanding an immigrant economy, the networks expand the economy in the destination locality. Expansion permits more immigrants to find work than could have done so had the general labor market been the only dispenser of employment. Naturally, the expansion of destination economies begins after the migration network has begun to land workers there. The longer the lag, the feebler the expansion. The length of this lag is variable and probably depends upon political restraints on immigrant enterprise. These political restraints have been much more prominent in Europe that in North America (Blaschke, Boissevain, Grotenbreg *et al.*, 1990) and they have attracted stinging criticism in Latin America (De Soto, 1989). Nonetheless, the network's enlargement of the target economy supports the 'cumulatively caused' migration of network theory. Therefore, migration networks are actually more important than theory acknowledges because they not only lower the social and economic costs of migration, as existing theory asserts, they also augment economic opportunities in destination economies.

The migration network enhances immigrant entrepreneurship in three principal ways. First, the network feeds low-cost coethnic labor to immigrant entrepreneurs just as it does to non-immigrant entrepreneurs.

Immigrant entrepreneurs routinely employ coethnics (including kin) at rates vastly above chance levels. Min (1989, p. 66) reported that 30% of employed Koreans found jobs in firms owned by fellow Koreans even though Koreans were only 1% of the Los Angeles County population. More tellingly, Hansen and Cardenas (1988, p. 233) compared the employment rolls of Mexican immigrant employers, native-born Mexican employers, and non-Mexican employers in Mexican neighborhoods of California and Texas. They found that Mexican immigrant employers were 'most likely to hire undocumented Mexican workers', and were also most likely to express very favorable evaluations of the quality of these workers, not just their cheapness. Next in line came the native-born Mexican employers. Last were the non-Mexican employers who employed the least undocumented labor and, when asked about it, stressed its cheapness, not its quality. This result shows that the migration network fed foreign-born Mexican workers to coethnic employers who knew how to get more work out of them and had more favorable opinions of them.

Information is a second support resource. Migration networks feed economic information to immigrant entrepreneurs and would-be entrepreneurs concerning the best industries to enter, pricing, technology, business methods, and the like (Light and Bonacich, 1988, Ch. 7). A migration network is a channel of communication along which all kinds of messages easily and inexpensively flow. Business information is just another message. Migration network messages are credible because of the relationships of mutual trust that link members (Gold, 1991, p. 241). This credibility is especially important in business. In many cases, the migration network appeals to the ethnic chauvinism of its participants. Chauvinism encourages participants to hoard useful information while concealing it from outsiders. Under these conditions, the network becomes the channel by which knowledgeable immigrants hoard and conceal information for the benefit and advantage of their ethnic group.

In addition to information, migration networks also provide other forms of mutual aid and assistance. Many immigrant entrepreneurs acquire their initial training in business during the course of an apprenticeship passed in the business of a coethnic (Bailey and Waldinger, 1991). Once established in business, they can call upon primary social relationships, embedded in the migration network, for help in business. Help can include purchasing at advantageous prices, dealing with public bureaucracies and courts, customer and supplier relations, financial and production management, labor relations, industrial engineering, quality control, marketing, and the introduction of new products or techniques (Light and Bonacich, 1988, Chs. 7-10); Light, 1985; Boissevain, Blaschke, Grotenbreg *et al.*, 1990). In some cases, immigration networks provide access to rotating credit associations and, through them, to business capital (Light, Im and Deng, 1990). In all these cases, the existing literature documents the utility of the entrepreneur's network connections when confronting standard and inescapable business problems (Kilby, 1971).

**Policy implications**

Maximization of immigration is rarely a policy objective among governments. Minimization is more common. This reservation arises most directly from fears that rapid immigrant influx will hurt employment and housing opportunities of non-immigrants. Even governments that frankly encourage immigration must protect non-immigrant workers from the direct and indirect competition of immigrants for scarce jobs and housing. If they do not, alarmed constituents will vote them out of office. In the modern world, racist and xenophobic attitudes sometimes hide behind the more acceptable and neutral language of economics, but for all that, the economic objections to rapid and massive immigration are real enough to merit sympathetic attention.

However, when governments do wish to maximize immigration, as, for example, Israel wants to maximize the immigration of Jews from the CIS, they have to accept the political risk of anti-immigrant backlash that a rapid influx encourages. Naturally, if the risk materializes, and an anti-immigrant government takes power, then the door of immigration will slam shut. When that happens, the total volume of immigration that has been successfully admitted may actually prove *less* than it would have been under a more restrained policy that persisted longer. For example, suppose a rapid influx policy introduced 500,000 immigrants a year for three years, after which, in the anti-immigrant backlash that ensued, immigration simply stopped. In that case, 1,500,000 immigrants would have entered the country. However, if only 250,000 a year had been admitted, and this restrained rate permitted immigration to continue for ten years instead of three, then 2,500,000 immigrants would ultimately have entered the country. In this sense, the more restrained policy would increase immigrant influx more in the long-run than the unrestrained policy.

Of the sources that engender an anti-immigrant backlash, none is more potent than unrestrained competition for scarce resources. To minimize anti-immigrant political backlash, and to maximize immigration, governments have, therefore, to maximize the supply of housing and work in their country. To this end, policy makers need simultaneously to maximize both the job and housing supply in the general labor market and in the immigrant economy — J+I in the discussion above. Policies that concentrate wholly upon the general labor market overlook the significant contribution that immigrant entrepreneurship can make to the enhancement of the job supply, the reduction of resource competition, and the political, as well as economic, acceptability of rapid immigration.

The immigrant economy is a small business economy. Most immigrant firms have no employees. Many also fall into the informal economy, a twilight zone difficult to measure and to control (Sassen-Koob, 1989; Light and Karageorgis, 1994). A modern welfare state experiences legal contradictions in encouraging a large immigrant economy, because immigrant firms violate labor, housing, health, tax, occupational, and safety regulations already in place (De Soto, 1989). For example, ambulatory food vendors prepare pies and sandwiches under unsanitary conditions prohibited to restaurants; unlicensed taxicabs and vans accept passengers without insurance or safety inspections; immigrant-owned garment factories pay seamstresses less than the minimum wage and offer them inadequate health protection or sanitary facilities; immigrant peddlers sell their wares without proper licenses; or, immigrant families occupy self-built shanties that violate plumbing and electrical codes. The welfare state's legal code, therefore, can collide with a large immigrant economy. If existing codes are enforced, the police close down many immigrant firms and evict shanty-dwellers from their shacks. As a result, the immigrant economy is smaller than it might be, thus increasing the resource competition of immigrants and non-immigrants in the general economy while depriving the immigrants of the jobs and housing they did enjoy.

An immigrant economy requires legal/political toleration in order to stretch the supply of work to the maximum. Therefore, a consistent policy of immigration maximization requires a welfare state to liberalize existing labor, occupational, housing, and industrial codes. In effect, these standing codes represent concealed obstacles to the government's policy of immigration maximization. Liberalized codes tolerate 'Third World' living and working conditions that fall below the minimum standard of decency previously institutionalized by the welfare state. However, the liberalization is only temporary. It is appropriate, once codes have been abruptly liberalized, to plan for their gradual restoration, thus putting legal pressure upon the immigrant economy to upgrade its sanitary conditions, wages, health protection, and working conditions to those prevailing in the general labor market.

## Notes

1. In this respect, network theorists share a more general tendency to ignore self-employment's effects when discussing the labor force changes produced by immigration. For example, see 'Aggregate Population and Labor Force Effects', Chapter 2 in Demetrios G. Papademetriou *et al.* (eds.), 1989. This chapter does not mention self-employment.
2. The immigrant economy also includes employment and self-employment in illegal enterprises, as does the mainstream economy. We distinguish illegal enterprise from predatory crime, which we exclude from this analysis even though it represents, strictly speaking, an earning opportunity. On this subject, see Light, 1974, 1977; Jones, 1988.
3. Earnings opportunities exclude transfer payments such as public welfare, private charity, or remittances to the immigrants from abroad. On welfare and immigration, see Peterson and Rom, 1989.
4. In exactly this sense, Simon (1989) has explained the growth of immigrant self-employment in Europe following hard upon the decline of wage earning jobs for immigrants; I expanded when J contracted, so that S was unaffected.
5. See Jones, 1988.
6. The literature reads as if all immigrant women became employees. Certainly most do. In general, women are less likely to become self-employed than men. Nonetheless, some immigrant women become entrepreneurs. A complete account of the gender-specific effect of the immigrant economy would certainly need to bring in the women entrepreneurs too. See Goffee and Scase, 1983.

## References

Aldrich, H. and Zimmer, C. (1986), 'Entrepreneurship through Social Networks', in Sexton, D. and Smilor, R. (eds.), *The Art and Science of Entrepreneurship*, Ballinger: Cambridge, MA, pp. 3-23.

Bailey, T. and Waldinger, R. (1991), 'Primary, Secondary, and Enclave Labor Markets: A Training Systems Approach', *American Sociological Review*, Vol. 56, pp. 432-45.

Birley, S. (1985), 'The Role of Networks in the Entrepreneurial Process', *Journal of Business Venturing*, Vol. 1, pp. 107-17.

Blaschke, J, Boissevain, J., Grotenbreg, H., Joseph, I., Morokvasic, M. and

Ward, R. (1990), 'European Trends in Ethnic Business', in Waldinger, R., Aldrich, H. and Ward, R. (eds.), *Ethnic Entrepreneurs*, Sage: Newbury Park, CA, pp. 79-105.

Boissevain, J., Blaschke, J., Grotenbreg, H., Joseph, I., Light, I., Sway, M., Waldinger, R. and Werbner, P. (1990), 'Ethnic Entrepreneurs and Ethnic Strategies', in Waldinger, R., Aldrich, H. and Ward, R. (eds.), *Ethnic Entrepreneurs*, Sage: Newbury Park, CA, pp. 131-156.

Boyd, M. (1989), 'Family and Personal Networks in International Migration: Recent Developments and New Agendas', *International Migration Review*, Vol. 23, pp. 638-70.

Bozorgmehr, M. (1992), Internal Ethnicity: Armenian, Baha'i, Jewish, and Muslim Iranians in Los Angeles, Doctoral Dissertation, University of California at Los Angeles: Los Angeles, CA.

Bozorgmehr, M. and Sabagh, G. (1991), 'A Comparison of Exiles and Immigrants: Iranians in Los Angeles', in Fathi, A. (ed.), *Iranian Exiles and Refugees Since Khomeini*, Mazda, Publishers: Costa Mesa, CA, pp. 121-44.

Castells, M. and Portes, A. (1989), 'World Underneath: The Origins, Dynamics, and Effects of the Informal Economy', in Portes, A., Castells, M. and Benton, L. (eds.), *The Informal Economy: Studies in Advanced and Less Developed Countries*, Johns Hopkins University Press: Baltimore, MD, pp. 11-40.

Dallalfar, A. (1989). Iranian Immigrant Women in Los Angeles: The Reconstruction of Work, Ethnicity, and Community, Doctoral Dissertation, University of California at Los Angeles: Los Angeles, CA.

Davila, A and Saenz, R. (1990), 'The Effect of Maquiladora Employment on the Monthly Flow of Mexican Undocumented Immigration to the US, 1978-1982', *International Migration Review*, Vol. 24, pp. 96-107.

De Soto, H. (1989), *The Other Path*, I.B. Tauris: London.

Fawcett, J.T. (1989), 'Networks, Linkages, and Migration Systems', *International Migration Review*, Vol. 23, pp. 671-80.

Fernandez-Kelly, M.P. and Garcia, A.M. (1989), 'Informalization at the Core: Hispanic Women, Homework, and the Advanced Capitalist State', in Portes, A., Castells, M. and Benton, L.A. (eds), *The Informal Economy: Studies in Advanced and Less Developed Countries*, Johns Hopkins University Press: Baltimore, MD, Chapter 13.

Goffee, R. and Scase, R. (1983), 'Business Ownership and Women's Subordination: A Preliminary Study of Female Proprietors', *The Sociological Review*, Vol. 31, pp. 625-48.

Gold, S. (1991), *Refugee Communities*, Sage: Newbury Park, CA.

Gregory, P. (1989), 'The Determinants of International Migration and

Policy Options for Influencing the Size of Population Flows', Working Paper of the Commission for the Study of International Migration and Cooperative Economic Development, No. 2, U.S. Commission for the Study of International Migration and Cooperative Economic Development: Washington, DC.

Grieco, M. (1987),'Family Networks and the Closure of Employment', in Lee, G. and Loveridge, R. (eds.), *The Manufacture of Disadvantage*. Open University Press: Milton Keynes (UK), pp. 33-44.

Hansen, N.H. and Cardenas, G.C. (1988), 'Immigrant and Native Ethnic Enterprises in Mexican American Neighborhoods: Differing Perceptions of Mexican American Workers', *International Migration Review*, Vol. 22, pp. 226-42.

Jones, Y.V. (1988), 'Street Peddlers as Entrepreneurs: Economic Adaptation to an Urban Area', *Urban Anthropology*, Vol. 17, pp. 143-69.

Kilby, P. (1971), 'Hunting the Heffalump', in Kilby, P. (ed.), *Entrepreneurship and Economic Development*, Macmillan: New York, pp. 1-40.

Light, I. (1972), *Ethnic Enterprise in America*. University of California Press: Berkeley and Los Angeles.

Light, I. (1974), 'From Vice District to Tourist Attraction: The Moral Career of American Chinatowns, 1880-1940', *Pacific Historical Review*, Vol. 43, pp. 367-94.

Light, I. (1977), 'The Ethnic Vice District, 1880-1944', *American Sociological Review*, Vol. 42, pp. 466-79.

Light, I. (1984), 'Immigrant and Ethnic Enterprise in North America', *Ethnic and Racial Studies*, Vol. 7, pp. 195-216.

Light, I. (1985), 'Ethnicity and Business Enterprise', in Stolarik, M.M. (ed.), *Making It in America*, Bucknell University: Cranbury, NJ, Chapter 1.

Light, I. and Bonacich, E. (1988), *Immigrant Entrepreneurs*, University of California Press: Berkeley and Los Angeles.

Light, I., Im, J.-K. and Deng, Z. (1990), 'Korean Rotating Credit Associations in Los Angeles', *Amerasia*, Vol. 16, pp. 35-54.

Light, I. and Karageorgis, S. (1994), 'The Ethnic Economy', in Smelser, N. and Swedberg, R. (eds.), *The Handbook of Economic Sociology*, Russell Sage Foundation: New York.

Massey, D.S. (1988), 'Economic Development and International Migration in Comparative Perspective', *Population and Development Review*, Vol. 14, pp. 383-413.

Massey, D.S. (1990), 'Social Structure, Household Strategies, and the Cumulative Causation of Migration',*Population Index*, Vol. 56, pp. 3-26.

Massey, D.S., Alarcon, R., Durand, J. and Gonzalez, H. (1987), *Return to Azatlan*, University of California Press: Berkeley and Los Angeles.

Massey, D.S. and Espana, F.G. (1987), 'The Social Process of International Migration', *Science*, Vol. 237, pp. 733-37.

Min, P.G. (1989), Some Positive Functions of Ethnic Business for an Immigrant Community: Koreans in Los Angeles, Final Report, Submitted to the National Science Foundation (U.S.): Washington, DC.

Morawska, E. (1989), 'Labor Migrations of Poles in the Atlantic Economy, 1880-1914', *Comparative Studies in Society and History*, Vol. 31, pp. 237-72.

Papademetriou, D.G., Bach, R.L., Johnson, K., Kramer, R.G., Lowell, B.L. and Smith, S.J. (1989), *The Effects of Immigration on the U.S. Economy and Labor Market*, U.S. Department of Labor, Bureau of International Labor Affairs: Washington, DC.

Pedraza-Bailey, S. (1985), 'Cuba's Exiles: Portrait of a Refugee Migration', *International Migration Review*, Vol. 19, pp. 4-34.

Peterson, P.E. and Rom, M. (1989), 'American Federalism, Welfare Policy, and Residential Choices', *American Political Science Review*, Vol. 83, pp. 711-28.

Phizacklea, A. (1988), 'Entrepreneurship, Ethnicity, and Gender', in Westwood, P. and Bhachu, P. (eds.), *Enterprising Women*, Routledge: London and New York, pp. 20-33.

Portes, A. and Jensen, L. (1989), 'The Enclave and the Entrants: Patterns of Ethnic Enterprise in Miami before and after Mariel', *American Sociological Review*, Vol. 54, pp. 929-49.

Sassen-Koob, S. (1989), 'New York City's Informal Economy', in Portes, A., Castells, M. and Benton, L.A. (eds.), *The Informal Economy: Studies in Advanced and Less Developed Countries*, Johns Hopkins University Press: Baltimore, MD, pp. 60-94.

Schmink, M. (1984), 'Household Economic Strategies: Review and Research Agenda', *Latin American Research Review*, Vol. 19, pp. 87-102.

Simon, J.L. (1989), *The Economic Consequences of Immigration*, Basil Blackwell and Cato Institution: New York and Oxford.

Stepick, A. (1989), 'Miami's Two Informal Sectors', in Portes, A., Castells, M. and Benton, L.A. (eds.), *The Informal Economy: Studies in Advanced and Less Developed Countries*, Johns Hopkins University Press: Baltimore, MD, Chapter 6.

Tilly, C. (1978), 'Migration in Modern European History', in McNeill, W.H. and Adams, R.S. (eds.), *Human Migration*, University of Indiana

Press: Bloomington, IN, pp. 48-72.

Wilpert, C. and Gitmez, A. (1987), *Revue Européenne des Migrations Internationales*, Vol. 3, pp. 175-96.

Zhou, M. and Logan, J.R. (1989), 'Returns on Human Capital in Ethnic Enclaves: New York City's Chinatown', *American Sociological Review*, Vol. 54, pp. 809-20.

# 2 The four Iranian ethnic economies in Los Angeles

*Ivan Light, Georges Sabagh, Mehdi Bozorgmehr and Claudia Der-Martirosian*

In contrast to an 'ethnic enclave economy', which is a territorial concentration of ethnic-owned firms in a locality (Portes and Jensen, 1989; Sanders and Nee, 1987; Zhou and Logan, 1989), the term ethnic economy refers to all ethnic-owned business firms and their coethnic personnel, irrespective of geographical location. An ethnic economy requires no territorial clustering. It exists wherever immigrants have grafted their own firms onto the mainstream economy of a host society, and its economic importance is primarily the partial independence of the general labor market that it affords its creators. An ethnic economy gives ethnics a choice between working within it, or working for wages or salaries in the general labor market (Light, Bhachu and Karageorgis, 1993; Portes and Manning, 1986).

Bonacich and Modell (1980, p. 110) defined the ethnic economy as coethnic self-employed plus their coethnic employees. In a slightly broader formulation, Reitz (1980) added all employees whose on-the-job language was their native tongue rather than English. In the narrower sense, then, the ethnic economy includes all the ethnic self-employed and their coethnic employees; and if one follows Reitz, it also includes employees of the general labor market who work in an ethnic ambiance.

Like its more celebrated twin, the ethnic enclave economy, the ethnic economy has attracted most attention because of its possible economic contribution to the welfare of coethnic participants.[1] In this paper, however, we shall not discuss the usual subjects that pertain to ethnic economies or ethnic enclave economies — economic causes or consequences — but instead, we will focus on the neglected subject of internal ethnicity in the ethnic economy.

Whatever else it is, the ethnic economy is ethnic. Therefore, the subject belongs in the field of ethnic groups. The study of ethnic groups is basically the study of group boundaries (Barth, 1969). These boundaries determine who is a coethnic. Ethnic boundaries expand and contract. In most cases, they also fit within larger ethnic identities and subsume smaller ones. Internal ethnicity exists when ethnic or immigrant groups themselves contain ethnic groups (Bozorgmehr, 1992, Ch. 1). Therefore, internal ethnicity is a boundary problem and, as such, a core concern of the voluminous literature on ethnicity. As is already very well understood, most immigrant minorities did not arrive in North America with an ethnic identity coincident with their national origin (Nahirny and Fishman, 1965, p. 312; Barton, 1975; Light, 1983, Ch. 12). Instead, most debarking immigrants defined themselves in terms of regional or local provenance, only later acquiring an ethnic identity based upon national origin. Thus, immigrants from Italy originally thought of themselves as Neapolitans, Calabrians, and Sicilians. Only later did their descendants accept an 'Italian American' ethnic identity (Dinnerstein and Reimers, 1975, p. 51).

Internal ethnicity requires one to examine the ethnic boundaries within the ethnic economy. Surprisingly, the ethnic economy literature offers slight precedent for so doing. The recent ethnic economy literature has inexplicably run away from the older ethnicity literature in which internal ethnicity is so prominent an issue. An exception is found in a study by Light (1972, pp. 66-67, 91-93, 106), which showed that the prewar Chinese and Japanese ethnic economies were actually formed from provenance-defined nuclei. Lacking comparable nuclei, native black internal migrants were less entrepreneurial than the immigrant Asians. More recently, Kim, Won and Fernandez (1989, p. 73) have reported big differences in 'business participation' among Gujerati and non-Gujerati Indians in Chicago, an internal ethnic distinction. However, for the most part, ethnic economy theorists have assumed that ethnic economies had unproblematic national-origin boundaries that complemented the national-origin identity of their creators. For example, Bonacich and Modell (1980) defined the Japanese American ethnic economy as economic activity carried on by Japanese Americans. Reitz (1980) similarly treated the Chinese and Ukrainian ethnic economies in Canada as economic activities carried on by Chinese or Ukrainian Canadians. Finally, Portes and Bach (1985) identified the Cuban ethnic enclave economy as an economy whose participants were born in Cuba.

National-origin definitions of the ethnic economy assume a national-origin ethnic identity, a hazardous assumption. For example, in the case of Japanese-Americans, the Japanese ethnic identity developed only after decades of residence in the United States and was still less than fully encompassing in 1966-68 when the Japanese American Research Project conducted its interviews. Originally, Japanese settlers in Hawaii and on the Pacific Coast identified themselves with prefectural origins, not with Japanese nationality. This identification gave rise to a fragmented Japanese community, internally organized into endogamous subethnic clusters. *Hiroshimakenjin* distinguished themselves from *Fukuokakenjin* and vice-versa (Light, 1972, Ch. 4; Lyman, 1986, Parts 1 and 2). If one had focused on the internal ethnic differences, then Bonacich and Modell's (1980) homogeneous Japanese ethnic economy might have been conceptualized instead as a broad framework that contained within it a plurality of subethnic economies.

Similarly, among contemporary Chinese immigrants to North America, those from Taiwan distinguish themselves from those from Hong Kong, and both from earlier Cantonese settlers (Zhou and Logan, 1989, p. 819). Even the dialect of these 'Chinese' is not mutually intelligible. If one acknowledges the internal ethnicity of Chinese in North America, then the 'Chinese ethnic economy' loses its monolithic structure, resembling instead a framework within which the real ethnic economies (Taiwanese, Hong Kongese, Cantonese) operate (Hamilton, 1977; Lai, 1988). When Reitz overlooked internal ethnicity among the Chinese, he simplified the ethnic economy concept, possibly weakening its universality. Zhou and Logan's (1989, p. 819) analysis of the Chinese enclave economy in New York's Chinatown also overlooked internal ethnicity, an oversight that may have glossed over gaping internal differences within the Chinese population.

In the case of Miami's Cubans, Portes (1987) acknowledges the pioneering contribution of regional *municipios* and of 12,000 Cuban Jewish families to the subsequent emergence of the Cuban ethnic enclave economy; however, in their earlier book, Portes and Bach (1985) ignored both. This research revealed nothing about internal ethnicity in the Cuban ethnic economy because Portes and Bach treated Cubans as an ethnically homogeneous category rather than a scaffolding for internal ethnic economies based on religion and provenance.

## Internal ethnicity

In these three exemplary cases of Japanese, Chinese and Cuban immigrants to the United States — important contributions to the literature — ethnic economy encounters internal ethnicity, a basic subject in ethnic research (Bozorgmehr, 1992; Cornell, 1988; Light, 1983, pp. 277-280). Internal ethnicity arises in many ways. In some cases, larger 'ethnic categories' develop as a result of aggregating the initially distinctive subgroups (Espiritu, 1989; Sarna, 1978). Internal ethnicity also arises when the immigrants' country of origin is ethnically heterogeneous, and/or there is migrant selectivity along ethnic lines (Bozorgmehr, 1992, Ch. 1). Finally, internal ethnicity arises from successive immigration of the same ethnic group from one society to another. When immigrant minorities have acculturated and partially assimilated one dominant culture, they accommodate to it. This accommodation changes them, but not so much as to obliterate their ethnic distinctiveness. When later they relocate again, experiencing the acculturational demands of yet another dominant society and culture, the self-same ethnic minorities experience an *ethnic* attachment to the foreign culture to which they had earlier assimilated. In effect, this foreign culture now becomes part of the ethnic culture that the new immigrants are reluctant to shed in response to novel acculturational demands. National origin is added to ethnic identity for ethnic groups from the same country, as well as for any one ethnic group with different national origins. Under these circumstances, internal ethnicity spontaneously arises from successive migration, not aggregation.

We will address here the influence of internal ethnicity on the ethnic economy developed by Iranian immigrants in Los Angeles, whose large ethnic economy is internally heterogeneous. The category 'Iranian' includes Muslims, the overwhelming majority in Iran; but it also includes Armenians, Baha'is, and Jews, members of ethno-religious minorities in Iran.[2] Therefore, the ethnic category Iranian conceals internal ethnicity of possible relevance to the functioning of the Iranian ethnic economy.

*Sources of data*

The data presented in this paper are from the Public-Use Microdata Sample of the 1980 census for Los Angeles County and from a sample survey of Iranians in Los Angeles that we completed in 1987-88 covering various aspects of the economic activities of Iranians in Los Angeles (Bozorgmehr, 1992, Ch. 2; Bozorgmehr and Sabagh, 1988).

Existing lists offered the best method to sample this sparse and dispersed immigrant population. The eight white-page telephone directories for Los Angeles County constituted our main sampling frame. Two hundred pages in each directory were randomly selected, and foreign-born

Iranian coders checked off Persian and Armenian names in each of the selected pages. Since Armenian Iranian surnames are indistinguishable from other Armenian names (most end in 'ian' or 'yan'), we extracted all Armenian names and screened the non-Iranians by telephone. The vast majority of Persian family names are distinctive, and given the recency of arrival of Iranians, we expected few surname changes in this population. In spite of this, a separate list of uncertain names was also created and later checked against a 1979 Immigration and Naturalization Service master list of 43,271 Iranian surnames to exclude non-Iranian names. As a supplement, we obtained and used community lists to insure the inclusion of a minimum number of respondents from each ethno-religious subgroup for statistical analysis, and to address the problem of unlisted telephone numbers.

The study questionnaire was developed in English and then translated into Persian and Armenian. Native speakers of Persian and Eastern-Armenian dialects conducted lengthy in-person interviews with 671 heads of households (201 Muslims, 195 Armenians, 188 Jews, and 87 Baha'is). Interviews were conducted from late August 1987 to early March 1988.[3]

**Iranians in Los Angeles**

Los Angeles is the largest center of expatriate Iranians in the United States (Bozorgmehr and Sabagh, 1988). Iranian immigrants and exiles in Los Angeles come from a religiously homogeneous country: 98% of Iran's population are Muslim, of which 93% are Shiite, and the rest Sunni. Armenians, Jews and Baha'is are ethno-religious minorities in Iran. As 'people of the Book,' Iran's Jews and Christian Armenians have occupied a tolerated, if socially and even juridically inferior, status. As alleged Muslim heretics, however, Iran's Baha'is are vulnerable to religious persecution under the revolutionary regime (Jones, 1984). Together, these three minorities represented less than 2% of Iran's population in 1976, the year of the last census before the Islamic revolution.

The Islamic revolution of 1978-79 intensified religious intolerance in Iran, causing an abrupt deterioration in the economic position and security of ethno-religious minorities. Baha'is in particular were singled out for death sentences, and their were homes looted, and their property confiscated. Unsurprisingly, minorities were over represented among those who have fled the Islamic Republic. Although the 1980 U.S. Census contains no information on religion, ancestry data indicates that 25% of Iranians in

Los Angeles were of Armenian ancestry at the time of the census. The other three-quarters included not only Baha'is, Jews, and Muslims, but also Assyrians and Zoroastrians. Armenians, Baha'is, and Jews were also much more numerous among Iranians in Los Angeles than they were in Iran's population (Sabagh and Bozorgmehr, 1987).

The Iranian community in Los Angeles therefore encompasses three major ethno-religious minorities (Armenians, Baha'is, Jews) who simultaneously have national (Iranian) and minority ethnic identities. This complexity unavoidably affects the Iranian ethnic economy in Los Angeles. Following Bonacich and Modell (1980), we defined the Iranian ethnic economy as Iranian self-employed plus their Iranian employees. However, we hypothesized that the so-called Iranian ethnic economy has only a shadow existence, and that real economic organization centers around four internal ethnic economies (Armenian, Baha'i, Jewish, Muslim), which are ethno-religious rather than broadly Iranian in character. If one discussed only the Iranian ethnic economy, overlooking the internal ethnic economies of the Baha'is, Jews, Armenians, and Muslims, one would interpret as unitary what may be, in fact, complexly federated.

*The Iranian ethnic economy*

The size of an ethnic economy is not a condition of its existence. Small ethnic economies are, for all their smallness, still ethnic economies. However, a principal discovery of the ethnic economy literature has been the surprisingly large share of total employment of an ethnic group that is accounted for by the ethnic economy. These results shocked analysts who believed that small business was no longer of economic importance. Among the Japanese American males studied by Bonacich and Modell (1980), 47% had found employment in the ethnic economy. Among the principal non-English, non-French Canadian ethnic minorities studied by Reitz (1980), up to one-third had found employment in the ethnic economy. Light and Bonacich (1988, pp. 3-4) estimated that the Korean ethnic economy in Los Angeles included 62% of Korean workers. Zhou and Logan (1989, p. 66) report an even higher rate of 75%.

Table 1 shows that Iranians in Los Angeles have developed an extensive ethnic economy based on self-employment. The 1980 U.S. census showed that only 8.8% of the adult labor force of Los Angeles County was self-employed compared to 25.2% of persons born in Iran (Sabagh and Bozorgmehr, 1987).[4] The Census defined the self-employed as proprietors, partners, employees of their own corporations, and unpaid family workers, a practice we followed in our study of 1988. Our sample of four Iranian ethno-religious groups found each significantly overrepresented in self-employment relative to the Los Angeles County labor force (Table 1). The least self-employed were the Armenians, 26% of whom were self-employed, which was still a three-fold over-representation in entrepreneurship relative to the County. The level of self-employment among Jews was an astounding 69.1%. This level represented an eight-fold overrepresentation in entrepreneurship. Taken together, Iranian immigrants in Los Angeles in 1987-88 exhibited 45.3% self-employment, a nearly six-fold overrepresentation.[5]

Table 1.
Percentage distribution, class of worker, and Indices of Dissimilarity of persons 16 years of age and over for Los Angeles, 1980, and unweighted sample of Iranians in Los Angeles, 1987-88

|  | LA County* 1980 (1) | IRANIANS IN LOS ANGELES, 1987-88 ||||| 
| --- | --- | --- | --- | --- | --- | --- |
|  |  | All Iranians (2) | Armenians (3) | Baha'is (4) | Jews (5) | Muslims (6) |
| *Class of Worker* | | | | | | |
| Wage & Salary | 91.2 | 54.7 | 74.0 | 56.0 | 30.9 | 59.3 |
| Self-Employed | 8.8 | 45.3 | 26.0 | 44.0 | 69.1 | 40.7 |
| Total | 100 | 100 | 100 | 100 | 100 | 100 |
| N | (185,276) | (971) | (273) | (109) | (288) | (300) |
| *Index of Dissimilarity* | | | | | | |
| All Iranians | 36.5 | -- | | | | |
| Armenians | 17.2 | 19.3 | -- | | | |
| Baha'i | 35.2 | 1.3 | 18.0 | -- | | |
| Jews | 60.3 | 23.8 | 43.1 | 25.1 | -- | |
| Muslims | 31.9 | 4.6 | 14.7 | 3.3 | 28.4 | -- |

* U.S. Bureau of the Census 1980.

Although each of the ethno-religious groups was overrepresented in self-employment, the four groups exhibited substantial variation in self-employment rates, such that changes in the proportion of the groups could affect the size of the Iranian ethnic economy. For example, if Muslims had been 98% of the Iranian community of Los Angeles and Armenians 2%, then the overall Iranian self-employment rate would have been 40.4%. If the internal ethnic proportions were reversed, the Iranian self-employment rate would be 26.3%. This variation suggests that the concept of an Iranian ethnic economy might overlook and conceal distinct, internal ethnic economies in the four subgroups, and that gross errors of interpretation could result.

As one assessment of this issue, we wanted to ascertain whether the self-employment of Iranians as a whole was more divergent from that of Los Angeles County than was the self-employment of Iranian subgroups from that of the larger Iranian group. If so, we would have evidence of an Iranian ethnic economy. To this end, we utilized the Index of Dissimilarity (ID) to measure the clustering of the various ethno-religious groups in self-employment. The results appear in the bottom panel of Table 1.[6] The widely-utilized ID is the leading measure of residential segregation, and it applies just as well to segregation by occupation (Massey and Denton, 1988). The ID ranges from 0 (no dissimilarity) to 100 (maximum dissimilarity), and is most easily understood as the percentage of a group that would have to change categories in order to yield the distribution of another group.

Using the results shown in the top panel of Table 1, the ID of each of the four ethno-religious groups (Armenian, Baha'i, Jewish, Muslim) can be computed relative, first, to the labor force of Los Angeles County, and then to the aggregate of employed Iranians. These results appear in the lower panel of Table 1. Combining the four Iranian ethno-religious groups, we obtain a mean ID of 36.5 relative to Los Angeles County. This score means that 36.5% of Iranians would have had to switch from self-employment to wage or salary employment in order to give the Iranians the same proportion in these two categories that existed in Los Angeles County's labor force.

Measuring each ethno-religious group relative to all Iranians, we then obtained the ID scores listed in column 2. Except for Armenians, each subgroup's ID was much lower relative to the total Iranian employed than relative to Los Angeles County. The unweighted mean ID of the four ethno-religious subgroups was 12.3, just one-third of the Iranian/Los Angeles ID. Only one-third as many workers would have to change categories to eliminate the difference between the Iranians and the four subgroups than would have to change categories in order to eliminate the difference between the Iranians and the labor force of Los Angeles County.

*Occupational and industrial clustering*

Economic clustering offers another test of the unity of the Iranian ethnic economy. Economic clustering is the concentration of group members in particular industries and occupations at levels far in excess of their representation in the general labor force (Reitz, 1980, pp. 135-136). Occupational and industrial clustering is now, and has long been, a common feature of immigrant and ethnic minorities (Koenig, 1943; Light, 1983, Ch. 12). Indeed, occupational and industrial clustering or segregation is itself a common measure of ethnic distance.

The four Iranian subgroups had obviously different occupational and industrial profiles. Compared to the other Iranians, Iranian Jews were more likely to be in wholesale and retail trades, especially apparel and jewelry: 43% were in these industries, and nearly 10% in apparel alone. Iranian Armenians concentrated in 'finance, insurance, and real estate', and 'business repair and service' (35% were in these two fields). Iranian Muslims concentrated in construction and durable goods manufacture (27%), while Baha'is were most common in durable goods manufacture, and 'other health and legal services' (27% of employed Baha'is). The modal occupation of Iranian Armenians was secretary (16.1%); of Iranian Baha'is, sales supervisor (18.2%); of Iranian Jews, sales supervisor (40.7%); of Iranian Muslims, engineer (16.9%).

To measure economic clustering, we again utilized the index of dissimilarity. In this case, however, we made use of all the two-digit occupational/industrial categories, combining where necessary, to achieve comparability of our Iranian sample and census categories. Results appear in Table 2. When Iranians are compared with the labor force of Los Angeles County with respect to occupational distribution, the ID is 44. This result means that 44% of the Iranians would have had to change categories in order to achieve an occupational distribution identical to that of Los Angeles County's labor force. The ID of 44 is higher than the ID of 36.5 which we obtained when comparing the self-employment of Iranians with that of Los Angeles County. This situation implies even more occupational clustering than clustering in self-employment.

When we compare the aggregate occupational distribution of Iranians with that of the four ethno-religious subgroups, we are also investigating the extent to which the four subgroups differ from all Iranians with respect to occupational distribution. These results appear in column 2 of the top panel of Table 2. Subgroup IDs relative to the aggregate labor force of Iranians are lower than subgroup IDs relative to the labor force of Los Angeles County. This discrepancy means that fewer people would have to change occupations to equalize the occupational distributions of the subgroups and the Iranian parent group than would have to change occupations to equalize the occupational distribution of Iranians and Los

Angeles County. If we use the ID, as it is frequently used, as an index of ethnic differentiation, we would therefore conclude that there was more ethnic distance between the Iranians and the non-Iranians than there was among the Iranians subgroups.

Table 2.
Indices of Dissimilarity of industrial and occupational clustering for persons 16 years of age and over, Los Angeles, 1980, and unweighted sample of Iranians in Los Angeles, 1987-88

|  | LA County* 1980 (1) | IRANIANS IN LOS ANGELES, 1987-88 ||||| 
|  |  | All Iranians (2) | Armenians (3) | Baha'is (4) | Jews (5) | Muslims (6) |
| --- | --- | --- | --- | --- | --- | --- |
| *Occupational* | | | | | | |
| All Iranians | 44 | -- | | | | |
| Armenians | 41 | 36 | -- | | | |
| Baha'is | 52 | 24 | 46 | -- | | |
| Jews | 62 | 35 | 63 | 45 | -- | |
| Muslims | 50 | 18 | 45 | 27 | 44 | -- |
| *Industrial* | | | | | | |
| All Iranians | 31 | -- | | | | |
| Armenians | 37 | 24 | -- | | | |
| Baha'is | 36 | 25 | 37 | -- | | |
| Jews | 47 | 23 | 48 | 46 | -- | |
| Muslims | 37 | 25 | 37 | 33 | 49 | -- |

* U. S. Bureau of the Census 1980.

If there were only one Iranian ethnic economy, the IDs for occupational distributions for each subgroup would be very small. As can be seen from the top panel of Table 2, this is clearly not the case. The range in these IDs is from 18 for the Muslims/All Iranians comparison to 63 for the Armenians/Jews comparison. To measure the average ID of the Iranian subgroups relative to all Iranians, we computed the unweighted mean of the IDs, which is 28.3.[7] If ID stands for ethnic differentiation, then the Iranian subgroups were two-thirds as different from one another with respect to occupational clustering as the Iranians were from the non-Iranians. This much difference is big enough to be called internal ethnic differentiation. Here is evidence that Iranians operated four internally-differentiated ethnic economies, not one unitary and undifferentiated Iranian ethnic economy.

The lower panel of Table 2 applies the same technique to industrial clustering. Comparing Iranians with Los Angeles County's labor force, we obtain an ID of 31. This result means that 31% of Iranians would have had to change industries in order to give Iranians an industrial distribution identical to that of Los Angeles County. As before, the Los Angeles/Iranian ID exceeds the Iranian/subgroup in every case. The unweighted mean of the subgroup IDs is 24.3. This unweighted mean is, however, 78% as large as the Los Angeles/Iranian ID. If the industrial segregation of Iranians in Los Angeles betokens ethnic economic segregation, then the industrial segregation of Iranian subgroups from the Iranian aggregate betokens 78% as great a segregation as the segregation of Iranians from non-Iranians. Surely this is segregation enough to warrant the label of internal ethnicity.

*Coethnicity in the employment relationship*

If an Iranian ethnic economy, rather than four semi-independent ethno-religious sub-economies, existed in Los Angeles County, then Iranians of one ethno-religious identity ought to work and cooperate as frequently with other Iranians as with Iranian co-religionists. To evaluate the importance of Iranian, as opposed to internal ethnic, ties in the ethnic economy, we distinguished two economic linkages for separate analysis. These were coethnicity in the employment relationship, and coethnicity in the partnership/co-owner relationship. First, following Bonacich and Modell (1980), we examined coethnicity in the employment relationship. Among employees, we distinguished those who reported that '90% or more' of the owners of their firms were Iranian co-religionists from those who reported that 90% or more of the owners were other Iranians or non-Iranian co-religionists.[8] Of these three, the first two categories correspond to an employment relationship belonging to what Bonacich and Modell defined as the ethnic economy. However, our data make it possible to ascertain what the balance was between Iranian and subethnic linkages in that ethnic economy.

The category of non-Iranian co-religionists means non-Iranian Jews, Muslims, Baha'i, and Armenians, with whom, in principle, Iranians of the same faith could cooperate in economic life; that is, an Iranian Jew could hire non-Iranian Jews. The non-Iranian co-religionist identity provides yet another potential ethnic linkage which would imply incorporation in a differently-defined ethnic economy.

Table 3 shows the ethno-religious identity that our employed Iranian respondents ascribed to their employers. We developed two measures of employer ethnicity: the more restrictive assigned an ethnic identity when employees attributed '90% or more' of their firm's owners to an ethno-religious category; while the less restrictive assigned an ethnic identity to the firm when employees reported that '50% or more' of owners were of that background. Naturally, the more restrictive 90% criterion reduced the percentage of employers who could be labeled Iranian co-religionists. Using a 50% criterion, 13.8% of employers were so identified; using a 90% criterion, only 12.4%. Conversely, the 50% criterion reduced the proportion working for non-Iranians in the general labor market from 91.1% to 87.4%. Other differences were equally small and did not materially affect the interpretation. Moreover, since, the 90% criterion minimized the extent of internal ethnicity, a conservative bias in this case, we decided to report only the 90% results in the interest of economy of space.

Among all working Iranians, only 43.2% were employees, the majority being self-employed (Table 3). Of the employed, 12.4% reported that 90% or more of their firm's owners were Iranian co-religionists. Only 2.5% of the employed reported that 90% or more of owners were non-Iranian co-religionists, and only 4% worked for other Iranians. The vast majority of employed Iranians, therefore — nearly 82% — were in the general labor market, and reported that 90% or more of owners were non-Iranians. Of course, for the Iranian minority, the general labor market might generate all of their employment in Los Angeles County if chance alone determined employment situs. Consequently, Table 3 shows that Iranians were appreciably more likely to find employment outside the general labor market than one would expect by chance, and that, outside that general labor market, Iranians were twice as likely to be employed by their Iranian co-religionists as by others. Although this tendency appears greatest for Jews and smallest for Baha'is, the small number of cases does not warrant generalizations about differences between subgroups.

Another measure of coethnicity in employment is coethnic workers. Reitz (1980) employed foreign language use at work to investigate this dimension. Language spoken at work is not a good indicator of ethnicity of co-workers for ethnically-diverse immigrants or ethnic groups such as Iranians. The use of Persian does not distinguish Persian-speaking Baha'is, Jews and Muslims. Although the use of the Armenian language distinguishes Armenian co-workers from other Iranians, it would not distinguish between Iranian Armenian and non-Iranian Armenian co-workers (Der-Martirosian, 1989).

**Table 3.**
**Ethnicity of employers of Iranian employees; unweighted sample of Iranians in Los Angeles, 1987-88**

|  | Armenians | Baha'is | Jews | Muslims | All Iranians |
|---|---|---|---|---|---|
| *90% Iranian Co-Religionists* | | | | | |
| Number | 13 | 0 | 6 | 6 | 25 |
| Percentage | 16.7 | 0 | 28.6 | 7.6 | 12.4 |
| *90% Other Iranians* | | | | | |
| Number | 4 | 2 | 0 | 2 | 8 |
| Percentage | 5.1 | 8.7 | 0 | 2.5 | 4.0 |
| *90% Non-Iranian Co-Religionists* | | | | | |
| Number | 4 | 0 | 0 | 0 | 4 |
| Percentage | 5.1 | 0 | 0 | 0 | 2.0 |
| *90% Non-Iranians* | | | | | |
| Number | 57 | 21 | 15 | 71 | 164 |
| Percentage | 73.1 | 91.3 | 71.4 | 89.9 | 81.6 |
| *Total reporting* | | | | | |
| Number | 78 | 23 | 21 | 79 | 201 |
| Percentage (Total) | 100.0 | 100.0 | 100.0 | 100.0 | 100.0 |
| *Self-Employed* | | | | | |
| Number | 61 | 34 | 127 | 83 | 305 |
| Percentage | 42.7 | 54.0 | 82.5 | 46.9 | 56.8 |

We defined coethnicity at work according to a conservative and a liberal criterion. The conservative criterion imputed ethnicity to a workplace when an employee identified 90% or more of co-workers as Iranian coethnics. The liberal criterion required only 50% of co-workers to be so identified. Naturally, the liberal criterion increased the proportion of coethnic workplaces while reducing the number of non-Iranian workplaces. For example, 5.4% of Iranian employees identified their workplace as one in which 90% or more of co-workers were Iranian co-religionists; and 8.4% so identified their workplace when we used the

50% criterion of coethnicity. Conversely, 91.1% of Iranian employees declared that 90% or more of their workmates were non-Iranians; while only 87.4% declared that 50% or more of their workmates were non-Iranians. As before, none of the differences was big enough to affect interpretation. Since the 90% criterion minimized internal ethnicity (a conservative bias), we decided to report it alone in order to economize space.

Workplace coethnicity depended only on the perceived ethnicity of co-workers. Even if the owner or owners were non-Iranians, as long as 90% of co-workers were Iranian coethnics, we still treated this respondent as employed in a coethnic workplace. The results shown in Table 4 are similar to those reported in Table 3. Almost 6% of employed Iranians reported that 90% or more of their coworkers were Iranian co-religionists.

Table 4.
Ethnic economies of heads of households defined by co-workers; unweighted sample of Iranians in Los Angeles, 1987-88.

| Ethnicity of Co-Workers | Armenians | Baha'is | Jews | Muslims | All Iranians |
|---|---|---|---|---|---|
| *90% Iranian Co-Religionists* | | | | | |
| Number | 8 | 0 | 3 | 1 | 12 |
| Percentage | 12.7 | 0.0 | 15.0 | 1.1 | 5.9 |
| *90% Other Iranians* | | | | | |
| Number | 1 | 1 | 0 | 1 | 3 |
| Percentage | 1.6 | 3.6 | 0.0 | 1.1 | 1.5 |
| *90% Non-Iranian Co-Religionists* | | | | | |
| Number | 2 | 0 | 0 | 1 | 3 |
| Percentage | 3.2 | 0.0 | 0.0 | 1.1 | 1.5 |
| *90% Non-Iranians* | | | | | |
| Number | 52 | 27 | 17 | 89 | 185 |
| Percentage | 82.5 | 96.4 | 85.0 | 96.7 | 91.1 |
| *Total Reporting* | | | | | |
| Number | 63 | 28 | 20 | 92 | 203 |
| Total Percentage | 100.0 | 100.0 | 100.0 | 100.0 | 100.0 |

This percentage was nearly four times as large as those who reported that more than 90% of co-workers were other Iranians. Of course, 91.1% indicated that 90% or more of their co-workers were non-Iranians, the general labor market indicator. This result is predictable in view of the small size of Iranian firms, the scant numbers of Iranians in Los Angeles, and the overwhelming power of the general labor market. Nonetheless, the results show an approximately nine-fold over representation of Iranian employees in coethnic workplaces.

Without taking account of internal ethnicity, one might stop here. However, Table 4 also shows that Iranian employees were three times more likely to report Iranian co-religionists than 'other Iranians' or 'non-Iranian co-religionists', the other ethnic ties, despite the much larger population of both these alternative ethnic categories.

*Coethnicity in partnerships*

Coethnicity in partnerships and co-ownerships means a tendency of self-employed Iranians to select Iranian co-religionists for these important business affiliations. Table 5 shows that most co-owners or partners were either relatives or Iranian co-religionists. Among the 203 Iranian business owners who had partners or co-owners, only 11 reported non-Iranian partners or co-owners. Since non-Iranians represented 99% of the Los Angeles labor force, Iranians were grossly overrepresented among the business partners of Iranians — an obvious ethnic effect.

However, internal ethnicity enhances our knowledge of Iranian business practices. Among all Iranians, Iranian co-religionists were seven times more common as partners or co-owners than were Iranians who were not also co-religionists. This ratio was highest for Jews and lowest for Baha'is, but internal ethnic selectivity operated in all four ethno-religious communities. While Iranian wage and salary workers relied mainly on employment in the general labor market (with non-Iranians for employers), the Iranian self-employed almost exclusively selected relatives and Iranian co-religionists for partners or co-owners.

The evidence proves that internal ethno-religious connections determined the partnership and co-ownership decisions of Iranian immigrants of all faiths. These decisions were not universalistic, as class theory would have it; but neither were they based on Iranian ethnicity. To have excluded internal ethnicity from our analysis would have been to distort and conceal the true ethnicity at work in this population.

**Table 5.**

**Coethnicity of respondent's partners and co-owners; unweighted sample of Iranians in Los Angeles, 1987-88**

|  | Armenians | | Baha'is | | Jews | | Muslims | | All Iranians | |
|---|---|---|---|---|---|---|---|---|---|---|
|  | N | % | N | % | N | % | N | % | N | % |
| No Partners | 25 | 40.9 | 11 | 32.3 | 18 | 14.2 | 48 | 57.8 | 102 | 33.4 |
| Iranian Co-Religionists* | 28 | 45.9 | 17 | 50.0 | 92 | 72.4 | 25 | 30.1 | 162 | 53.1 |
| Other Iranians | 3 | 4.9 | 5 | 14.7 | 10 | 7.9 | 5 | 6.0 | 23 | 7.6 |
| Non-Iranian Co-Religionists | 4 | 6.6 | 0 | 0.0 | 3 | 2.4 | 0 | 0.0 | 7 | 2.3 |
| All Others | 1 | 1.6 | 1 | 2.9 | 4 | 3.1 | 5 | 6.0 | 11 | 3.6 |
| Total Self-Employed | 61 | 100 | 34 | 100 | 127 | 100 | 83 | 100 | 305 | 100 |

* Includes relatives.

## Conclusion and discussion

The vast majority of Iranian employees worked in the general labor market: 81% of Iranian employees had mostly non-Iranian employers, and 91% of them had mostly non-Iranian co-workers. In view of the fact that Iranians constituted less than 1% of the labor force in Los Angeles County in 1980, these proportions are unsurprising.

Iranian employees found jobs in the Iranian ethnic economy 20 times more frequently than chance would predict. Of those employed for wages or salary outside the general labor market, jobs in the Iranian ethnic sub-economies were much more common than jobs in the Iranian ethnic economy. Ethnic economy employees reported three times as many Iranian co-religionists as employers than they did other Iranian owners, even though the other Iranians were always more numerous than the Iranian co-religionists. Similarly, employees of the Iranian ethnic economy reported twice as many Iranian co-religionists as co-workers than they did other Iranians as co-workers.

The Iranian ethnic economy had only a shadow existence. Occupation and industrial clustering distinguished the Iranian subgroups from one another almost as strongly as they distinguished Iranians from non-Iranians. Iranian workers were much more likely to find a job in a firm owned by an Iranian co-religionist than in a firm owned by other Iranians. Similarly, when selecting a partner or co-owner, Iranians chose Iranian co-religionists in preference to other Iranians or non-Iranian co-religionists. Given a choice between a non-Iranian co-religionist and an Iranian co-religionist, the immigrants selected the Iranian co-religionist. Given a choice between an Iranian immigrant and an Iranian co-religionist, they chose the co-religionist. The result was the formation of four ethnic economies with only a veneer of all-Iranian solidarity to weld them together. In effect, there were four Iranian sub-economies rather than one Iranian ethnic economy in Los Angeles.

The ethnic economy literature has been insensitive to internal ethnicity, a central issue in the theoretical literature on ethnicity. Yet, the ethnic economy is ethnic, and ethnic boundaries are always problematic. Ethnic boundaries structure ethnic economies. When it exists, internal ethnicity fragments an ethnic economy, leaving only shadow linkages to connect the separate segments.

We do not claim that, in overlooking internal ethnicity, all previous studies of the ethnic economy erred, although we have shown that internal ethnicity was an ignored and possibly influential factor in three important research efforts. Nonetheless, the case of Iranians certainly shows that mechanical and thoughtless application of the concept of 'ethnic economy' risks error if it overlooks internal ethnicity. Therefore, internal ethnicity ought to be considered in future research on the ethnic economy.

**Notes**

\* This paper is based on research supported by grant #SES-8512007 from the National Science Foundation. The authors acknowledge this support with thanks. However, the authors bear sole responsibility for errors of interpretation, fact, or method.

1 Self-employment is the core of an ethnic economy, and the self-employed usually earn more than wage and salary workers. Even if employees do not earn as much in the ethnic economy as they sometimes do in outside employment, they choose to work in an ethnic economy because whatever the mainstream economy offers them (possibly unemployment), they find less attractive. Additionally, the rewards of work are intrinsic as well as extrinsic,

so that a strictly pecuniary evaluation of comparative wages in the ethnic economy and outside does no justice to the subjective preferences of actors. Finally, non-economic values and attitudes affect peoples' choices of workplaces. Some workers prefer lower wages in a convenient and culturally comfortable workplace to higher wages in a mainstream factory or office.

2   The category Iranian also includes Christian Assyrians and Zoroastrians, whom we did not include in our survey because of their small numbers (Bozorgmehr and Sabagh, 1989).
3   A more detailed discussion of our survey methodology is given in Bozorgmehr and Sabagh (1989).
4   Calculated from Table 2 in Sabagh and Bozorgmehr (1987), this percentage is for Iranians who were non-students in 1980, and is comparable to the population included in our 1987-88 survey (Bozorgmehr and Sabagh, 1989).
5   Strictly speaking, the causes of this remarkable self-employment are not at issue in this paper. However, to assuage the inevitable curiosity, we note that most Iranians were well-endowed with class resources upon arrival in the United States. They had money, higher educational credentials, entrepreneurial working experience in Iran, knowledge of English, and previous experience in the United States (Bozorgmehr and Sabagh, 1988). These advantages certainly encouraged their entrepreneurship.
6   These indices are equal to the differences in percents between the groups.
7   This is equal to $(36 + 24 + 35 + 18)/4$.
8   In some cases, employees worked for multiple-owned firms whose owners might mix persons of diverse ethno-religious backgrounds. Therefore, we defined coethnicity in an employment relationship as reporting that 90% or more of the owners of one firm were coethnics.

**References**

Barth, F. (1969), *Ethnic Groups and Boundaries: The Social Organization of Cultural Difference*, Little, Brown: Boston.

Barton, J.J. (1975), *Peasants and Strangers*, Harvard University Press: Cambridge, MA.

Bonacich, E. and Modell, J. (1980), *The Economic Basis of Ethnic Solidarity*, University of California Press: Berkeley and Los Angeles, CA.

Bozorgmehr, M. (1992), Internal Ethnicity: Armenian, Baha'i, Jewish, and Muslim Iranians in Los Angeles, Doctoral Dissertation, University of California at Los Angeles: Los Angeles, CA.

Bozorgmehr, M. and Sabagh, G. (1988), 'High Status Immigrants: A Statistical Profile of Iranians in the United States', *Iranian Studies*, Vol. 21, pp. 5-36.

Bozorgmehr, M. (1989), 'Survey Research among Middle Eastern Immigrant Groups in the United States: Iranians in Los Angeles', *Middle East Studies Association Bulletin*, Vol. 23, pp. 23-34.

Cornell, S. (1988), 'The Transformations of Tribe: Organization and Self-Concept in Native American Ethnicities', *Ethnic and Racial Studies*, Vol. 11, pp. 27-47.

Der-Martirosian, C. (1989), Ethnicity and Ethnic Economy among Armenian Iranians in Los Angeles, Masters Thesis, University of California at Los Angeles: Los Angeles, CA.

Dinnerstein, L. and Reimers, D. (1975), *Ethnic Americans*, Bod and Mead: New York.

Espiritu, Y. (1989), 'Beyond the Boat People: Ethnicization in America', *Amerasia*, Vol. 15, pp. 49-67.

Hamilton, G.G. (1977), 'Ethnicity and Regionalism: Some Factors Influencing Chinese Identities in Southeast Asia', *Ethnicity*, Vol. 4, pp. 337-51.

Jones, A.K. (1984), 'Iranian Refugees: The Many Faces of Persecution', an Issue Paper, U.S. Committee for Refugees: Washington, DC.

Kim, K.C., Won, M.H. and Fernandez, M. (1989), 'Intra-Group Differences in Business Participation: Three Asian Immigrant Groups', *International Migration Review*, Vol. 23, pp. 73-95.

Koenig, S. (1943), 'Ethnic Factors in the Economic Life of 1943 Urban Connecticut', *American Sociological Review*, Vol. 8, pp. 193-7.

Lai, D. (1988), *Chinatowns*, University of British Columbia Press: Vancouver.

Light, I. (1972), *Ethnic Enterprise in America*, University of California Press: Berkeley and Los Angeles, CA.

Light, I. (1983), *Cities in World Perspective*, Macmillan: New York.

Light, I., Bhachu, P. and Karageorgis, S. (1993), 'Migration Networks and Immigrant Entrepreneurship', in Light, I. and Bhachu, P. (eds.), *Comparative Immigration and Entrepreneurship*, Transaction Press: New Brunswick, NJ, Ch. 2.

Light, I. and Bonacich, E. (1988), *Immigrant Entrepreneurs*, University of California Press: Berkeley and Los Angeles, CA.

Lyman, S.M. (1986), *Chinatown and Little Tokyo*, Associated Faculty

Press: Millwood NY.

Massey, D.S. and Denton, N.A. (1988), 'The Dimensions of Residential Segregation', *Social Forces*, Vol. 67, pp. 281-315.

Nahirny, V. and Fishman, J.A. (1965) 'American Immigrant Groups: Ethnic Identification and the Problems of Generations', *Sociological Review*, Vol. 13, pp. 311-26.

Portes, A. (1987), 'The Social Origins of the Cuban Enclave Economy in Miami', *Sociological Perspectives*, Vol. 30, pp. 340-72.

Portes, A. and Bach, R.L. (1985), *Latin Journey*, University of California Press: Berkeley and Los Angeles, CA.

Portes, A. and Jensen, L. (1989), 'The Enclave and the Entrants: Patterns of Ethnic Enterprise in Miami before and after Mariel', *American Sociological Review*, Vol. 54, pp. 929-49.

Portes, A. and Manning, R.D. (1986), 'The Immigrant Enclave: Theory and Empirical Examples', in Nagel, J. and Olzak, S. (eds.), *Competitive Ethnic Relations*, Academic Press: Orlando, FL, pp. 47-64.

Reitz, J.G. (1980), *The Survival of Ethnic Groups*, McGraw Hill: Toronto.

Sabagh, G. and Bozorgmehr, M. (1987), 'Are the Characteristics of Exiles Different from Immigrants? The Case of Iranians in Los Angeles', *Sociology and Social Research*, Vol. 71, pp. 77-84.

Sanders, J. and Nee, V. (1987), 'Limits of Ethnic Solidarity in the Enclave Economy', *American Sociological Review*, Vol. 52, pp. 745-73.

Sarna, J.D. (1978), 'From Immigrants to Ethnics: Towards a Theory of "Ethnicization" ', *Ethnicity*, Vol. 5, pp. 370-8.

Zhou, M. and Logan, J.R. (1989), 'Returns on Human Capital in Ethnic Enclaves: New York City's Chinatown', *American Sociological Review*, Vol. 54, pp. 809-20.

# 3 Issues in the absorption of older immigrants in employment

*Judah Matras*

Resumption of immigration to Israel in very large numbers, which also includes very substantial numbers and percentages of middle-aged and elderly immigrants, in a period of high unemployment and reductions in the work force by means of constrained or early retirement engenders a new confrontation with the problems of absorption in employment of the oldest immigrants. Past experience indicates that the problems of relatively older immigrants in obtaining employment are not only problems of their own and their families' economic absorption and material welfare in the years following their immigration to Israel; but, rather, involve as well the question of their status and situations in later life; their entitlements to income maintenance, health care, and welfare services; their abilities to enter or create family, community, and other social and support networks; and patterns of family and community as they enter old age.

Despite the centrality of the absorption of immigrants in sociology and the other social sciences in Israel, and despite the fact that the topic of migrant adjustment and assimilation in new personal and social settings is a classic sociological topic abroad as in Israel, the number of studies addressing problems of age differentiation in absorption, adjustment, and assimilation processes is small. To be sure there is some attention to the adjustment of children, on the one hand, and of elderly migrants, on the other, to new residential and social settings; however, such studies have frequently lacked firm empirical anchorage. In Israel, reference to the absorption of older immigrants has been primarily in the context of studies of the ageing and elderly. This is not surprising, since large proportions of the elderly Jewish population immigrated to Israel in old age or as middle-aged adults (see Wiehl, Nathan and Avner, 1970). In this paper, some findings of national census and survey data on absorption of older immigrants in employment in Israel in the recent past are reviewed, and some implications for absorption of the new wave of older immigrants in employment are considered.

## Labor force participation and employment

The early studies of immigrant absorption in Israel noted both the difficulties encountered by middle-aged and older immigrants in finding employment in Israel, and the tendencies of middle-aged and older immigrants to forego the hope of ever finding employment and to abandon its search. These difficulties and tendencies were noted in Israeli official statistics as early as the first national labor force surveys in the 1950s and in the first Israeli national census in 1961, and are documented in great detail by Avner (1970) through low rates of labor force participation among older immigrants. Avner observed high rates of unemployment among older immigrants in the early years of statehood. Some older immigrants may have found that adjustment to new work situations was too difficult at their age; others may have encountered age discrimination on the part of employers or been disqualified for employment because of a poor command of Hebrew language. Widespread tenure and job protection arrangements may have helped some new immigrants to prolong employment, but these may also have reduced the prospects of finding regular employment because of employers' reluctance to become entangled in various 'social payments' to workers who might retire after only a short period (Ibid., p. 157). Of the total male population of 65 and older in 1966, about one-fifth had never worked in Israel at all; and these comprised about one-third of the entire 'retired' population. More than one-third of those who immigrated at ages 50+ never worked in Israel at all (Ibid., Table VI/16). On the other hand, limitations on provisions for income maintenance for older immigrants forced many to remain in the labor force even beyond the normal retirement age, so that, altogether, rates of labor force participation of Jewish men 65+ have been higher than those of other Western countries. Labor force participation and employment of older immigrants to Israel from countries of Asia and Africa was much lower than that of immigrants of European origin; those who had been blue-collar workers abroad and those with relatively less education were much less likely to find employment (and subsequently to 'retire' without ever having been employed in Israel) than were men with secondary or higher education and men previously employed in clerical or managerial positions (Ibid.).

As mentioned above, many of the older persons arriving in the post-statehood waves of immigration from the USSR also had difficulties in finding or holding employment in Israel despite overall successes in the socio-economic absorption of the later immigration waves. Shuval, Marcus and Dotan (1975) reported that, of recent Russian immigrant Jews aged 55 or over when interviewed in 1971, only about 40% were fully-employed; and of the 60% not fully employed, almost half said that they had sought full employment without success, many for more than a year.

Special tabulations carried out by the Central Bureau of Statistics (1989a, Table 1) on data obtained in the 1983 Census of Population and Housing for Jewish immigrants from the USSR in the years 1970-83 are shown in Table 1. The data are classified for immigrants by period of arrival and by age at the time of immigration, and the row headings also show the approximate ages of the immigrants at the time of the 1983 Census. Thus, in the top panel, we note that of those men aged 18-19 at the time of immigration in 1970-74, more than 93% were employed in the 1983 Census, when they were aged between 29 and 42 years old (Column 1). By comparison, of those aged 45-54 who arrived in the same period and who were between 54-67 years old at the time of the 1983 Census, only about 82% were employed. Among immigrants of the same period who were aged 55-64 or 65+ at the time (about 64-77 or 74+, respectively, at the time of the 1983 Census) much smaller fractions were employed: less than one-third (32.8%) of those immigrating at ages 55-64, and less than one-tenth (9.8%) of those immigrating at ages 65 or over. Obviously persons in the latter two groups may have had employment in Israel and then retired, since almost all were already beyond the normal retirement age by the time of the 1983 Census.

But the pattern of low employment percentages among men immigrating at ages 55-64 or 65+ is repeated among those immigrating in the later periods of 1975-77, 1978-70, or 1980-83 (Column 1, Table 1). In all groups, those immigrating at ages 55-64 were much less likely to be employed at the time of the 1983 Census than were those immigrating at younger ages; and the percentages employed among those immigrating at ages 65+ were very low indeed.

The CBS *Survey on Absorption of Immigrants* is another source of data on employment of older immigrants in the 1970s (CBS, 1986, Table 10). This survey collected data on Eastern European immigrants of both sexes

## Table 1.

**Male Jewish immigrants aged 18+ from the USSR, 1970-83, by period of immigration and age at immigration: percent employed, percent with post-secondary schooling or academic degree, and percent not able to speak Hebrew in 1983 (as reported in the 1983** *Census of Population*)

| Age at Immi-gration | No. | Age in 1983 | 1983 Census Data Reports (%) | | |
|---|---|---|---|---|---|
| | | | (1) | (2) | (3) |
| **1970-74:** | 23,445 | | 77.8 | 22.8 | 28.6 |
| 18-29 | 7,390 | 29-42 | 93.1 | 25.2 | 5.7 |
| 30-44 | 7,465 | 39-57 | 92.6 | 27.0 | 18.2 |
| 45-54 | 4,205 | 54-67 | 82.2 | 20.1 | 44.7 |
| 55-64 | 2,490 | 74-77 | 32.8 | | |
| 65+ | 1,895 | 77+ | 9.8 | 12.9 | 69.8 |
| **1975-77:** | 6,265 | | 72.7 | 26.8 | 38.3 |
| 18-29 | 1,860 | 24-37 | 89.5 | 23.8 | 13.2 |
| 30-44 | 1,735 | 36-52 | 92.5 | 30.5 | 21.8 |
| 45-54 | 915 | 51-62 | 89.6 | 26.8 | 44.5 |
| 55-64 | 735 | 61-72 | 56.6 | | |
| 65+ | 1,000 | 73+ | 3.1 | 15.9 | 77.8 |
| **1978-79:** | 8,670 | | 69.1 | 25.1 | 43.0 |
| 18-29 | 2,340 | 22-34 | 80.6 | 19.0 | 17.8 |
| 30-44 | 2,685 | 34-49 | 93.7 | 34.6 | 26.5 |
| 45-54 | 1,080 | 49-59 | 82.4 | 30.0 | 51.2 |
| 55-64 | 1,135 | 59-69 | 52.8 | | |
| 65+ | 1,430 | 69+ | 7.1 | 18.2 | 79.2 |
| **1980-83:** | 3,535 | | 64.9 | 31.3 | 47.2 |
| 18-29 | 780 | 18-32 | 69.9 | 22.7 | 9.9 |
| 30-44 | 1,025 | 30-47 | 89.8 | 41.0 | 29.0 |
| 45-54 | 515 | 45-57 | 82.5 | 35.6 | 51.0 |
| 55-64 | 595 | 55-67 | 62.2 | | |
| 65+ | 620 | 65+ | 6.0 | 26.2 | 78.4 |

(1) % employed
(2) % with post-secondary schooling or academic degree
(2) % not able to speak Hebrew

*Source*: Israel Central Bureau of Statistics, 1989a. *Immigrants from the USSR 1970-1983.* Special Series No. 846. Jerusalem. Tables 1,3.

who arrived in the periods 1972/3 to 1974/5 and 1978/9 to 1979/80 (corresponding to the Hebrew years 5732-5735 and 5739-5740, respectively) that were recorded one year after immigration and again 3 years after immigration for all immigrants class'fied by age at entry to Israel (and in particular, for those aged 55-70 at the time of entry). In the findings of this survey, the percentages belonging to the labor force (employed or actively seeking employment) among the older immigrants are very much lower than those among the total, and decline from the first to the third years subsequent to immigration. Part of this decline is due to the fact that some of these older immigrants have experienced disabilities or loss or deterioration of health, while others have been able to retire from employment; but some part of this decline is probably due to discouragement over the inability to find satisfactory employment and termination of the search for employment. Among older immigrants in both periods, the unemployment rate (the percent not employed among those in the labor force) was much higher than those for the totals of all ages, and they *increased* from the first to the third years. By contrast, among younger immigrants the percentages not employed were much more moderate one year after arrival and, moreover, decreased dramatically by the third year.

An indicator of educational attainment, the percent of those who completed an academic degree in post-secondary schooling, is shown for each of the age-at-immigration groupings of Russian immigrant men in Column 2 of Table 1. In general, these percentages are very high; considerably higher than both those of previous immigrant groups and those of the resident population of Israel. Yet the data in the respective rows of Table 1 show that those who immigrated at ages 55 or over consistently included smaller percentages with higher education or academic degrees compared to the younger immigrants. Thus, in all the periods shown, the older immigrants were relatively disadvantaged from the point of view of the levels of their completed education. Moreover, the educational experience of older immigrants was typically considerably less recent than that of those immigrating at younger ages.

Compounding a relative academic disadvantage when compared to younger immigrants, those immigrating at older ages have consistently been much less successful in learning and using the Hebrew language. In the data shown in Column 3 of Table 1, it is clear that, regardless of period of immigration and length of time in Israel prior to the 1983 Census, those who immigrated at ages 55 or over lag considerably behind those who immigrated at younger ages, and very large percentages of the older men who immigrated even as much as 10-13 years prior to the

Census (e.g., almost 70% of those who immigrated at ages 55+ during the 1970-74 period) reported that they still did not speak Hebrew. Shuval, Marcus and Dotan (1975) noted that, among the Russian immigrants to Israel whom they studied, those immigrating at young ages made rapid progress in learning Hebrew, while those immigrating at ages 45-64 progressed much more slowly and those who immigrated at ages 65 or over progressed almost not at all.

Earlier in the paper, mention was made of the fact that there has been relatively little investigation of age differentiation in processes of socio-economic absorption of migrants generally, and of immigrants to Israel in particular. A partial qualification to this generalization is in the investigation of the acquisition and adoption of the Hebrew language. There has been extensive study and publication of national census and survey data on knowledge and use of Hebrew by immigrants, as well as of fluency in languages in the population generally. A consistent finding of these studies has pointed to the relatively low percentage of older immigrants who report successful acquisition and extensive use of Hebrew, even though younger immigrants are very successful indeed. The consistency of this finding, which also applies to middle-aged and older immigrants from the USSR who arrived with relatively high levels of educational attainment and past occupational skills, suggests that part of the effort to render them fluent enough in Hebrew to be able fully to perform socially and occupationally may be misplaced. In all cases, the possibilities of providing employment for older immigrants, or of helping older immigrants find employment, *not conditional* on their mastery of the Hebrew language must be explored more fully.

### Economic branches and occupations

That recent immigrants from Eastern Europe, and from the former USSR in particular, have included very high proportions of persons trained and previously employed abroad in scientific, academic, and professional occupations is fairly well known. This is borne out in the data from both of the sources noted above. Thus, for example, among male immigrants from the USSR of 1978-79 and 1980-83 who, in the 1983 Census, reported their occupations in 1978 (in the USSR, for the most part), some 37% of those immigrating in 1978-79 and 46% of those immigrating in 1980-83 reported having been employed either as 'scientific and academic' or as 'other professional, technical, and related' workers (CBS, 1989a, Table 1). Among Eastern European immigrants who arrived in 1972-75 and in

1978-80 and were studied one year and three years after arrival, 39% and 46%, respectively, reported having been previously employed abroad in scientific, academic, or professional occupations (CBS, 1986, Table 4). There were very few employed as service workers or in agricultural occupations. Less well known, however, is that the occupational composition of the immigrants abroad was quite dissimilar among the different age groups. Relatively fewer of those immigrating at older ages (i.e., smaller percentages) had previously been employed in scientific, academic, and professional occupations. On the other hand, relatively more of them had been employed in clerical and administrative, and in sales or commercial, occupations. The very oldest groups (those immigrating at ages 65+) also included substantial percentages previously employed abroad as unskilled workers. Thus, from the point of view of the status or level of occupational training and experience abroad, the older immigrants have been disadvantaged by comparison with those immigrating at younger ages.

The Israel CBS *Survey on Absorption of Immigrants* also showed the occupational distributions of Eastern European immigrants in Israel one year and three years after arrival in 1972-75 and in 1978-80, respectively (CBS, 1986). Altogether, the numbers of those employed increased somewhat from the first year after immigration to the third year. These immigrants were, in their first years in Israel as they had been abroad, very highly concentrated in scientific, academic, and professional occupations, with 29-33% reporting such employment. The percentages employed in the 'skilled and unskilled workers in industry, mining, building, and transport' occupational category are even higher, including almost half of those employed in the Israel in the first year after immigration. Between the first and third years, the percentages in this occupational category declined substantially, but they remain high compared both to those of the immigrants in other occupational categories and to the occupations in which the resident Jewish population is employed in Israel. Conversely, the percentages of immigrants employed in clerical, administrative, and managerial occupations are initially (after the first year) small, even though they increased substantially between the first and third years; and they remain low compared both to those of the immigrants in other occupational categories and to the occupations of the resident Jewish population. Older immigrants are much less highly concentrated in the scientific, academic, and professional categories, but have a relatively higher representation in clerical, administrative, and managerial occupations. The division of older workers among the skilled and unskilled workers in industry, mining, and building and the 'other' occupational categories differs greatly between those who immigrated in the early half of the 1970s and those arriving in the second half of the decade.

The CBS *Survey of Absorption of Immigrants* (1988) data indicate that the composition of employed immigrants by economic branches is consistent with the occupational distributions. There are concentrations in industry, mining, and manufacturing (which are generally high, but decline after the first year, though they remain high compared to the resident population) and in public and community service branches (which are lower than in the resident population, though they increase considerably between the first and third years). There is little employment in personal services branches, and only very moderate employment in sales, commerce and in business or financial service branches. As Ofer, Vinokur, and Bar-Haim (1980) have noted, the immigrants from the USSR in the 1970s represent an important positive economic increment in Israeli society in that, compared to the resident population, their rates of labor force participation have been high; the quality, training, and skill levels, and the human capital invested in their labor input, are high; and their employment has been relatively concentrated in industrial or 'production', rather than in service, branches of the economy. The pattern of absorption of older immigrant workers into the respective economic branches is not entirely consistent among subgroups for which data are available. However, there was evidently a greater tendency for the older immigrants to find employment in personal service, and in commerce, business, and finance branches of the economy, compared to younger immigrant workers.

Immigrant workers of all ages are almost all employees, with less than 3% reporting themselves self-employed. Workers immigrating to Israel at older ages are much more likely than younger immigrants to be employed part time. They are also more likely to express satisfaction with their employment, while younger workers are more likely to express dissatisfaction (bottom panel, Table 1). There do not appear to be systematic age-related differences in the degrees of satisfaction expressed concerning wages, nor in the extent of anxiety reported concerning the possibility dismissal. But Ofer, Vinokur, and Bar-Haim (1980) reported that, among respondents in the sample of USSR immigrants which they studied, older men (aged 55-64) were considerably more likely to report satisfaction with their jobs than were younger employees; but they were also much less likely than younger immigrant employees to report close relationships between their jobs in Israel and those they had in the USSR, and somewhat more likely than younger employees to report undergoing loss of occupational status in the transition from employment in the USSR to employment in Israel.

## Occupational mobility and change among immigrants

In an early study of employment of older immigrants in Israel, Avner (1970) reported that, among men who immigrated at 50 or more and were employed in Israel, only about half continued to work in the same occupational category in Israel in which they were employed abroad. Most of the others, and particularly those with low education, experienced downward occupational mobility, mainly in the direction of agriculture and services. Avner conjectured that an ability to change occupations was an important factor influencing the prospects of finding work after immigration. On the other hand, it is possible that the decision to retire (for those who worked in Israel) was also influenced by the experience of downward mobility, which Avner found more frequent among those elderly retirees who had at some time been employed in Israel than among those still employed (Ibid., pp. 187-9). In a somewhat later study, Sabatello (1979) also found that three years after arrival in Israel just slightly over half of the immigrant men in the labor force were employed in the same occupational categories as they had been in their countries of origin prior to immigration; but older employed immigrants (55+) were considerably more likely than younger ones (30-54) to have changed occupations.

Data from the 1983 Census of Population on occupational change during the five-year period preceding the census confirm that similar mobility has occurred among those immigrating to Israel in 1978-83 (CBS, 1989b, Tables 18, 19). Of male immigrants who were employed abroad in 1978 and were employed in Israel at the time of the census in 1983, about 59% *changed* occupations. Just under half of these changes (45% of those changing occupations) represented major changes of occupational categories (e.g. from clerical to skilled manual occupations), or from professional to sales occupations, etc. In general, the lower the educational attainment of the immigrants, the more frequent were the changes of occupation connected with immigration to Israel, but changes of occupation were also very common among those with secondary and higher educational attainment: of immigrant men with 0-8 years of schooling, about 79% changed occupations in the transition, compared to 68% of those with 9-12 years of schooling, and 40% with 13 or more school years completed (Ibid., Table 18, middle panel).

Relatively high proportions of both men and women who had been scientific and academic employees abroad were able to find employment in the same occupations in Israel (78% of the men and 65% of the women). Among women, but much less so among the men, who had been employed in other professional or in technical occupations abroad, relatively high proportions found employment in similar occupations in Israel (65% of the women, but only 54% of the men). Among men, but much less so among women, who had previously been employed in skilled manual occupations in industry, transport, or construction, a large percentage (69% of the men, compared to only 53% of the women) found employment in similar occupations in Israel. Among immigrant workers previously employed abroad in *any* of the other occupational categories, the proportions obtaining employment in the same occupations in Israel were substantially smaller, and the frequencies and percentages of change of occupation in Israel were much higher (Ibid., Table 19).

Of special interest to us in the present context is the finding, from the 1983 census data cited, that, among immigrants previously employed abroad and who were employed also in Israel, change of occupation was most frequent among the oldest immigrants (those 65 and over and reporting employment in 1983) and substantially more frequent among those aged 55-64 or 45-54 than among workers in the 35-44 age group. More than two-thirds (67%) of the immigrants aged 65+ reporting employment and more than 60% of those in the 55-64 and 45-54 age groups were in occupations different from those in which they were employed abroad, compared to just under 52% among those aged 35-44 who reported occupational change (Table 2). Moreover, among those changing occupations, the older workers were much more likely to have experienced changes in major occupational categories rather than simply moving among the subcategories of the same major occupational group (CBS, 1989b, Table 18). Thus, in 1983, among employed male immigrants from the USSR who had immigrated during the period 1980-83 at ages 55 or over, about 26% were employed as scientific, academic, or other professional workers in Israel, compared to 42% who had been employed in these occupations abroad; about 34% were employed as industrial workers in Israel, compared to only 29% who had been employed in such occupations abroad; and 25% were employed in 'other occupations' in Israel, including personal service, sales, banking, and finance, compared to just under 16% employed in such occupations in the USSR. Among employed female immigrants from the USSR who had immigrated during the period 1980-83 at ages 55 and over, the change in occupational composition was even more dramatic. While more than 53% had been employed in scientific, academic, or other professional occupations abroad, in Israel in 1983 the percentage of women in the same occupational groups was only 33%. In Israel in 1983, about 28% were employed in clerical or administrative occupations, compared to just under 17% employed in such occupations abroad five years earlier; and 31% were employed in Israel as industrial workers, compared to only 14% in such occupations previously (Ibid., Table 1).

Table 2.
Jews 25+ who immigrated in 1978-83 and were employed in Israel in 1983, by sex and age groups: percent changing occupations in Israel

| Age | Both Sexes | Men | Women |
| --- | --- | --- | --- |
| Total Sample | 57.5 | 58.8 | 55.5 |
| 25-34 | 58.9 | 62.1 | 55.2 |
| 35-44 | 52.2 | 51.6 | 53.1 |
| 45-54 | 59.6 | 60.3 | 58.6 |
| 55-64 | 60.9 | 62.1 | 58.5 |
| 65+ | 67.2 | 67.2 | 66.7 |

The social scientific literature on job mobility and occupational change has consistently shown a negative relationship between age and mobility. Data from the Israel 1983 Census point to a similar relationship in Israel, except that elderly Jewish men (65+) change jobs frequently in order to continue in employment beyond retirement age (e.g., move to different part-time jobs), and accordingly report somewhat higher rates of job mobility than do the middle-aged (45-54 or 55-64) (CBS, 1989b, Table 8). But, aside from this deviation, job mobility and occupational change are typically much more frequent among younger persons — and especially among unmarried younger persons — than among middle-aged or older workers. The conjecture of Avner, noted earlier, that the ability to change occupations, even at older ages, is an important factor influencing the prospects of finding work after immigration, seems to be borne out in subsequent data for immigrants to Israel generally and for those from the USSR in particular. The deviation this implies from the more familiar age-related patterns of change and mobility highlights the importance of intervention and measures to ease or facilitate moves, changes, and accommodations among older persons wishing to continue or renew employment in a social, economic, and political setting and environment so different from those of their lifelong employment histories.

## Occupations of recent immigrants from the former USSR

The dramatic pace and magnitude of recent Jewish emigration from the former USSR to Israel is matched by the astonishing proportions of both men and women who had been employed abroad and the even more astonishing concentration of immigrants in scientific, academic, and professional occupations abroad. The occupational distribution abroad of immigrants from the former USSR in the first nine months of the year 1990 is shown in Table 3. The data are based upon the reports of the immigrants on arrival.

Of the total of some 28,500 male immigrants aged 19-65 who arrived during the period 1 January through 30 September 1990, all but 8% reported previous employment in the former USSR. About 68% reported previous employment in scientific, academic, or other professional or technical occupations. The largest group (about 11,500, or 44%) were employed in the scientific and academic occupations category, including large numbers of engineers (about 8,000), many physicians (about 1,400), and mathematicians, economists, and teachers and researchers in the exact sciences and humanities. The next largest group (about 7,400, or 28%) were employed in the other professional and technical occupations category, including large numbers of engineering and general technicians (over 4,000), teachers, computer programmers, musicians, and artists and photographers.

### Table 3.
### Jewish Immigrants aged 19-65 arriving in Israel from the USSR, 1 January 90 to 30 September 90, by sex, age group, and major occupation group abroad

|  | Total | BY AGE GROUP | | | | |
|---|---|---|---|---|---|---|
|  |  | 19-24 | 25-34 | 35-44 | 45-64 | 65+ |
| *MALES* | | | | | | |
| Total | 28,542 | 2,863 | 8,183 | 9,418 | 7,614 | 464 |
| Not Employed | 2,275 | 1,227 | 125 | 40 | 521 | 362 |

Table 3 (cont'd)

|  | Total | BY AGE GROUP | | | | |
|---|---|---|---|---|---|---|
|  |  | 19-24 | 25-34 | 35-44 | 45-64 | 65+ |
| **EMPLOYED ABROAD** | | | | | | |
| Total | 26,267 | 1,636 | 8,050 | 9,378 | 7,093 | 102 |
| *Occupation Group* | | | | | | |
| 0  Scientific, Academic | 11,554 | 218 | 3,625 | 4,486 | 3,187 | 38 |
| 1  Other Professions, Technical | 7,390 | 755 | 2,285 | 2,581 | 1,741 | 28 |
| 2  Managers, Administrators | 83 | 4 | 16 | 32 | 30 | 1 |
| 3  Clerical | 134 | 7 | 32 | 40 | 53 | 2 |
| 4  Sales | 358 | 16 | 97 | 101 | 139 | 5 |
| 5  Service | 510 | 80 | 164 | 151 | 115 | -- |
| 6  Agricultural | 25 | 4 | 2 | 6 | 13 | -- |
| 7  Skilled, Semi-skilled | 2,385 | 215 | 618 | 810 | 735 | 7 |
| 8  Manual | 3,108 | 278 | 1,058 | 946 | 813 | 13 |
| 9  Unskilled Manual | 720 | 59 | 161 | 225 | 267 | 8 |
| *Percent Distributions* | | | | | | |
| Total | 100.0 | 100.0 | 100.0 | 100.0 | 100.0 | 100.0 |
| Scientific, Academic | 44.0 | 13.3 | 45.0 | 47.8 | 44.9 | 37.2 |
| Other Professions, Technical | 28.1 | 46.2 | 28.3 | 27.5 | 24.5 | 27.4 |
| Managerial, Admin, Clerical | 0.8 | 0.6 | 0.6 | 0.8 | 1.2 | 3.0 |
| Sales, Service, Agricultural | 3.4 | 6.1 | 3.3 | 2.8 | 3.8 | 5.0 |
| Skilled, Semi-Skilled, Manual | 21.0 | 30.2 | 20.8 | 18.7 | 21.8 | 19.6 |
| Unskilled Manual | 2.7 | 3.6 | 2.0 | 2.4 | 3.8 | 7.8 |

Table 3 (cont'd)

| | | | BY AGE GROUP | | | |
|---|---|---|---|---|---|---|
| | Total | 19-24 | 25-34 | 35-44 | 45-64 | 65+ |
| **FEMALES** | | | | | | |
| Total | 28,879 | 3,432 | 9,220 | 9,405 | 6,822 | |
| Not Employed | 2,129 | 1,120 | 196 | 126 | 687 | |
| **EMPLOYED ABROAD** | | | | | | |
| Total | 26,750 | 2,312 | 9,024 | 9,279 | 6,135 | |
| *Occupation Group* | | | | | | |
| 0  Scientific, Academic | 10,556 | 414 | 3,669 | 3,953 | 2,520 | |
| 1  Other Professions, Technical | 10,682 | 1,251 | 3,537 | 3,705 | 2,189 | |
| 2  Managers, Administrators | 84 | 8 | 30 | 25 | 21 | |
| 3  Clerical | 1,839 | 158 | 566 | 582 | 533 | |
| 4  Sales | 780 | 63 | 254 | 230 | 233 | |
| 5  Service | 1,483 | 255 | 562 | 457 | 209 | |
| 6  Agricultural | 17 | 2 | 10 | 2 | 3 | |
| 7  Skilled, Semi-skilled | 116 | 20 | 38 | 26 | 32 | |
| 8  Manual | 817 | 114 | 280 | 184 | 239 | |
| 9  Unskilled Manual | 376 | 27 | 78 | 115 | 156 | |
| *Percent Distributions* | | | | | | |
| Total | 100.0 | 100.0 | 100.0 | 100.0 | 100.0 | |
| Scientific, Academic | 39.4 | 17.9 | 40.7 | 42.6 | 41.2 | |
| Other Professions, Technical | 39.9 | 54.1 | 39.2 | 39.9 | 35.8 | |
| Managerial, Admin., Clerical | 7.2 | 7.2 | 6.6 | 6.5 | 9.1 | |
| Sales, Service, Agricultural | 8.5 | 13.8 | 9.1 | 7.4 | 7.3 | |

Table 3 (cont'd)

|  | Total | BY AGE GROUP | | | | |
|---|---|---|---|---|---|---|
|  |  | 19-24 | 25-34 | 35-44 | 45-64 | 65+ |
| Skilled, Semi-Skilled, Manual | 3.5 | 5.8 | 3.5 | 2.3 | 4.1 |  |
| Unskilled Manual | 1.4 | 1.2 | 0.9 | 1.2 | 2.5 |  |

Source: Ministry of Absorption/Jewish Agency Data Bank

About 21% of the immigrant men (about 5,500) previously employed reported skilled and semi-skilled manual occupations in industry and service branches, including drivers (about 1,300), workers in building and construction industries, machinists, shoemakers, carpenters and woodworkers, mechanics, electricians, and tailors. Relatively few of the men had been employed in unskilled manual occupations or sales or service occupations, and even fewer in managerial, clerical, or agricultural jobs. About half of those not previously employed were students, primarily in the 19-24 age group, and most of the rest reported themselves as 'pensioners'.

An important feature of the data of Table 3 for the male immigrants is the relative absence of sharp age differentiation. Those of the youngest age group (19-24) who reported employment were considerably less likely to report scientific and academic occupations and considerably more likely to report skilled and semi-skilled manual occupations than were older men; but a large fraction of the men in this age group were still students when they emigrated. The number of men aged 65 years who reported employment is small, and the 45-64 age group is probably too broad a category to allow assessment of any special features of the occupational histories of middle-aged and older workers. But, for the most part, they are also very highly concentrated in the scientific, academic, and professional occupations.

All but 7% of the 29,000 female immigrants aged 19-64 and arriving in the first nine months of 1990 reported previous employment in the USSR. The women immigrants had been, if anything, even more concentrated (no less than 79%!!) in scientific, academic, and professional employment than the men, though not necessarily in the same occupations. In the bottom part of Table 3, we note that about 39% (representing about 10,600 immigrant women) had been employed in jobs in the scientific and academic category and almost 40% (some 10,700 women) in the other professional and technical occupations category. The former category includes about 5,000 engineers, some 1,800 physicians and dentists, and 1,400 economists as well as chemists, biologists, mathematicians, physicists, and lawyers. The latter category includes some 3,000 teachers, 2,500 technicians, 2,000 nurses, and over 1,500 musicians and performing and applied artists, and many computer programmers, writers, and accountants.

In contrast to the men, very few of the women had been employed in skilled or semi-skilled manual occupations (including the more than 600 women previously employed in the needle trades). Relatively more had been in clerical occupations, in service occupations, or in sales occupations. There are more than 1,100 bookkeepers, a large number who were employed as secretaries or clerks, about 1,300 hairdressers or cosmeticians, and many (over 700) salespersons and agents among the women immigrants. The majority of the women not previously employed had been students, mostly in the 19-24 age group; but a number reported themselves as housewives, and these were mostly women in the 45-64 age group.

Age differentiation in the occupational distributions among the women immigrants, as among the men, reflects primarily the fact that a large proportion of those in the 19-24 age group were still students at the time of emigration. Thus, in this age group, the percentage in the scientific and academic occupations is strikingly lower than in all other age groups, while the percentages in all the other occupational groups are notably higher. Among women age 45-64, the percent reporting not having been employed is high compared to those in the (post-student) 25-44 age groups; and among those who had been employed, there are about the same percent reporting scientific and academic occupations, somewhat fewer reporting other professional and technical occupations and somewhat more reporting occupations in all the other white collar and in the manual occupational groups. As in the case of the men, the breadth of the age groupings does not yet permit us to consider the special characteristics of the middle-aged or older women workers.

**Concluding remarks**

Even in the past period of relatively easy and successful absorption in employment of the immigrants from the USSR in the 1970s and early 1980s, older immigrants were relatively disadvantaged. As a result, their rates of labor force participation were relatively lower, and the percentages of those changing occupations and the percentages in part-time employment were both higher. At the present time, the situation of older immigrants willing and able to work in the formal sector is likely to be even more problematic because of the number of unemployed generally in the labor force, because of the anticipated rise in the number of new immigrants among the unemployed, and because of the sharp competition expected for each job opening, both from other new immigrants — mostly younger and with more attributes that are attractive to employers — and from veteran resident job-seekers, for the most part Hebrew-speakers and knowledgeable and experienced in the Israeli labor market.

On the basis of past experience, we may surmise that a large part of the employment of the oldest immigrants in the near future will entail shifts from the occupations in which they were employed abroad to other occupations in Israel; and unlike the case of the occupational shifts of younger persons in occupations and employment in the industrial and production branches of the economy, probably many of the occupational changes of the older workers will be in the direction of commerce and services. Obviously it is important that government and public bodies find or create information and mediation services, as well as retraining opportunities, that can encourage such shifts and ease the difficulties of both employees and employers. But this is not likely to suffice to absorb the large number of middle-aged and older immigrants who wish and need to be absorbed in employment both because of their immediate economic needs and because they must build and fortify their status and entitlements as elderly and pensioners in the not-very-distant future.

Just as it did not happen in the past, it would appear that there is no chance in the near future that, in a climate of rationalization, reductions in work force, and international competition, the private and profit-making sectors of the Israeli economy will be able to employ and absorb the large number of older immigrants; and they are certainly not likely to prefer them to the younger workers competing for the same jobs. In the absence of employment for older immigrants, it will be necessary to keep in place — and perhaps continue indefinitely — the schemes and arrangements for income maintenance, essential services, and basic welfare which they receive as new immigrants, or else to replace these with alternative arrangements, even though these immigrants represent a potential work and productive force with extensive and high-level experience and the willingness and ability both to support themselves and to bring positive contributions to the economy and society. Thus, society has a key interest, and also a potential economic payoff, in creating employment — including, possibly, in the public sector — that would also give jobs to the oldest workers among the new immigrants.

Created or subsidized employment, including employment in community, health, educational, and cultural services, which, presumably, would not be generated or economically viable under 'pure market conditions', would contribute not only as a substitute for transfers and various income maintenance schemes, but also to expansion and deepening of the human, educational, and cultural infrastructure of all the regions of the State and of all the strata of the society. In all those towns and settlements, and in those quarters and neighborhoods of the largest cities, in which community services are presently very thin, superficial, and undeveloped, there is both a need and now an opportunity to expand and enhance them by means of this 'new' source of manpower. Clearly the development of plans and procedures for the retraining or preparation of the workers themselves will require time and resources. But, the potential of such plans and procedures should be viewed as exceeding by far any immediate benefits. Examples of job creation and protected employment in Israel in the 1950s and 1960s might be used as starting points. It would also be useful to study the proposals, plans, and experiences of other societies in terms of full employment policies, preparation and implementation of job creation for different strata and levels of employees and in the different economic sectors, and development and equalization of public services in a modern welfare state.

## References

Avner, U. (1970), 'Work and Retirement', in Wiehl, H., Nathan, T. and Avner, U. (eds.), *Investigation of the Family Life Living Conditions and Needs of the Non-institutionalized Urban Jewish Aged 65+ in Israel. Part 2*, Ministry of Social Welfare: Jerusalem, Chapter 6.

CBS (1986), *Survey of Immigrant Absorption: Immigrants of the Seventies, the First Three Years in Israel. Immigrants of 1972/73 — 1974/75 and 1978/79 — 1979/80*, Special Publications Series No. 771, Israel Central Bureau of Statistics: Jerusalem.

CBS (1989a), *Immigrants from the USSR, 1970-1983*, Special Publications Series No. 846, Israel Central Bureau of Statistics: Jerusalem.

CBS (1989b), *Labour Mobility. Data from the Sample Enumeration. 1983 Census of Population and Housing Publications No. 23*, Israel Central Bureau of Statistics: Jerusalem.

Ofer, G., Vinokur, A. and Bar-Haim, Y. (1980), *Economic Absorption and*

*Contribution of Immigrants from the USSR in Israel*, Maurice Falk Institute of Economic Research in Israel: Jerusalem. [Hebrew]

Sabatello, E.F. (1979), 'Patterns of Occupational Mobility Among New Immigrants to Israel', presented to ISA Research Committee on Social Stratification, Jerusalem 1976.

Shuval, J.I., Marcus, E.J. and Dotan, J. (1975), 'Age Patterns in the Integration of Soviet Immigrants in Israel', *Jewish Journal of Sociology*, Vol. 17, p. 2.

Wiehl, H., Nathan, T. and Avner, U. (eds.) (1970), *Investigation of the Family life, Living Conditions, and Needs of the Non-Institutionalized Urban Jewish Aged 65+ in Israel*, Final Report, Parts 1 & 2, Ministry of Social Welfare: Jerusalem.

# 4 Social networks, local opportunities and entrepreneurship among immigrants in Israel

*Eran Razin*

The study of entrepreneurship in general, and entrepreneurship as a path of economic absorption of immigrants in particular, has long been neglected in Israel, with few, exploratory exceptions (Ben-Porath, 1986; Nahon, 1989; Yaar, 1986). However, since 1989, the urgent need to accommodate and absorb the new immigration wave from the former USSR, in the face of economic stagnation and limited public resources, aroused interest in entrepreneurship as a path to absorption. The aim of this paper is to evaluate past experiences on immigrant entrepreneurship in Israel, in light of international experience, and the new needs and expectations in Israel. It is based on an extensive study of location and entrepreneurial activity of ethnic groups in Israel, parts of which have been published elsewhere (Razin, 1989; 1990a,b).

**Shifting attitudes toward entrepreneurship in Israel —
From evil to blessing**

The resurgence of the small-business economy in many Western countries since the 1970s (Storey, 1988; Brock and Evans, 1989) did not appear in Israel until more than a decade later. Because of a socialist bias, which has been characterized by deep antagonism, and even hostility, toward the self-employed sector, the Israeli political-economic system has not been very receptive to small entrepreneurs. Small-business owners were perceived as unproductive middlemen who lived by exploiting the industrial and agricultural workers. Calls for public policies concerning the small-business sector have frequently focused a perceived need to reduce suspected tax-evasion by the self-employed, which might give them an unjust advantage over salaried employees. Hence, the potential and actual role of self-employment in the process of absorption of immigrants has hardly received any attention. The drive to self-employment in Israel was also delayed by the lack of large-scale unemployment until the mid-1980s.

Greenwood (1990) emphasized the unfavorable climate for entrepreneurship which has made Israel one of the few non-Communist countries where Jews do not gravitate to small business. Among the 'nightmares' experienced by Israeli small businesses, one can include the severe consequences of military reserve service on sole proprietors, inferior treatment by welfare state mechanisms, the government's dominant role in the capital markets, which dried up most traditional sources of financing for small businesses, difficult access to vital information on procedures required for establishing a business, and all the other bureaucratic evils that discriminate against small businesses in favor of large private and public corporations and non-profit organizations.

In recent years, a gradual change in attitude in favor of the small business sector has occurred in Israel. This change was provoked in part by a political-ideological shift. The right-wing Likud Party, which assumed power in 1977, was at least officially more committed to free-enterprise ideology than the Labor Party, which had led Zionist and Israeli politics until then. Pressures originating from infiltration of 'new right' ideologies from Britain and the United States were perhaps of even greater impact. The change was also a consequence of the new economic realities of stagnation and crisis in many of Israel's largest industrial corporations and public organizations during the late 1980s, as well as of rising unemployment and increasing pressures on the government's budget.

The diffusion of planning perceptions and practices from Western countries had an additional role in inducing a change in attitudes toward entrepreneurship. Advocates of small-business-oriented policies in Israel (Avraham, 1985; Razin, 1988b; Greenwood, 1990) have been guided by the revival of interest in the role of small firms in job-creation and economic development in European and North American planning literature (Birch, 1987; Giaoutzi, Nijkamp and Storey, 1988; Piore and Sabel, 1984; Storper and Scott, 1989). Calls for emphasizing small-business formation, while grounded in recent professional literature and experience of Western countries, have roots in two very different ideologies, however. Many advocates viewed the promotion of the small-business economy in the context of conservative free-market ideology. Thus, promoting entrepreneurship has been perceived as part of a wider action to enhance competition, reduce bureaucratic red-tape, and remove rigidities in the labor market by cutting down the strength of labor unions. Others have advocated entrepreneurship, from a belief in a liberal-socialist ideology of 'development from below' (Stohr, 1981), and have stressed the need for greater control of local communities over their economic fate, and the reduction of their dependence on externally-controlled firms and externally-operated development policies. Hence, promoting entrepreneurship has been considered a means of reducing inter-regional and interethnic inequalities, as well as a tool to enhance the efficiency of market mechanisms.

Consolidation of positive attitudes toward entrepreneurship has been slow. Small-business development was disregarded for a long time by Israeli policy-makers, since it did not offer highly visible and quick influence on local economies. A few pioneering efforts were implemented during the 1980s, most notably a technological incubator project initiated in the Galilee by a private industrialist with government support (Arner, 1989), and loan funds for small businesses initiated in two development towns by the Jewish Agency's Project Renewal (Klausner and Shamir-Shinan, 1988). Only shrinking opportunities in alternative strategies for economic development (Razin, 1990c) and the immense pressures created by the new wave of mass immigration have prompted policy-makers to grasp any opportunity for job creation which does not place a heavy burden on the public budget. Hence, by 1991, numerous loan funds and incubator projects, aimed at assisting various types of entrepreneurs, have been in various phases of formation.

This new action raises two questions: *what is the effectiveness of public measures in promoting entrepreneurship; and, what is the specific entrepreneurial potential among immigrants in Israel?* As to the first question, entrepreneurial development policies, dealing with access to capital, management skills, information on supplier and buyer markets and the political climate facing small firms, can be cost effective in generating jobs within the confines of their limited resources. However, these policy tools cannot influence those fundamental characteristics of a community that promote entrepreneurship, such as the presence of an entrepreneurial culture and information networks. Such policies mainly have a significant effect where entrepreneurship is already rooted (Mokrey, 1988). To answer the second question, specific immigrant communities, as well as Israel's absorbing environment, must be examined in light of the international experience. Assessing the myth of entrepreneurial immigrant groups in the United States may serve as a starting point in such an analysis.

*Issues in the study of entrepreneurship among immigrants*

The extensive literature on immigrant entrepreneurs deals largely with the issue of why certain immigrant groups utilize the entrepreneurial mobility route more than others (Light, 1972; Bonacich and Modell, 1980; Portes and Bach, 1985; Fratoe, 1986; Waldinger, Aldrich and Ward, 1990). Some authors have stressed cultural factors or a perceived status of sojourners, whereas others have emphasized availability of human and financial resources. Discrimination, language difficulties, and lack of local contacts have been considered disadvantages that hamper the ability to penetrate well-paying, salaried jobs and drive able immigrants into entrepreneurship. A tradition of enterprise has also been considered as playing a major role among certain groups, such as Jews and Chinese; however, the experience of Koreans in the United States, who have tended to come from non-entrepreneurial middle-class backgrounds, suggests that such a tradition is not necessarily a precondition. In the case of the Koreans, a combination of obstacles to advancement as salaried employees, and high levels of human capital, which could not be satisfied by unskilled, low-paid jobs, have led to their inclination toward self-employment. High educational levels assisted in the acquisition of formal aspects of management skills through courses offered by various Korean voluntary associations (Light and Bonacich, 1988). Ethnic solidarity and extensive informal ethnic entrepreneurial networks, channeling new immigrants to small-business niches formed by earlier arrivals, also appear to have been crucial elements in the development of a thriving ethnic sub-economy.

Examination of the differing inclination of immigrant groups into entrepreneurship has led to a second question: is entrepreneurship among immigrants always a glamorous path for economic advancement, or can it frequently be only a no-choice, dead-end alternative based on self-exploitation? For professionals and industrialists, it is certainly an alternative for advancement, but is it always so for peddlers, or for grocery store owners in depressed areas? Most of the North American literature emphasizes the positive role of even the most petty enterprise as a first step leading to subsequent mobility of the business owner, his children, and grandchildren. Nevertheless, the risk involved in self-employment, the unpublicized fate of many losers, as well as negative implications for health, psychological well-being, and family life have also been documented (Light and Bonacich, 1988). Moreover, the British literature has been more pessimistic about the ability of petty enterprise to lead immigrants to bright futures (Ladbury, 1984; Werbner, 1984; Jones, McEvoy and Paulson-Box, 1990).

The next issue of interest is the impact of immigrant entrepreneurs on host economies. Do immigrant entrepreneurs boost local economic development, or do they merely serve their own communities, fill existing niches, or even displace locals? Immigrants creating a new local economic niche, as well as those investing large sums brought from abroad, obviously create jobs and contribute to local economic growth. Those who seem to fill existing niches, particularly retailers, may displace others, but they may also revitalize declining areas, as well as free local labor and resources for other sectors of the economy. Negative implications of immigrant entrepreneurs on host economies include the expansion of gray and illegal elements in the economy, as well as the creation of competition with the weaker elements of society. My aggregate studies, made in California, Canada, and Israel, suggest that the large mass of immigrant entrepreneurs fill existing niches in the local economy. Thus, the existence of large non-entrepreneurial groups, such as blacks and Latin Americans in American metropolitan areas, opens more opportunities for entrepreneurial immigrant groups to reach extraordinarily high rates of self-employment (Razin, 1988a; 1990b). Such aggregate analysis, however, is not sensitive enough to identify the contribution of immigrant entrepreneurs who create new niches in the economy. It is a small number of entrepreneurs who can have the greater impact on the economy.

Another issue concerns the influence of location, particularly local opportunities and localized supportive networks, on entrepreneurship among immigrants. The tendency of immigrant entrepreneurs to serve as middleman minorities has been emphasized in sociological studies. Additional opportunities created by local economies, local socio-ethnic composition, and localized networks can be of importance in channeling immigrant entrepreneurs into specific niches.

*Ethnicity and entrepreneurship in Israel — Major issues*

Entrepreneurship in Israel has played a different role in the mobility routes of immigrants of various countries of origin. The major socio-ethnic divide in Israeli society between Jews of Eastern (Middle Eastern and North African) and Western (European and American) origins has been most distinctive — a distinction that also appears in entrepreneurial behavior (Nahon, 1989). As a working hypothesis, it was assumed that immigrants of European countries of origin would have had a greater propensity to utilize self-employment as a gateway to the Israeli labor market. As a group, they have enjoyed better qualifications, as well as a tradition of petty enterprise brought from Europe, and closer ethnic and cultural familiarity with the pre-1948 mainstream Jewish population. In Israel, they joined an ethnic group that was both politically and economically dominant, and the offspring of the European immigrants, therefore, would have been expected to exit petty entrepreneurial occupations and enter white-collar salaried jobs or larger businesses and those requiring white-collar professional qualifications.

Immigrants of Middle Eastern and North African origins, on the other hand, were disadvantaged in their new host society, lacking the 'right' contacts and familiarity with the dominant culture. Arriving as part of a large, penniless mass to a country with a centralist political system influenced by socialist ideology, these immigrants did not find a favorable climate for starting their lives in the new country as small scale entrepreneurs in an informal sector/marginal economy. Their dependence on the government for housing and basic services also discouraged and reduced the ability of these immigrants to take an independent path of economic advancement. Only subsequent generations, who grew up in Israel and had become familiar with Israeli realities, could be expected to gravitate to self-employment as a route to overcome obstacles created by their inferior levels of formal education.

I contend, then, that entrepreneurs of Eastern and Western origins differ in their personal attributes (human capital and personal resources), socio-ethnic networks, and local opportunities to support their business ventures. Those of Western origin enjoyed higher levels of human capital, consisting of formal education, professional skills and relevant experience, as well as superior personal resources. Eastern origin Jews, on the other hand, had to compensate for their relative inferiority by relying more on socio-ethnic supportive networks. It has been documented that such networks may in fact be more selective, instrumental, and effective among Western origin groups (Maman, 1991). Eastern origin immigrants, particularly Moroccans, have been disadvantaged also in terms of availability of local opportunities due to their relative dispersion to non-metropolitan development towns, which offer small and undiversified local markets. Their dispersal might also be expected to hamper the evolution of supportive entrepreneurial networks, and limit them mainly to immediate kinship ties. This role of location deserves, therefore, close examination, since it is a major factor that can be directly influenced by public policy.

It can also be argued that wide variations in entrepreneurial behavior exist within the two broad groups of Eastern and Western origin immigrants. These variations have become particularly evident among the Eastern origin groups, which occupy both extremes of the most and the least entrepreneurial groups in Israel (Razin, 1992). One reason for these differences are that the Eastern origin Jews have retained their ethnic identities and ethnic-based networks to a larger extent than have those groups originating from Western countries.

## Methodology

The analysis consists of two parts. The first examines the experience of those who immigrated to Israel from ten major countries: Iraq, Yemen, Iran, Turkey, Morocco, Poland, Romania, Bulgaria, Greece, and Czechoslovakia. For each country of origin, three age cohorts were analyzed: those born abroad between 1918 and 1927 who immigrated to Israel between 1948 and 1954; those born abroad between 1933 and 1942 who immigrated between 1948 and 1954; and, those born in Israel during the period 1948-1954 whose father was born in one of the countries specified above. The first two cohorts distinguish those arriving as adults, probably with prior working experience, from those coming as children who first began working in Israel. The third cohort includes the first Israeli-born generation who began entering the labor market during the 1970s. These were either children of immigrants arriving during the 1948-1954 years of mass-immigration, or of immigrants who arrived earlier. These definitions gave 27 specific cohorts, whose changing role in the labor market was examined in the population censuses of 1961, 1972, and 1983.

The second part of the analysis examines business formation in blue-collar and distribution activities, which are frequently utilized as an upward mobility route by immigrants lacking qualifications and contacts to advance as employees. This part is based on a survey conducted by the author in 1989-1990 of 421 small-businesses in one city within the Tel-Aviv metropolis (Holon) and four non-metropolitan towns of varying sizes and distances from metropolitan areas (Yavne, Ashqelon, Ofaqim, and Kiryat Shemona). Whereas the census data analysis is mainly intended to identify the differing role of self-employment in the economic mobility routes of immigrants of various origins, the survey enables identification of the roles of various determinants of business formation among the different origin groups. The analysis refers to countries of origin and years of entry into Israel as far as the size of sample permits. The role of location has been discussed in greater detail elsewhere

(Razin, 1992); nevertheless, implications of spatial variations of entrepreneurship, as well as the distinction between local and non-local business owners are considered.

## Self-employment among immigrant groups — Trends of change through the generations

Immigrants who arrived in Israel between 1948 and 1954 came to a new and economically weak country which, in these few years, had absorbed mass immigration outnumbering its previous population. The role of self-employment in their short-term absorption, as well as in their long-term occupations, varied substantially between those of Eastern and European origins. Among Eastern-origin groups, those immigrating as children (born 1933-1942) tended to become self-employed more than those immigrating as adults (born 1918-1927). By contrast, among European-origin groups, those immigrating as children tended to become self-employed less than those coming as adults (Table 1).

### Table 1.
### Israel's urban population — percent self-employed among selected population cohorts, 1961-1972-1983

| Country of birth/father's country of birth | Born 1918-1927 Migrated to Israel 1948-1954 | | | Born 1933-1942 Migrated to Israel 1948-1954 | | | Born in Israel 1948-1954 |
|---|---|---|---|---|---|---|---|
| | 1961 | 1972 | 1983 | 1961 | 1972 | 1983 | 1983 |
| Iraq | 14.1 | 17.0 | 15.7 | 5.6 | 19.5 | 19.7 | 12.3 |
| Yemen | 7.7 | 7.0 | 4.7 | 4.3 | 11.2 | 8.2 | 9.4 |
| Iran | 11.7 | 19.2 | 12.3 | 6.7 | 21.8 | 20.7 | 12.9 |
| Turkey | 25.1 | 24.7 | 16.5 | 9.3 | 22.1 | 18.0 | 12.1 |
| Morocco | 8.1 | 13.0 | 9.1 | 2.7 | 11.9 | 15.0 | 12.4 |
| Poland | 23.2 | 23.3 | 17.2 | 5.7 | 15.8 | 14.5 | 9.8 |
| Romania | 19.1 | 25.2 | 22.6 | 5.4 | 16.0 | 14.3 | 9.6 |
| Bulgaria & Greece | 21.6 | 26.8 | 19.9 | 4.9 | 15.4 | 18.3 | 11.4 |
| Czechoslovakia | 21.9 | 26.7 | 18.9 | 2.7 | 11.8 | 14.8 | 11.7 |

*Source:* Censuses of Population and Housing, Israel Central Bureau of Statistics.

Hence, among adult immigrants, those of Eastern origin were less entrepreneurial than Europeans, the Yemenites and Moroccans being particularly non-entrepreneurial. Among those immigrating as children, the Eastern-origin groups, with the exception of Yemenites, were more entrepreneurial than Europeans.

The declining propensity of European-origin groups to become self-employed is clearly evident in data for the first Israeli-born generation (Table 1). Variations among Eastern-origin groups seemed to diminish among the Israeli-born generation, and all groups, except for Yemenites, had a greater propensity to become self-employed than Europeans. It should be noted that the relatively low rates of self-employment among the Israeli-born generation are a function of their young age in 1983.

Entrepreneurial activities performed by immigrants differed widely between Eastern- and European-origin groups. In the total sample, those immigrating as children had a higher propensity than older immigrants to own large businesses employing at least three salaried workers (Table 2). However, unlike the trends for the self-employed described above, young European immigrants retained a much higher propensity to engage in large businesses than young Eastern immigrants. This gap between European- and Eastern-origin groups also persisted among the first Israeli-born generation, although its magnitude can be evaluated only when data for the 1990s become available.

Table 2.

Israel's urban population — percent self-employed with 3+ salaried workers[1] among selected population cohorts, 1961-1972-1983

| Country of birth/father's country of birth | Born 1918-1927 Migrated to Israel 1948-1954 | | | Born 1933-1942 Migrated to Israel 1948-1954 | | | Born in Israel 1948-1954 |
|---|---|---|---|---|---|---|---|
| | 1961 | 1972 | 1983 | 1961 | 1972 | 1983 | 1983 |
| Iraq | 0.4 | 1.3 | 2.1 | 0.3 | 2.4 | 2.9 | 1.4 |
| Yemen | 0.2 | 0.1 | 0.4 | 0.3 | 1.0 | 0.4 | 0.7 |
| Iran | 0 | 1.6 | 0.7 | 0 | 2.2 | 3.1 | 1.6 |
| Turkey | 0.2 | 1.5 | 0.8 | 0 | 1.8 | 2.3 | 1.9 |
| Morocco | 0 | 0.7 | 0.6 | 0 | 1.9 | 1.7 | 1.0 |
| Poland | 1.4 | 4.1 | 3.2 | 0.3 | 2.6 | 4.2 | 1.8 |
| Romania | 0.9 | 3.1 | 3.0 | 0.4 | 3.3 | 3.6 | 2.0 |
| Bulgaria & Greece | 0.7 | 2.6 | 2.7 | 0.4 | 3.0 | 4.4 | 1.6 |
| Czechoslovakia | 2.0 | 4.0 | 2.3 | 0 | 4.3 | 5.6 | 2.6 |

[1] Percent of the total working population of each cohort.

*Source:* Censuses of Population and Housing, Israel Central Bureau of Statistics.

Whereas the propensity to become self-employed appears to be somewhat influenced by inter-ethnic convergence, it is in the industrial composition of the self-employed that gaps have persisted and perhaps even widened. Among the self-employed immigrants of Eastern origin, those arriving as children tended to be involved in retail trades less often than those immigrating as adults; instead, they engaged more in other blue-collar and distribution activities (manufacturing, car repair shops, construction, transportation). A clear trend of moving from retail to other blue-collar activities, which mostly do not require high levels of formal education, has continued among the first Israeli-born generation (Table 3). There has also been a modest increase in the proportion of self-employed in white-collar occupations, but holders of these occupations have remained a small minority among Eastern-origin entrepreneurs.

Table 3.
The self-employed among 24 population cohorts by major industries, 1961-1972-1983 (in percentages)[1]

| Country of birth/father's country of birth | Born 1918-1927 Migrated to Israel 1948-1954 | | | Born 1933-1942 Migrated to Israel 1948-1954 | | | Born in Israel 1948-1954 | | |
|---|---|---|---|---|---|---|---|---|---|
| | Blue-collar | Retail | White-Collar | Blue-collar | Retail | White-Collar | Blue-collar | Retail | White-Collar |
| *Iraq* | | | | | | | | | |
| 1961 | 30.6 | 53.3 | 8.3 | 49.0 | 38.1 | 6.8 | | | |
| 1972 | 30.6 | 50.7 | 7.7 | 52.7 | 30.6 | 6.5 | | | |
| 1983 | 24.3 | 47.3 | 17.6 | 47.3 | 32.6 | 9.7 | 47.6 | 29.1 | 11.5 |
| *Iran* | | | | | | | | | |
| 1961 | 38.3 | 47.1 | 0 | 51.6 | 39.4 | 6.0 | | | |
| 1972 | 41.0 | 48.0 | 0 | 53.5 | 30.3 | 4.3 | | | |
| 1983 | 24.3 | 66.7 | 3.0 | 40.7 | 42.7 | 5.3 | 37.5 | 28.4 | 17.0 |
| *Turkey* | | | | | | | | | |
| 1961 | 52.0 | 39.4 | 0.8 | 67.3 | 28.8 | 0 | | | |
| 1972 | 41.7 | 42.5 | 2.4 | 54.4 | 25.3 | 3.7 | | | |
| 1983 | 50.0 | 41.6 | 1.7 | 49.1 | 29.2 | 8.5 | 54.7 | 20.5 | 7.7 |
| *Morocco* | | | | | | | | | |
| 1961 | 46.0 | 40.0 | 2.0 | 60.0 | 12.0 | 4.0 | | | |
| 1972 | 25.5 | 61.7 | 5.4 | 50.4 | 28.3 | 9.6 | | | |
| 1983 | 37.9 | 44.4 | 11.1 | 40.7 | 32.9 | 9.3 | 48.6 | 21.5 | 17.4 |

Table 3 (cont'd)

| Country of birth/father's country of birth | Born 1918-1927 Migrated to Israel 1948-1954 | | | Born 1933-1942 Migrated to Israel 1948-1954 | | | Born in Israel 1948-1954 | | |
|---|---|---|---|---|---|---|---|---|---|
| | Blue-collar | Retail | White-Collar | Blue-collar | Retail | White-Collar | Blue-collar | Retail | White-Collar |
| *Poland* | | | | | | | | | |
| 1961 | 56.9 | 29.6 | 3.8 | 79.1 | 9.3 | 4.6 | | | |
| 1972 | 50.9 | 28.4 | 8.0 | 51.7 | 12.3 | 18.1 | | | |
| 1983 | 43.5 | 29.3 | 11.8 | 47.4 | 11.7 | 24.1 | 25.9 | 13.3 | 40.1 |
| *Romania* | | | | | | | | | |
| 1961 | 52.1 | 31.8 | 5.1 | 66.1 | 11.3 | 8.0 | | | |
| 1972 | 41.7 | 36.6 | 7.1 | 45.6 | 23.0 | 16.4 | | | |
| 1983 | 26.1 | 44.6 | 10.2 | 39.0 | 28.4 | 23.9 | 29.8 | 22.1 | 32.6 |
| *Bulgaria & Greece* | | | | | | | | | |
| 1961 | 45.3 | 34.9 | 9.3 | 83.4 | 8.3 | 4.2 | | | |
| 1972 | 41.8 | 34.5 | 11.8 | 54.9 | 14.0 | 16.1 | | | |
| 1983 | 37.8 | 32.1 | 18.8 | 42.1 | 21.4 | 28.2 | 47.6 | 20.4 | 18.4 |
| *Czechoslovakia* | | | | | | | | | |
| 1961 | 60.6 | 17.9 | 5.6 | — | — | — | | | |
| 1972 | 43.2 | 34.1 | 10.6 | — | — | — | | | |
| 1983 | 31.8 | 34.8 | 13.6 | — | — | — | 30.2 | 9.3 | 34.9 |

<sup>1</sup> 100% - All self-employed among each cohort in the relevant year.
— A sample of less than 30.
Notes: Blue-collar — manufacturing, construction, car repair shops, transportation.
Retail — retail and restaurants.
White-collar — business and public services.
Other (not specified in the Table) — wholesale, personal services, agriculture.
*Source:* Censuses of Population and Housing, Israel Central Bureau of Statistics.

Among self-employed European immigrants, retail trades were less dominant from the start. Europeans immigrating as children tended less than older immigrants to engage in retailing, the major trend being toward professional white-collar services rather than to other blue-collar and distribution activities. The retreat from retail to white-collar self-employment occupations has continued in the first Israeli-born generation (Table 3). The share of white-collar business owners increased over time and through the generations, and among the Israeli-born generation they were the largest group of self-employed in three of the European-origin groups — Poles, Romanians, and Czechoslovakians (Table 3). Blue-collar occupations were still dominant among all Israeli-born groups of Eastern origin, as well as among Bulgarians and Greeks. Retailing was dominant among many of the groups immigrating as adults, and blue-collar occupations were dominant among nearly all groups immigrating as children. Hence, the gaps in this respect persisted and even widened.

### Paths to business ownership — Personal attributes and ethnic networks

The small-business survey confirmed the census analysis indicating the major role of ethnicity in explaining variations in entrepreneurship. Some of the basic differences between the businesses of Eastern- and Western-origin groups can be seen in Table 4, which presents data for business owners in blue-collar activities (manufacturing, car repair shops, repairs and maintenance of mechanical equipment), and distribution (wholesale, retail, food services, personal services). Businesses of the Western-origin group were larger, older, and a higher proportion of them was incorporated. In blue-collar activities, businesses of Western-origin entrepreneurs tended to have sub-contracting relationships with other firms which were more spread out geographically.

Table 4.
**Business owners in blue-collar and distribution activities by ethnic origin and selected characteristics of the business and its owner, 1989/90 (in percentages)**

|  | BLUE-COLLAR[1] | | DISTRIBUTION[2] | |
|---|---|---|---|---|
|  | Asia, Africa[3] | Europe, America[4] | Asia, Africa | Europe, America |
| *Number of employees* | | | | |
| 1 | 8.0 | 2.7 | 41.3 | 34.4 |
| 10+ | 18.0 | 32.0 | 3.2 | 8.6 |
| *Year of establishment* | | | | |
| 1938-1969 | 12.0 | 30.7 | 6.4 | 26.9 |
| 1980-1990 | 61.0 | 41.3 | 76.0 | 55.9 |

Table 4 (cont'd)

|  | BLUE-COLLAR[1] | | DISTRIBUTION[2] | |
| --- | --- | --- | --- | --- |
|  | Asia, Africa[3] | Europe, America[4] | Asia, Africa | Europe, America |
| *Status of business* | | | | |
|   Private | 45.0 | 30.7 | 75.4 | 74.2 |
|   Partnership | 26.0 | 13.3 | 15.1 | 14.0 |
|   Incorporated firm | 29.0 | 56.0 | 9.5 | 11.8 |
| *Sub-contractor* | 23.2 | 44.0 | - | - |
| *Offering sub-contracts* | 26.3 | 48.0 | - | - |
| *Sex* (% females) | 2.0 | 1.3 | 28.6 | 23.7 |
| *Age* | | | | |
|   22-44 | 71.0 | 41.3 | 69.0 | 51.1 |
|   45+ | 7.0 | 37.3 | 12.7 | 35.9 |
| *Total* (absolute number) | 100 | 75 | 126 | 93 |

[1] Manufacturing, car repair shops, repairs and maintenance of mechanical equipment.
[2] Retail, wholesale, food services, personal services.
[3] Immigrants and children of immigrants from Asia and Africa.
[4] Immigrants and children of immigrants from Europe and America.

Source: Field survey conducted in Holon, Yavne, Ashqelon, Ofaqim and Kiryat Shemona. The table does not include second generation native Israelis. Only selected categories of some variables are presented in the Table.

The businesses of Western-origin entrepreneurs were also more concentrated in Holon, whereas businesses of Eastern-origin owners were more dominant in non-metropolitan towns (Table 5), in line with the greater concentration of these groups in these towns.

Table 6 includes factors which point to the determinants of business-formation. It reveals that entrepreneurs of Western origin tended to rely more on formal education, experience gained from their parents, and personal financial resources. Entrepreneurs of Western origin had superior levels of education, including a higher percentage of vocational high-school graduates. Skills acquired from parents and family tradition more frequently influenced their entrepreneurial decision. A relatively high percentage of them had self-employed parents, and thus they tended somewhat more than others to become self-employed by inheriting businesses. As much as 25% of the business owners of Western origin in blue-collar activities had self-employed parents engaged in similar activi-

**Table 5.**
**Business owners included in the small business survey by ethnic origin and location of business, 1989/90 (in percentages)**

|  | BLUE-COLLAR | | | DISTRIBUTION | | |
|---|---|---|---|---|---|---|
|  | Holon | non-metro towns[1] | Total (abs.no.) | Holon | non-metro towns | Total (abs.no.) |
| *Asia-Africa (total)* | <u>51.0</u> | <u>49.0</u> | <u>100</u> | <u>27.8</u> | <u>72.2</u> | <u>126</u> |
| Iraq | 73.3 | 26.7 | 15 | 57.9 | 42.1 | 19 |
| Iran | 57.1 | 42.9 | 7 | 44.4 | 55.6 | 18 |
| Morocco | 30.3 | 69.7 | 33 | 12.5 | 87.5 | 32 |
| Others | 57.8 | 42.2 | 45 | 21.1 | 78.9 | 57 |
| *Europe-America (total)* | <u>77.3</u> | <u>22.7</u> | <u>75</u> | <u>36.6</u> | <u>63.4</u> | <u>93</u> |
| USSR | 81.8 | 18.2 | 11 | 36.8 | 63.2 | 19 |
| Poland | 89.5 | 10.5 | 19 | 55.0 | 45.0 | 20 |
| Romania | 54.5 | 45.5 | 11 | 17.9 | 82.1 | 28 |
| Others | 76.5 | 23.5 | 34 | 42.3 | 57.7 | 26 |
| *Total*[2] | 62.6 | 37.4 | 182 | 33.8 | 66.2 | 231 |

[1] Yavne, Ashqelon, Ofaqim and Kiryat Shemona.
[2] Including second generation native Israelis (Jews, Arabs, and a Samaritan).
Note: The proportions of businesses of each type in Holon and in non-metropolitan towns is a function of sampling. Thus, only ethnic groups within each industry (blue-collar, distribution) should be compared.
Source: Field survey.

ties, whereas self-employed parents of business-owners of Eastern origin were fewer and engaged mostly in retail trades.

While Western-origin entrepreneurs relied more on personal resources to finance the establishment of their businesses, entrepreneurs of Eastern origin tended to rely more on loans from family members and banks and compensation payments received when quitting salaried jobs. Eastern-origin business owners tended to form partnerships with other family members, and nearly 50% of them had self-employed brothers and sisters, compared to a figure of 15% for Western-origin entrepreneurs. Eastern-origin entrepreneurs depended somewhat more on experience as salaried employees, and, in the case of blue-collar activities, also on vocational training. They stressed financial considerations slightly more often as a motive for becoming self-employed, choosing a specific activity for which they expressed some kind of interest or love, and quoting place of

## Table 6.
### Business owners in blue-collar and distribution activities by ethnic origin and selected characteristics related to the business formation process, 1989/90[1] (in percentages)

|  | BLUE-COLLAR | | DISTRIBUTION | |
|---|---|---|---|---|
|  | Asia, Africa | Europe, America | Asia, Africa | Europe, America |
| *The business owner* | | | | |
| Established business by himself | 48.5 | 36.0 | 66.7 | 67.7 |
| Established business with partners | 42.4 | 48.0 | 22.2 | 20.4 |
| Inherited/joined family business | 1.0 | 6.7 | 2.4 | 8.6 |
| *Why self-employed?* | | | | |
| Independence/challenge | 34.7 | 43.1 | 26.0 | 23.9 |
| To make money | 29.6 | 22.2 | 20.3 | 17.4 |
| Family tradition | 3.1 | 5.6 | 4.9 | 12.0 |
| *Why this industry?* | | | | |
| I like it | 15.3 | 6.7 | 26.0 | 16.3 |
| Profession/skills | 63.3 | 65.3 | 31.7 | 38.0 |
| Family tradition | 3.1 | 10.7 | 11.4 | 13.0 |
| *Why this town?* | | | | |
| Place of residence[2] | 47.4 | 28.4 | 57.7 | 45.2 |
| *Sources of entrepreneurial skills*[3] | | | | |
| Parents | 6.1 | 4.0 | 12.7 | 22.8 |
| Experience as salaried employee | 59.6 | 54.7 | 23.0 | 18.5 |
| Army | 7.1 | 4.0 | 4.0 | 2.2 |
| Vocational high-school | 26.3 | 33.3 | 3.2 | 9.8 |
| Higher education | 3.0 | 8.0 | 4.8 | 6.5 |
| Vocational training | 20.2 | 10.7 | 11.1 | 15.2 |
| *Self-employed father* | 30.3 | 38.4 | 35.2 | 38.0 |
| *Self-employed brothers* | 49.5 | 16.4 | 43.2 | 14.3 |
| *Highest level of education* | | | | |
| Elementary school | 19.4 | 5.4 | 19.8 | 15.2 |
| Partial secondary education | 35.7 | 17.6 | 34.9 | 26.1 |
| Full secondary education | 30.6 | 52.7 | 34.1 | 37.0 |
| A university degree | 4.1 | 8.1 | 5.6 | 9.8 |
| Other post-secondary training | 8.2 | 14.9 | 5.6 | 10.9 |

Table 6 (cont'd)

|  | BLUE-COLLAR | | DISTRIBUTION | |
|---|---|---|---|---|
|  | Asia, Africa | Europe, America | Asia, Africa | Europe, America |
| *Initial sources of financing*[3] | | | | |
| Family | 31.9 | 17.6 | 37.3 | 19.5 |
| Bank loans | 28.7 | 26.5 | 45.2 | 33.3 |
| Personal resources | 76.6 | 88.2 | 61.1 | 75.9 |
| *Use of lay-off compensation payments* | 23.0 | 19.4 | 18.7 | 13.3 |
| *Total* (absolute number) | 100 | 75 | 126 | 93 |

[1] See all notes to Table 4.
[2] Including love for the place, Zionism.
[3] More than one source is possible. Thus percentages add up to more than 100%.

residence as a major location factor. On the other hand, Western-origin entrepreneurs in blue-collar activities emphasized challenge and desire for independence more often as motives for becoming self-employed, their choice of industry was based slightly more on their education and qualifications, and the choice of location on various site advantages.

Examination of origin groups shown in Table 5 was restricted in its scope due to the small sample. Nevertheless, interethnic variations were visible, particularly in blue-collar activities. The data reveals that among Western-origin groups, Poles enjoyed the most advantageous paths to self-employment, whereas Romanians had the least advantages. Poles were most concentrated in the metropolitan city of Holon, where they operated the largest businesses and had the highest proportion of incorporated firms. As many as 47.4% of the Polish blue-collar business owners had self-employed parents, in many cases in a similar industry. Few of them (10.5%) utilized loans from family members, and few of those in distribution activities were female (10.0%). Romanians, on the other hand, were relatively dispersed (see Table 5). Of the Romanian blue-collar business owners, only 20% had self-employed parents. In addition, they had somewhat lower levels of education than other Western-origin entrepreneurs, and among those operating in distribution (mainly retail establishments), as many as 32.1% were female. Among immigrant entrepreneurs from the USSR, who mostly arrived during the 1970s, dominant features were few self-employed parents, very few blue-collar business-owners with previous experience as self-employed, and infrequent use of loans from family members. Given these characteristics, their low inclination to self-employment (Razin, 1990b) is not surprising.

Among the Eastern-origin groups, Iraqis were the most likely to deviate in the direction of the European group patterns, whereas Moroccans were at the other extreme. Iraqis were more concentrated in Holon than other Eastern-origin entrepreneurs (Table 5), they operated relatively large businesses, and many of them (35.7% among blue-collar business owners) had been self-employed before establishing their present business. However, Iraqis still had lower levels of human capital than Western-origin groups and depended more on family cooperation. Moroccan entrepreneurs, conversely, were the most dispersed (Table 5), and few of the blue-collar business owners among them had self-employed parents (21.9%), or had been previously self-employed (12.9%). Over 30% of them depended on loans from family members to establish their businesses. Moroccan business owners in distribution had the highest proportion of females (37.5%), indicating the role of small retail establishments in the employment mobility of Moroccan women.

The influence of length of stay in Israel on entrepreneurship has already been pointed out in the previous section. Additional insights are provided by the survey. The superior levels of education of Western-origin business owners were independent of length of stay in Israel, and were still evident among those born in Israel. Hence, among the Israeli-born blue-collar business owners, 73.7% of Western origin had completed high-school, compared with only 44.7% of those of Eastern origin.

Among the foreign-born, those of Western origin more frequently based their entrepreneurial venture on previous skills. This was no longer true for the Israeli-born; but among these, the Western-origin entrepreneurs had a clear advantage of family tradition, and their choice of industry was based in 21.1% of the cases on family succession. Hence, among those immigrating to Israel between 1948 and 1966 who operated businesses in blue-collar activities, the proportion having self-employed parents was similar for Western- and Eastern-origin groups (30% and 29.1%, respectively); while among the Israeli-born, the Western-origin group had a clear advantage (47.4% versus 28.9%). The Israeli-born of Western origin also enjoyed more ample opportunities to reach their first clients through previous business contacts. Finally, whereas among the foreign-born business owners in distribution, Western-origin entrepreneurs had a slightly higher proportion of females (23%) as compared to female entrepreneurs of Eastern-origin (18.1%), among the Israeli-born, the proportion of females was much higher among the Eastern-origin group (42.6%) than among the Western-origin group (27.3%). This clearly indicates the use of retail proprietorship as a route for advancement by women of Eastern origin.

**The role of location**

Metropolitan areas, particularly the Tel-Aviv metropolis, offered more self-employment opportunities than non-metropolitan development towns (Razin, 1990a; 1990b). Hence, the direction of immigrants, particularly of Eastern origin, to the development towns could have negatively influenced their ability to advance through the small-business economy. Still, large ethnic concentrations in non-central locations could also serve to increase the potential of business formation for members of a specific immigrant group beyond the general potential for business formation in a particular location. Thus, spatial variations in rates of self-employment among the Israeli-born of Moroccan origin, Israel's most dispersed origin group, were small.

Determinants of business formation in the metropolitan city (Holon) differed from those in the non-metropolitan towns studied (Razin, 1992). Entrepreneurs in non-metropolitan towns depended much more on narrow family and social networks, whereas those in Holon enjoyed better opportunities to gain relevant experience as salaried employees, as well as useful business contacts and a much broader range of business formation opportunities. A significant number of women apparently operated retail establishments in the non-metropolitan towns due to the lack of attractive salaried jobs in these towns. Entrepreneurs in Holon also had superior professional qualifications and financial resources. Hence, the combination of Eastern-origin population and non-metropolitan location created the most restricted paths to entrepreneurship. These paths were characterized by a high dependence on kinship and social networks for advancement through self-employment in locations where such opportunities and supportive networks were least available (Razin, 1992).

In the periphery, place of residence had the overwhelming role in business location decisions, particularly among business owners of Eastern origin. In Holon, on the other hand, a higher proportion of business owners migrated from other localities or commuted from fairly large distances (in blue-collar activities); business owners in Holon more often quoted availability of a suitable site and proximity to clients as location factors (Razin, 1992).

Local and non-local business owners in Holon's industrial estate differed substantially. Non-local owners had larger and older businesses, were engaged more frequently in sub-contracting relationships, and more of their businesses were formed as partnerships. The non-locals had superior levels of education, a higher proportion had self-employed parents, and their entrepreneurial venture was more frequently based on previous skills (Table 7). Local business owners — those residing in Holon and adjacent Bat Yam — had inferior entrepreneurial resources, depended more on kinship ties, and operated smaller and simpler businesses.

Table 7.

Owners of manufacturing, car repairs and maintenance of mechanical equipment businesses in Holon by place of residence of owner and selected characteristics of the business, its owner, and the business-formation process, 1989/90 (in percentages)

|  | Holon, Bat Yam | Other Localities |
|---|---|---|
| *Number of employees* | | |
| 1-3 | 44.1 | 26.8 |
| 4+ | 55.9 | 73.2 |
| *Year of establishment* | | |
| 1938-1979 | 47.5 | 62.5 |
| 1980-1990 | 52.5 | 37.5 |
| *Sub-contractor* | 27.1 | 39.3 |
| *Offering sub-contracts* | 35.6 | 41.1 |
| *Country of origin of owner* | | |
| Asia-Africa | 55.9 | 32.7 |
| *The business owner* | | |
| Estab. business by himself | 49.2 | 33.9 |
| Estab. business with partners | 40.7 | 48.2 |
| Inherited/joined family business | 1.7 | 7.1 |
| *Why this industry?* | | |
| I like it | 15.3 | 5.4 |
| Profession/skills | 62.7 | 73.2 |
| *Self-employed father* | 28.8 | 41.1 |
| *Self-employed brothers* | 39.0 | 28.6 |
| *Highest level of education* | | |
| Elementary school | 17.2 | 10.9 |
| Partial secondary education | 27.6 | 10.9 |
| Full secondary education | 37.9 | 58.2 |
| A university degree | 3.4 | 9.1 |

Table 7 (cont'd)

|  | Holon, Bat Yam | Other Localities |
|---|---|---|
| Other post-secondary training | 13.8 | 9.1 |
| *Initial sources of financing*[1] | | |
| Family | 27.1 | 10.9 |
| Bank loans | 25.4 | 12.7 |
| Personal resources | 81.4 | 76.4 |
| *Reaching first clients* | | |
| Kinship, social relations | 19.6 | 6.0 |
| Previous business contacts | 33.9 | 36.0 |
| Without any promotion | 5.4 | 26.0 |
| *Total* (absolute number) | 59 | 56 |

[1] More than one source is possible. Thus percentages add up to more than 100%.

It could be argued that the above differences between local and non-local business owners are largely a consequence of the greater tendency of Eastern-origin groups to reside in Holon and Bat Yam (Table 7). Hence, another Table (not shown here) showed Western- and Eastern-origin business owners in Holon's industrial estate separately. The superior entrepreneurial resources of non-local commuters were largely independent of ethnic origin. Nevertheless, the difference between locals and non-locals was most marked among the Western-origin business owners, and smaller among the Eastern-origin group. Hence, business owners of Western origin who operated their businesses in the metropolitan city of Holon, and resided elsewhere in the metropolis or its vicinity, enjoyed a most advantageous position with regards to determinants of entrepreneurship.

## Conclusions and policy implications

The findings generally support the major arguments of the paper: while significant differences exist among immigrants of specific countries of origin in their inclination to entrepreneurship and in the determinants of entrepreneurship, the separation into Eastern- and Western-origin groups is of major significance in predicting entrepreneurial behavior. Immigrants of Eastern origin initially had a lower propensity to become self-employed than those of Western origin. However, subsequent generations of Eastern origin increasingly turned to self-employment as a mobility route for those possessing inferior levels of formal education, including women. It is uncertain whether this route has reduced the gap between Eastern- and Western-origin groups, since the latter have progressed as well to white-collar salaried jobs or to large businesses and businesses requiring white-collar professional qualifications. Western-origin business owners enjoyed superior levels of human capital and personal resources, whereas those of Eastern origin had to compensate for their inferiority by a greater reliance on kinship and socio-ethnic ties. However, it seems that Eastern-origin business owners did not have an advantage even in access to effective social networks. They usually could not depend on a tradition of enterprise in the family or business-oriented contacts to the same extent as Western-origin entrepreneurs.

The Eastern-origin entrepreneurs, particularly Moroccans, also suffered from a disadvantageous position with respect to local opportunities, since they have been more dispersed to non-metropolitan development towns. The Eastern-origin immigrants who resided in these non-metropolitan towns had the least favorable determinants of entrepreneurship. In contrast, those possessing the most favorable determinants were Western origin business owners from the Tel-Aviv area who established their businesses in Holon's thriving industrial area as a result of conscious location choice. However, despite the implied inferiority of Eastern-origin business owners, it has been shown elsewhere (Razin, 1989; 1990a) that even non-professional self-employment occupations have led to a reduction of spatial and inter-ethnic disparities. It might well be that penetration of Eastern-origin groups into blue-collar self-employment activities will gradually lead to improved determinants of entrepreneurship, influencing the younger generations.

The option of entrepreneurship has recently emerged for the first time in Israel as a major goal of public policies intended to assist the absorption of the present immigration wave from the former USSR. It is unlikely that many of these immigrants will be able to form intensive entrepreneurial sub-economies in narrow niches, since their numbers are too large relative to Israel's indigenous population. These newcomers possess substantial human capital combined with great difficulties in advancing as salaried employees because of the present economic realities in Israel. Nevertheless, lack of a tradition of enterprise or extensive ethnic entrepreneurial networks will weaken their prospects of successful entrepreneurship. These prospects will also be influenced by specific public policies that promote access to management skills and capital, as well as by the housing policy.

During the 1950s and 1960s, the policy of dispersing population through the establishment of new non-metropolitan development towns enabled

Israel to settle mainly the poorer Eastern-origin immigrants in peripheral areas, where they remained relatively immobile geographically. Spatial adjustment in order to utilize non-local job opportunities was limited (Razin, 1991), and this initial residential pattern of immigrant groups had a long-term impact even on the first Israeli-born generation. Thus, the population dispersal policy restricted the prospects of immigrants to advance through entrepreneurship.

Excessive dispersal of immigrants may impair prospects for the evolution of supportive ethnic networks and reduce the availability of entrepreneurial opportunities. This does not imply that unlimited concentration in metropolitan areas is optimal from the point of view of job generation through entrepreneurship. Opportunities for a large mass of immigrants in small-businesses geared primarily to local markets are limited even in the Tel-Aviv metropolis, while some opportunities do exist in non-metropolitan towns. Still, both the formation of supportive networks and the identification of entrepreneurial opportunities depend on the pre-existence of a significant local market. Immigrants settled in completely new and isolated towns or in small and peripheral towns will not be able to form informal networks or identify opportunities in a new unfamiliar economy, and will thus depend to a greater extent on direct government action for job provision, even in an age of advanced transportation and telecommunications systems.

## Acknowledgments

This study was supported by grants from the Israel Foundation Trustees and the Fund for Basic Research administered by the Israel Academy of Sciences and Humanities.

## References

Avraham, M. (1985), *With Their Own Resources: A New Look at Investment Required for Economic Development in Israel's Development Towns*, Jewish Agency, Project Renewal: Jerusalem.

Arner, A. (1989), 'The Development of an Industrial Park in a Rural Area — The Case of Tefen', in Weitz, R. et al. (eds.), *The Regional Operation from the Lakhish Region to Region 2000*, Settlement Study Centre: Rehovot, pp. 92-112. [Hebrew]

Ben-Porath, Y. (1986), 'Self-Employed And Wage Earners in Israel: Findings from the Census of Population 1972', in Schmelz, U.O. and Nathan, G. (eds.), *Studies in the Population of Israel*, Magnes: Jerusalem, pp. 245-80.

Birch, D. (1987), *Job Creation in America: How Our Smallest Companies Put the Most People to Work*, Free Press: New York.

Bonacich, E. and Modell, J. (1980), *The Economic Basis of Ethnic Solidarity*, University of California Press: Berkeley, CA.

Brock, W.A. and Evans, D.S. (1989), 'Small Business Economics', *Small Business Economics*, Vol. 1, pp. 7-20.

Fratoe, F.A. (1986), 'A Sociological Analysis of Minority Business', *The Review of Black Political Economy*, Vol. 15, pp. 5-29.

Giaoutzi, M., Nijkamp, P. and Storey, D.J. (1988), *Small and Medium Size Enterprises and Regional Development*, Routledge: London.

Greenwood, N. (1990), *The Nightmares of Israeli Small Business*, Policy Studies, Division for Economic Policy Research: Jerusalem.

Jones, T.P., McEvoy, D. and Paulson-Box, E. (1990), 'South Asian Retailers in Canada: Montreal, Toronto and Vancouver', presented at the Annual Meeting of the Canadian Association of Geographers, Edmonton, Canada, June.

Klausner, D. and Shamir-Shinan, L. (1988), *Local Organization for Economic Development*, The Jerusalem Institute for Israel Studies: Jerusalem. [Hebrew]

Ladbury, S. (1984), 'Choice, Chance or No Alternative? Turkish Cypriots in Business in London', in Ward, R. and Jenkins, R. (eds.), *Ethnic Communities in Business*, Cambridge University Press: Cambridge, pp. 105-24.

Light, I. (1972), *Ethnic Enterprise in America.*, University of California Press: Berkeley, CA.

Light, I. and Bonacich, E. (1988), *Immigrant Entrepreneurs, Koreans in Los Angeles, 1965-1982*, University of California Press: Berkeley, CA.

Maman, D. (1991), *Ethnicity, Social Status and Social Networks — Preliminary Findings*, The Jerusalem Institute for Israel Studies: Jerusalem. [Hebrew]

Mokrey, B.W. (1988), *Entrepreneurship and Public Policy, Can Government Stimulate Business Startups?* Quorum Books: New York.

Nahon, Y. (1989), *Self-Employed Workers — the Ethnic Dimension.*, The Jerusalem Institute for Israel Studies: Jerusalem. [Hebrew]

Piore, M.J. and Sabel, C.F. (1984), *The Second Industrial Divide*, Basic Books: New York.

Portes, A. and Bach, R.L. (1985), *Latin Journey, Cuban and Mexican Immigrants in the United States*, University of California Press:

Berkeley, CA.

Razin, E. (1988a), 'Entrepreneurship among Foreign Immigrants in the Los Angeles and San Francisco Metropolitan Regions', *Urban Geography*, Vol. 9, pp. 283-301.

Razin, E. (1988b), 'The Role of Ownership Characteristics in the Industrial Development of Israel's Peripheral Towns', *Environment and Planning A*, Vol. 20, pp. 1235-52.

Razin, E. (1989), 'Relating Theories of Entrepreneurship among Ethnic Groups and Entrepreneurship in Space — The Case of the Jewish Population in Israel', *Geografiska Annaler*, Vol. 71B, pp. 167-81.

Razin, E. (1990a), 'Spatial Variations in the Israeli Small-Business Sector: Implications for Regional Development Policies', *Regional Studies*, Vol. 24, pp. 149-62.

Razin, E. (1990b), 'Immigrant Entrepreneurs in Israel, Canada and California', ISSR Working Papers in the Social Sciences, UCLA, Institute for Social Science Research: Los Angeles.

Razin, E. (1990c), 'Urban Economic Development in a Period of Local Initiative: Competition among Towns in Israel's Southern Coastal Plain', *Urban Studies*, Vol. 27, pp. 685-703.

Razin, E. (1991), 'Geographical Mobility of Selected Age Cohorts of Immigrant Groups in Israel: Implications for Occupational Mobility', presented at the British-Israeli Workshop on Migration and Development, Shefayim, Israel, June.

Razin, E. (1992), 'Paths to Ownership of Small Businesses among Immigrants in Israeli Cities and Towns', *The Review of Regional Studies*, Vol. 22, pp. 277-96.

Stohr, W.B. (1981), 'Development from Below: The Bottom-Up and Periphery-Inward Development Paradigm', in Stohr, W.B. and Taylor, D.R. (eds.), *Development from Above or Below?* John Wiley & Sons: Chichester (UK), pp. 39-72.

Storey, D.J. (1988), 'The Role of Small and Medium-Sized Enterprises in European Job Creation: Key Issues for Policy and Research', in Giaoutzi, M., Nijkamp, P. and Storey, D.J. (eds.), *Small and Medium Size Enterprises and Regional Development*, Routledge: London, pp. 140-60.

Storper, M. and Scott, A.J. (1989), 'The Geographical Foundations and Social Regulation of Flexible Production Complexes', in Wolch, J. and Dear, M. (eds.), *The Power of Geography: How Territory Shapes Social Life*, Unwin Hyman: Winchester, MA, pp. 21-40.

Waldinger, R., Aldrich, H. and Ward, R. (eds.), (1990), *Ethnic Entrepreneurs*, Sage: Newbury Park, CA.

Werbner, P. (1984), 'Business on Trust: Pakistani Entrepreneurship in the

Manchester Garment Trade', in Ward, R. and Jenkins, R. (eds.), *Ethnic Communities in Business*, Cambridge University Press: Cambridge (UK), pp. 166-88.

Yaar, E. (1986), 'Differences in Ethnic Patterns of Socioeconomic Achievements in Israel — A Neglected Aspect of Structured Inequality', *Megamot*, Vol. 29, pp. 393-412. [Hebrew]

# 5 Ethnic conflict and social cohesion among Israeli adolescents

*Richard E. Isralowitz and Ismael Abu Saad*

Since 1989, the population of Israel has increased by almost 10% due to the influx of immigrants from Eastern Europe, particularly the former Soviet Union. This immigration has had both positive and negative influence on the attitudes of veteran citizens toward the newcomers in terms of ethnic conflict and social cohesion (Isralowitz and Abu Saad, 1992a). These attitudes have important consequences since they provide the context within which individual and group behavior takes place (Ehrlich, 1973, p. 8; Fishbein and Ajzen, 1975). As pointed out by McAllister and Moore (1988, p. 1),

> for the 'in' group which expresses prejudice, it may result in a whole range of socioeconomic, cultural and political policies, formal and informal, directed against the minority group. For the 'out' group, which is the target of the prejudice, it can result in greater ethnic self-identification and cultural maintenance, and consequently a weak commitment to integration within the host society.

The effects of immigration on Israeli society have been well-documented (Eisenstadt, 1954; Selzer, 1965; Smooha, 1978; Swirski, 1981; Halper, 1987); however, a considerable void exists in understanding the issue from the perspective of adolescents. This article examines and discusses the attitudes of high school age youth toward immigrants from the Soviet republics and their absorption process in Israel. This article is based on an exploratory study which was designed to assess the extent of social cohesion and conflict being expressed by two groups of young people with different educational status (i.e., regular and vocational education) yet with similar socio-economic background characteristics, including ethnic origin.

**Background**

Adolescence is a period of change, transition, and upheaval. During this period, the attitudes and behavior of young people are related to the developmental life tasks and circumstances they face. These tasks consist of: 1) the development of a system of values, beliefs, and goals which will guide behavior; 2) the establishment of personal identity and self-image; 3) the development of interpersonal skills and relationships with peers of the same and opposite sex; and, 4) the establishment and clarification of one's goals and roles in terms of occupation, sex, marriage, and family, and future life-style (Blum and Singer, 1983).

Explanations of the relationship between value development and behavior have been provided from a number of perspectives: the importance of differential associations (Sutherland, 1947); the effects of lower class culture (Kvaraceus and Miller, 1959); neighborhood values (Shaw and McKay, 1942); and, the importance of the concept of anomie (Merton, 1957), among others. The important point derived from these 'classical' approaches is that the social environment of a youth is a major source of that person's value orientation.

Various sociological theories of rational behavior and the role of social institutions have been used to examine the dynamics of value orientations, ethnic conflict, and social class mobilization. For example, Rex *et al.* in Britain (1975 with Tomlinson; 1986 with Mason), and Bell (1975) in the United States, have applied the Weberian notion of 'social closure' to show how ethnic conflict can arise out of interest divergences in competitive situations of an economic and social nature. Ethnic mobilization and even prejudice can appear as a rational strategy to maximize resource allocation in certain situations.

Another approach to understanding ethnic conflict argues that racism is a key factor in the analysis of the problem. Racism is viewed as a central aspect of

> . . . social hierarchy in capitalist societies, which must be analyzed in conjunction with political power, class relations, and gender divisions. Racism is derived from historical developments of industrial societies and is perpetuated through the cultural, social and economic structures of contemporary society. The strength and form of racism in a parti-

cular society is linked to economic and social changes, which appear to threaten the security of certain social groups (Cope, Castles and Kalantzis, 1990, pp. ii-iii).

Specific to Israel, Bar Yosef (1959), Frankenstein (1953), and Kleinberger (1969) identify cultural differences or deficiencies of immigrants as a major factor of ethnic conflict and the lack of social cohesion. Another approach is characterized by the work of people such as Eisenstadt (1954) and Smooha (1978), who focus on the inherent tensions between the reality of ethnicity and ethnic inequalities in the country, as well as formal ideologies, backed by normative pressures and institutionalized policies, that 'aim at creating a melting pot' (Halper, 1987, p. 112).

Like every society, Israel has a variety of subgroups differentiated by ascribed attributes or characteristics which belong, or are imputed, to individuals, often by birth, such as race, religion or the degree of religiosity, or language. In turn, many of these groups have traditionally viewed one another with a greater or lesser degree of suspicion or prejudice. According to McAllister and Moore, (1988, p. 1),

> Occasionally this suspicion or prejudice has been based on some objective knowledge of the group in question, exemplified by knowledge or contact with a particular individual or group of individuals. This has been referred to as the 'kernel of truth' hypothesis (Klineberg, 1950). More often, however, prejudice has been based on stereotypes which bear little relation to the objective reality.

The large numbers of immigrants from the Soviet Union and Ethiopia who have arrived since 1990 are examples of subgroups affected by this social process.

**The study**

*Subjects*

This study was based on a sample of 227 Israeli-Jewish, male, high school youth, 17 and 18 years of age. The study cohort included 127 adolescents from a general high school with a diverse studies curriculum including college preparatory courses, and 100 youth from a vocational high school. In Israel, students in a vocational school are viewed as less scholastically oriented and more prone to under achievement, problem behavior, and lower self-concept. The sample of respondents was drawn from selected classes in each school and represent the total population of youth present on the day the questionnaire was distributed. Both high schools where the study was conducted are from an Israeli 'development' town which is typified by an unemployment rate of 20%, semi-skilled to unskilled labor, and a population that is 75% Sephardi — i.e., Jewish people originally from North African or Middle-Eastern countries that are predominantly Moslem and Arabic-speaking.

Because the study is exploratory and based on data collected in one region of the country at one point in time, generalization of the findings is limited.

*Method*

Based on the work of Robbins (1989, p. 368-370), a number of factors were considered for this study. Among them were: functional and dysfunctional conflict (i.e., conflict may be good and used to support the goals of an individual and/or group and improve performance, or conflict may be destructive and hinder performance); the conflict paradox (i.e., some conflict has been proven to be beneficial to performance, yet, tolerance or acceptance of conflict tends to be rejected in most cultures with anti-conflict values and an emphasis on getting along with others); the conflict process (i.e., certain conditions such as poor communication and misunderstanding, structure including factors of group size, degree of a person's work specialization role and reward systems, as well as personal factors including age, socio-economic status, education, and ethnicity create opportunities for conflict to arise); perceptions of conflict; and, conflict-related behaviors such as competition, collaboration aimed at problem-solving and clarifying differences, avoidance by withdrawing or suppressing the conflict, accommodation by placing the opponent's interests above one's own, and compromise (a willingness to give up or sacrifice something to avoid conflict and achieve important goals).

A questionnaire developed for this study included measures of conflict, group relations, and socio-demographic variables. Subjects were asked to use a 5-point Likert-type scale to respond to 25 statements. The five choices were: 1) does not reflect my opinion at all; 2) does not reflect my opinion; 3) no opinion; 4) reflects my opinion; and, 5) strongly reflects my opinion. The demographic variables included: sex, parents' marital status, age, father and mother's education, ethnicity, place of residence, parents' employment status, and religious orientation. The statistical methods used to process the collected data were factor analysis and t-tests using the Statistical Package for Social Sciences (SPSSX) developed by Nie and others (1975).

**Results**

Table 1 depicts the results of factor analysis on the 25 items of intergroup conflict, using the Varimax Rotation procedure with Kaiser Normalization. Using a loading of >0.40 as the threshold for inclusion, the items were distributed among five primary factors, including:

Factor 1   'Dysfunctional Conflict' (e.g., immigration is a negative condition affecting peoples' lives and ability to get along).

Factor 2   'Security-Based Cooperation' (e.g., people should be involved with the immigration process to reduce conflict; and, job and economic security are important factors if people are to support the immigration process).

Factor 3   'Religious Leadership' (e.g., religious leaders have an influence on improving inter-group relations toward immigration).

Factor 4   'Functional Conflict' (e.g., immigration has a positive influence on peoples' ability to solve their problems and be creative in addressing their needs).

Factor 5   'Media Impact' (e.g., information about immigration through the media is helpful and a positive influence in terms of people's attitudes and understanding toward immigration).

The five factors have an eigenvalue greater than 1.0 and accounted for 45% of the total item variance. All factors were found to be acceptable in terms of reliability determined through the use of the appropriate statistical computation (i.e., Cronbach Alpha coefficient).

**Table 1.**
**Dimensions of intergroup conflict and Factor Analysis, Varimax Rotation**

| ITEM | | FACTORS | | | | |
|---|---|---|---|---|---|---|
| | | 1 | 2 | 3 | 4 | 5 |
| 1 | Soviet immigration is crippling the country's ability to meet the needs of its citizens. | .40 | .14 | .45 | -.12 | -.07 |
| 2 | The government is making an effort to help immigrants. | .44 | -.03 | -.14 | .09 | .00 |

Table 1 (cont'd)

| ITEM | | FACTORS | | | | |
|---|---|---|---|---|---|---|
| | | 1 | 2 | 3 | 4 | 5 |
| 3 | A lack of openness and trust exists between the government and the people over Soviet immigration. | .10 | .02 | .46 | -.01 | -.00 |
| 4 | Information (e.g., newspapers, television, etc.) on why people need to help Soviet immigrants is good. | .08 | .05 | .07 | .05 | .12 |
| 5 | Information (e.g., newspapers, television, etc.) about the importance of Soviet immigration is poor. | -.04 | .03 | .00 | .06 | .17 |
| 6 | Government assistance to Soviet immigrants comes at the expense of Israeli citizens. | .54 | -.03 | .36 | -.13 | -.05 |
| 7 | Soviet immigration should be limited. | .43 | -.41 | .30 | .03 | -.11 |
| 8 | Soviet immigration will limit my ability to obtain a job with prestige. | .63 | -.10 | .21 | -.00 | .02 |
| 9 | Soviet immigration will restrict my ability to receive public services (e.g., treatment, day care, etc.). | .30 | -.27 | .56 | -.11 | .07 |
| 10 | Soviet immigration will cause conflict over available resources (job, housing, university acceptance, etc.) between Israeli citizens. | .38 | .22 | .39 | -.29 | -.12 |
| 11 | Limited resources, as a result of Soviet immigration, will lead to violent, destructive or irrational behavior among people. | .22 | -.00 | .59 | -.21 | -.07 |
| 12 | Soviet immigration is important to the future of Israel. | -.32 | .55 | -.15 | .14 | .13 |
| 13 | Soviet immigration is obstructing peace between Arabs and Jews in Israel. | .37 | -.36 | .29 | .15 | -.13 |
| 14 | Soviet immigration will promote attempts by government to improve the quality of Israeli citizens lives. | -.01 | .04 | -.13 | .63 | .09 |

Table 1 (cont'd)

| ITEM | 1 | 2 | FACTORS 3 | 4 | 5 |
|---|---|---|---|---|---|
| 15 My family and friends believe Soviet immigration is a threat to their ability to succeed in life. | .56 | -.21 | .28 | -.00 | -.01 |
| 16 My family has a role in helping with the absorption of Soviet immigrants. | -.45 | .17 | -.00 | .20 | .16 |
| 17 Teachers have a role in reducing conflict and promoting people's understanding of Soviet immigration. | -.25 | .45 | -.00 | .05 | .35 |
| 18 Religious leaders have a role in reducing conflict and promoting Soviet immigration. | -.05 | .14 | -.03 | .13 | .84 |
| 19 Religious leaders have the ability to improve people's attitudes toward Soviet immigrants. | -.06 | .08 | -.08 | .12 | .84 |
| 20 Too much communication in the media about Soviet immigration is a reason for conflict between Israeli citizens and new immigrants. | .44 | -.01 | .25 | -.03 | .01 |
| 21 The more people are involved with Soviet immigration the more conflict between citizens will be reduced. | -.18 | .52 | .09 | .22 | .03 |
| 22 If people were more secure in their jobs there would be less conflict between citizens and Soviet immigrants. | .06 | .67 | .02 | .00 | .07 |
| 23 Conflict exists between Israeli citizens and Soviet immigrants because Soviet immigrants are receiving too many rewards and benefits. | .51 | .11 | .21 | -.01 | -.07 |
| 24 I deserve at least the same benefits being received by a new immigrant because I am a citizen of Israel. | .65 | -.09 | .14 | -.03 | -.13 |
| 25 Good relationships between citizens and Soviet immigrants will promote cooperation. | -.16 | .60 | -.09 | .25 | -.02 |
| Eigenvalue | 3.7 | 2.5 | 2.0 | 1.6 | 1.3 |

Table 2 contains the means and standard deviations of the intergroup conflict dimensions.

**Table 2.**
**Means and Standard Deviations of the**
**Intergroup Conflict Dimensions (N = 227)**

| Dimensions | Mean | S.D. |
|---|---|---|
| 1. Dysfunctional Conflict | 21.94 | 7.73 |
| 2. Security-based Cooperation | 20.62 | 6.48 |
| 3. Religious Leadership | 5.92 | 3.27 |
| 4. Functional Conflict | 11.31 | 4.54 |
| 5. Media Impact | 14.35 | 4.85 |

Table 3 compares the attitudinal dimensions of youth in a general high school and those in a vocational education program.

**Table 3.**
**Mean, Standard Deviation and T-Values for the intergroup conflict dimensions comparing general and vocational high school students**

| Dimensions | General High School (N=127) | | Vocational High School (N=100) | | t-Value | Prob. |
|---|---|---|---|---|---|---|
| | Mean | S.D. | Mean | S.D. | | |
| 1. Dysfunctional Conflict | 26.00 | 5.44 | 25.95 | 5.59 | .48 | .64 |
| 2. Security-Based Cooperation | 21.97 | 4.20 | 19.73 | 4.59 | 3.83 | .00 |
| 3. Religious Leadership | 6.29 | 2.60 | 6.02 | 2.22 | 0.83 | .40 |
| 4. Functional Conflict | 11.40 | 3.77 | 11.97 | 3.37 | -1.18 | .23 |
| 5. Media impact | 10.13 | 2.26 | 10.54 | 2.35 | -1.35 | .18 |

'Security-based cooperation' was the only factor found to differentiate the two study groups. Vocational education students tend to have a more negative view of the immigration of Russian Jewish people to Israel. They, more than their general high school peers, expressed the belief that the number of new immigrants permitted into the country should be limited; and that good relations between Israeli citizens and new immigrants will not necessarily promote cooperation; teachers do not have a role in reducing conflict and promoting understanding of Russian immigration; and, having contact with Russian immigrants will not help reduce inter-group conflict. These youths were also less inclined to believe that job security among Israeli citizens would reduce their feelings of conflict toward immigrants.

**Discussion**

This study reveals that a dual perspective of ethnic conflict and social cohesion tends to exist among high school youth enrolled in general and vocational studies. In other words, youth with the same socio-economic background characteristics, but different educational status, have different attitudes toward immigrants.

In one sense, the findings of this study relate to issues of institutional service provision and blockage of opportunities for success (Cloward and Ohlin, 1961; Cressey, 1970), the failure of schools to provide adequate education (Polk and Schafer, 1972), the negative effects of labeling by institutions (Becker, 1963; Thorsell and Klemke, 1972), and the consistently high unemployment rates of youth (Hahn, Danzberger and Lefkowitz, 1987; Natriello, 1987). These issues call attention to the importance of 'institutional arrangements in society which can make it nearly impossible for some youth to either acquire needed skills or to have effective access to employment opportunities' (Blum and Singer, 1983, p. 12).

The school drop-out rate for Jewish students in Israel is estimated to be less than 10%, a relatively low figure compared to that of inner-city youth in the United States. However, the failure of the Israeli school system to provide basic education (Elkana, 1991) and adequate vocational programs, the increasing number of youth rejected by the army (a vital path for job training, work, and government benefits) because of poor educational attainment, and the ongoing inability of the country to absorb young people into the labor market tend to be factors associated with a sub-population of Israeli youth most likely to express conflict with new immigrants.

In both the United States and Israel, the influx of immigrants willing to work long hours for low wages has most affected young people who are least skilled and have the lowest levels of educational attainment (Lueck, 1992). For example, young Russian immigrants often do hard physical jobs in supermarkets and outdoor markets, packing, unpacking and lifting boxes... many of these youngsters work because they need to help the family financially... Russians are willing to work at any job as long as they get money... they will do hard physical work whereas an Israeli teenager would think twice about it... (Sudilovsky, 1992a).

Catapano (1992), citing the work of economists and various research institutes, states that immigrants do jobs that native-born workers do not want.

The importance of the peer group is another factor to consider regarding ethnic and social cohesion attitudes among youth. The peer group can effectively set normative standards for the behavior of its members — they may demand conformity with group norms of selected behavior (Blum and Singer, 1983). Preliminary evidence from a related study on conflict shows that the peer group, particularly that consisting of employed and unemployed, low socio-economic status young adults, is a significant predictor of negative attitudes among Israeli citizens toward immigrants (Isralowitz and Abu Saad, 1992b).

For teen-age immigrants, the absorption process can be a difficult one — perhaps even harder than it is for their parents. The complexity of adolescence is compounded by being uprooted from familiar surroundings and transplanted to a country whose basic social structure is a puzzle to them. For some immigrant youth, being the target of ostracism and negative attitudes by Israeli-born youth creates a sense of emotional entrap-ment.

On one hand, they are angry and want to lash out at their parents for having brought them to Israel where they feel out of place. On the other hand, they feel protective of their parents as they see fathers and mothers — who once held positions as doctors and engineers — sweeping floors and cleaning apartments while struggling to learn a new language and culture (Sudilovsky, 1992b, p. 1).

Some reactions to this situation have been delinquency, prostitution, running away, dropping out of school, drinking, and/or gang-like behavior.

In conclusion, Israeli society is a complex configuration of multiple groups and interests — Jews and Arabs, religious and secular. It is an organizational structure whose groups are often in conflict primarily because individual goals are not consistent with the goals of the organization. It is not surprising, therefore, that the study findings reveal that immigration — a change effort — is viewed by certain young people as a source of inter-group conflict. According to Schein (1965, p. 80):

> This problem exists because as groups become more committed to their own goals and norms, they are likely to become competitive with one another and seek to undermine their rivals' activities, thereby becoming a liability to the organization as a whole. The overall problem, then, is how to establish high-productive, collaborative relations.

Israel is a nation with limited resources which is experiencing a period marked by economic and social constraints. At the same time, it wants to absorb large numbers of immigrants. Religious and educational institutions may have an important role in shaping the attitudes and values of youth toward each other; however, few constructive in-roads for improving social cohesion and social conflict are expected unless major policies and programs are implemented to address issues such as improved education and employment opportunities for young people.

**References**

Bar Yosef, R. (1959), 'The Moroccans: Background to the Problem', in Eisenstadt, S.N., Bar Yosef, R. and Adler, C. (eds.), *Integration and Development in Israel*, Israel Universities Press: Jerusalem, pp. 419-28.

Becker, H. (1963), *Outsiders: Studies in the Sociology of Deviance*, Free Press: London.

Bell, D. (1975), 'Ethnicity and Social Change', in Glazer, N. and Moynihan, D.P. (eds.), *Ethnicity: Theory and Experience*, Harvard University Press: Cambridge, MA, pp. 141-74.

Blum, A. and Singer, M. (1983), 'Substance Abuse and Social Deviance: A Youth Assessment Framework', in Isralowitz, R.E. and Singer, M. (eds.), *Adolescent Substance Abuse*, Haworth Press: New York, pp. 7-21.

Catapano, T. (1992), 'Immigrants Don't Take Jobs of the Poor', *New York Times*, June 14, p. 6 IE.

Cloward, R. and Ohlin, L. (1961), *Delinquency and Opportunity*. Free Press: Glencoe, IL.

Cope, B., Castles, S. and Kalantzis, M. (1990), *Immigration, Ethnic Conflicts and Social Cohesion*, Center for Multicultural Studies, University of Wollongong: Wollongong, Australia; and Australian Government Publishing Service: Canberra (Australia).

Cressey, D. (1970), 'Organized Crime and Inner-City Youth', *Crime and*

*Delinquency*, Vol. 16, pp. 132-5.

Ehrlich, H. (1973), *Racial and Ethnic Relations*, Prentice-Hall: Englewood Cliffs, NJ.

Eisenstadt, S. (1954), *The Absorption of Immigrants*, Routledge and Kegan Paul: London.

Eisenstadt, S. (1983), 'Israel's New Majority', *Commentary*, Vol. 74, No. 3, pp. 33-9.

Elkana, Y. (1991), 'Needed Accountability', *Jerusalem Post*, October 25, p. 6.

Fishbein, M. and Ajzen, I. (1975), *Belief, Attitude, Intention and Behavior*, Addison-Wesley: Reading, MA.

Frankenstein, C. (1953), 'The Problem of Ethnic Differences in the Absorption of Immigrants', in Frankenstein, C. (ed.), *Between Past and Future*, Szold Foundation: Jerusalem, pp. 13-32.

Halper, J. (1987), 'The Absorption of Ethiopian Immigrants: A Return to the Fifties', in Ashkenazi, M. and Weingrod, A. (eds.), *Ethiopian Jews and Israel*, Transaction: New Brunswick, NJ, pp. 112-39.

Hahn, A., Danzberger, J. and Lefkowitz, B. (1987), *Dropouts in America*, Institute for Educational Leadership: Washington, DC.

Isralowitz, R. and Abu Saad, I. (1992a), 'Soviet Immigration: Ethnic Conflicts and Social Cohesion in Israel', *International Journal of Group Tensions*, Vol. 22, No. 1, pp. 126-34.

Isralowitz, R. and Abu Saad, I. (1992b), *Ethnic Conflict and Social Cohesion Among Israeli Development Town Residents*, Unpublished Research Study, Hubert H. Humphrey Institute for Social Ecology, Ben-Gurion University of the Negev: Beer-Sheva (Isr).

Klineberg, O. (1950), *Tensions Affecting International Understanding*, Social Science Research Council: New York.

Kleinberger, A. (1969), *Society, Schools and Progress in Israel*, Pergamon Press: Oxford.

Kvaraceus, W. and Miller, W. (1959), *Delinquent Culture, Culture and the Individual*, National Education Association: New York.

Lueck, T. (1992), 'New York's Teenagers Face Worst Job Market in Decades', *New York Times*, June 2, p. 1.

Merton, R. (1957), 'Social Structure and Anomie', in Merton, R. (ed.), *Social Theory and Social Structure*, Free Press: Glencoe, IL, pp. 131-60.

McAllister, I. and Moore, R. (1988), *Ethnic Prejudice in Australian Society: Patterns, Intensity and Explanations*, University of New South Wales (paper published on behalf of the Office of Multicultural Affairs): Australia.

Natriello, G. (ed.) (1987), *Social Dropouts: Patterns and Policies*,

Teachers College Press: New York.

Nie, N., Hull, H., Jenkins, J., Steinbrenner, K. and Bent, D. (1975), *Statistical Package for the Social Sciences*, McGraw-Hill: New York.

Polk, D. and Schafer, W. (1972), *Schools and Delinquency*, Prentice-Hall: Englewood Cliffs, NJ.

Rex, J. and Tomlinson, S. (1975), *Colonial Immigrants in a British City*, Kegan Paul: London.

Rex, J. and Mason, D. (1986), *Theories of Race and Ethnic Relations*, Cambridge University Press: Cambridge (UK).

Robbins, S. (1989), *Organizational Behavior*, Prentice-Hall: Englewood Cliffs, NJ.

Schein, E. (1965), *Organizational Psychology*, Prentice-Hall: Englewood Cliffs, NJ.

Selzer, M. (1965), *The Outcasts of Israel: Communal Tensions in the Jewish State*, The Council of the Sephardi Community: Jerusalem.

Shaw, C. and McKay, H. (1942), *Juvenile Delinquency in Urban Areas*, University in Chicago Press: Chicago, IL.

Smooha, S. (1978), *Israel: Pluralism and Conflict*, Routledge and Kegan Paul: London.

Sudilovsky, J. (1992a), 'No Jobs, No School, No Fun', *Jerusalem Post*, August 2, p. 5.

Sudilovsky, J. (1992b), 'The New Rebels: Soviet Immigrant Youth', *Jerusalem Post*, July 31, p. 1 B.

Sutherland, E. (1947), *Principles of Criminology*, Lippincott: New York.

Swirski, S. (1981), *Orientals and Ashkenazi in Israel: The Ethnic Division of Labor*, Makhberot LeMekhkor Ulebikoret: Haifa. [Hebrew]

Thorsell, B. and Klemke, L. (1972), 'The Labeling Process: Reinforcement and Deterrent?' *Law and Society Review*, Vol. 6, pp. 393-403.

# 6 Social cohesion and intergroup conflict in the Negev: Jewish and Arab attitudes toward the absorption of Russian immigrants

*Ismael Abu Saad and Richard E. Isralowitz*

Israel is a nation in which massive immigration has created an ethnically diverse population. During 1990-1991, the number of Soviet immigrants to Israel was approximately 370,000, reaching nearly the number of immigrants who had settled in the country over the entire previous forty years (Goldscheider, 1992; Rosenbaum-Tamari and Dimian, 1991). In the modern era, a crucial dimension of immigration patterns relates to reception by the host society. Throughout its history, Israel has maintained a strong commitment to the absorption of Jewish immigrants. Nevertheless, in an already ethnically diverse society, the influx of new immigrants may increase competition over available resources, such as employment opportunities, housing, health, education, and social services, and, in turn, increase intergroup competition and conflict (Goldscheider, 1992; Lewin-Epstein and Semyonov, 1986).

Israel's current population is composed primarily of Jews (82%) — made up of two main ethnic groups of approximately equal size: Jews of European or American origin and Jews of Asian or African origin — and an Arab minority (18%) (Rekhess, 1993). These three groups are organized into a dualistic system of ethnic stratification (Semyonov and Lewin-Epstein, 1987). As stated by Semyonov and Tyree (1981, p. 653):

> The duality occurs on two levels: Jews and non-Jews (mainly Arabs); and, within the Jewish population, Jews of European or American origin (largely Ashkenazim) and Jews of Asian or African origin (largely Sephardim). In this social system, the Jewish population and the European-Americans comprise, respectively, the upper status

groups...A general awareness of these distinctions has led to a popular view of a tripartite ethnic order, with European-American Jews on top, Asian-African Jews in the middle, and Arabs on the bottom.

The majority of the Jewish population in Palestine before the establishment of Israel was of European-American origin. Most of the Asian-Africans arrived from Moslem countries in the Middle East and North Africa in the late 1940s and early 1950s. Their orientation to life was traditional, with only minimal exposure to the modern, westernized culture that had developed during the pre-state decades of settlement in Israel. Thus, they were faced with multiple disadvantages upon their arrival, including cultural estrangement, limited education, and the lack of socio-economic resources, skilled occupations and personal connections to the existing power structures in the country (Semyonov and Lewin-Epstein, 1987). Although the two Jewish ethnic groups are almost equal in size, European-Americans hold the higher positions in all dimensions of social stratification, including income, occupation, education, political power, standard of living and place of residence (Alder and Hodge, 1983; Selzer, 1965; Semyonov and Lewin-Epstein, 1987; Shavit, 1984; Smooha, 1976; Swirski, 1985).

The vast majority of Asian-African Jews lack capital assets, and thus have provided a pool of cheap labor for lower-level positions in the society's occupational stratum. According to Swirski (1985, 1990), their development is dependent on the planning of the 'larger society', which is controlled by the values, aspirations and actions of the dominant Ashkenazi (European-American) group. This group is, in part, represented by kibbutzim members (93% of whom are of European-American origin), who in spite of their quite low percentage in the Israeli population (3%), have played a prominent leadership role in areas of public service, government and the military (Curtis, 1973; Remba, 1973).

While there have been many changes in Israeli society over time, the ethnic stratification has remained relatively stable. Swirski (1990) cited a survey of Jewish males born in 1954 (Matras, Noam and Bar-Chaim, 1984) which revealed that 89% of Asian-African Jews did not pass the matriculation exams, which students take upon completion of high school, and must pass if they want to go on to higher education. Only 9% of Asian-African Jews went on to post-secondary education, compared to 43% of European-American Jews. In contrast, 48% of Asian-African Jews were employed in full-time jobs by the age of 17. Fifty-six percent (56%) of Asian-African Jews were employed in blue-collar occupations, compared to 35% of European-American Jews. In their longitudinal study of ethnic group occupational mobility, Semyonov and Lewin-Epstein (1987) found that European-American and Asian-African Jews were equally likely to improve their occupational status; thus, the gap between these groups has remained the same over time.

Arabs in Israel form the third level in the ethnic stratification. As a result of the establishment of Israel as a State in 1948, a high percentage of the Arab population, including most of its leadership, became refugees in the surrounding countries. Those remaining in the country became a minority population subject to Jewish economic and cultural domination (Landau, 1993; Peres, 1971; Rekhess, 1993). According to Smooha (1984, p. 10),

> The Arabs of Israel face multiple handicaps: lower status in the class structure, insufficient westernization in a European transplant society, being non-Jewish and non-Zionist in a society designed for Jews and Zionists, and being considered a security risk in a state under siege.

Israeli Arab citizens have experienced social and economic deprivation, as evidenced by levels of education, unemployment, poverty, workforce stratification, government social and health services, and numerous other elements related to living conditions (Al-Haj, 1992; Grossman, 1993; Landau, 1993; Lustick, 1980; Rekhess, 1993; Semyonov and Lewin-Epstein, 1987). Lustick (1980, p. 24) characterizes the overall position of Arab citizens of Israel as 'an isolated and peripheral group, whose demands for a greater share in the country's resources are seldom if ever registered in the national political arena'. The economic underdevelopment of the Arab sector remains one of the most striking characteristics of the country's social and economic structure (Lustick, 1980). Furthermore, the current Arab leadership in Israel has expressed their fears that the status of the Arab minority will be further marginalized as a consequence of the large-scale Soviet Jewish immigration (Al-Haj, 1992).

The lack of social cohesion in Israel, along with the extent of competition and conflict among various ethnic groups, is clearly related to these 'social gaps'. Swirski (1985, 1990) believes that this is a permanent feature of Israeli society, and that those of Asian-African background are being kept dependent upon those of European-American background. Halper (1985) notes that, although various agents of socialization (e.g., the military) have succeeded in bringing the children of Jewish immigrants from Eastern and Western backgrounds closer together, a significant gap still remains between the two groups, and is even evident among the second generation of these immigrant groups in Israel (Semyonov and Lewin-Epstein, 1987). Furthermore, the Arab citizens of Israel, as a whole, remain lower in all aspects of socio-economic status than the Jewish population (Grossman, 1993; Landau, 1993; Rekhess, 1993; Semyonov and Lewin-Epstein, 1987).

**Social conflict and cohesion: A conceptual framework**

Social theorists and researchers have developed a variety of approaches to defining and understanding conflict. It has been regarded as a failure of leadership (Barnard, 1962), and, in the context of government and political bureaucracies, as a result of human shortcomings such as cowardice, stupidity or greed (Weber, 1968). According to classical management theorists, it is a failure of adequate control, planning and execution. For the human theorists, it is a failure of leadership, a lack of participative process and decision making, and/or a temporarily constructive phenomenon that shows up areas where more work needs to be done (Perrow, 1986).

According to Morgan (1986), conflict arises whenever interests collide. The natural reaction to conflict in social contexts is usually to view it as a dysfunctional force that can be attributed to some regrettable set of circumstances or forces. It may be personal, interpersonal, or between rival groups or coalitions. It may be built into a society's structural roles, attitudes and stereotypes, or arise over a scarcity of resources. It may be explicit or covert. Whatever the reasons for it or the form it takes, its source lies in a real, or perceived, divergence of interests.

Burns (1961) has pointed out that modern social organization tends to promote conflict to the extent that it is organized as a system of simultaneous competition and collaboration. People must collaborate in pursuit of common goals and tasks, yet are often pitted against each other in competition for limited resources, status and opportunities.

Dahrendorf (1958) noted that the structural-functional approach in sociology, with its orientation toward problems of integration, neglects conflict processes, and suggests that models of social structure should include recognition of the built-in conflict associated with the dichotomy of positive and negative dominance roles. Coser (1956), for example, pointed out that conflict can have both dysfunctional and functional consequences. It can lead to heightened morale within subsystems or subgroups; and, it can lead to solutions which move more in an integrative than a compromise direction.

From yet another perspective, Robbins (1989, 1974) suggests that it is the result of: 1) imperfect or distorted communication and misunderstandings; 2) structural conditions, such as the heterogeneity of society, the extent of inclusion and participation, the power structure, the reward system, etc.; and 3) personal-behavioral variables in response to individual role satisfaction and goal achievement.

Within the context of Israeli society, the issue of conflict between various subgroups (i.e., Jews and Arabs, European-American Jews and Asian-African Jews, veteran Israelis and new immigrants, etc.) is essentially very similar to that in other multicultural societies; that is, an effort is made toward accommodation of conflicting population sections (Smooha, 1984; Swirski, 1990). This view of intergroup relations and social cohesion, can be characterized as the conflictual-pluralistic perspective (van den Berghe, 1978). It focuses on the pluralistic-inequality structure and its repercussions for internal stability. This perspective does not assign a priori precedence to either ethnicity or class; but, rather, it analyzes their interaction within society. It traces the sources of political stability/instability to the underlying forces of political organization and economic dependence (Smooha, 1984). The conflictual-pluralistic perspective has been used by Lustick (1980), Smooha (1978, 1984), Tessler (1980) and Swirski (1985, 1990) to gain insight into Israeli society.

This article examines and discusses the attitudes of Jewish and Arab Israeli citizens toward immigrants from the Soviet Union and the absorption process. It is based on a study that was designed to assess the extent of social cohesion and conflict being expressed by people with varying interests, social status and ethnic origins.

**The study**

*Subjects*

This study, conducted in 1991, was based on a random sample of Jewish (491) and Arab (115) citizens of Israel from the Negev region. The Jewish population included low-income residents of Beer-Sheva (primarily of Asian-African origin), middle- to high-income residents of a suburban community, and residents of kibbutzim. The later two groups consisted primarily of people of European-American origin. The Arab population included a representative cross-section of this ethnic group in the Negev. The study, like that of adolescents described in Chapter 5, is exploratory and based on data collected in one region of the country at one point in time. Generalization of the findings is thus limited.

*Method*

A questionnaire was developed based on the organizational behavior and intergroup conflict work of Robbins (1989). It included measures of conflict, group relations, and socio-demographic variables. Subjects were asked to use a 5-point Likert-type scale, ranging from (1) 'does not reflect my opinion at all' to (5) 'strongly reflects my opinion', to respond to 44 statements. The demographic variables included: sex, marital status, age, profession, education, father's and mother's education, ethnicity, place of residence and employment status. The statistical methods used to process the collected data were factor analysis and t-tests — two widely used measures.

The purpose of factor analysis, according to Kerlinger (1973, p. 150), '... is to help the researcher discover and identify the units or dimensions, called factors, behind many measures'. The construct validity of the instrument was examined through a factor analytic procedure. Two criteria were used in order to determine the number of factors: 1) the eigenvalue of each factor should be equal to or greater than 1.0 (eigenvalue is the total amount of variance accounted for by a factor, or the amount of explained variance due to a factor); and, 2) the loading of each item in the factors should be greater than or equal to 0.4.

The t-test compares sample means, and tests the significance of the differences between the means (Nie, Haadlai, Jenkins *et al.*, 1975).

*Findings*

Table 1 shows the results of factor analysis on the 44 items of intergroup conflict using the Varimax Rotation procedure with Kaiser Normalization. Using a loading of >0.40 as the threshold for inclusion, the items were distributed among seven primary factors:

Factor 1   'Dysfunctional Conflict' (e.g., immigration is a negative condition affecting people's lives and ability to get along).

Factor 2   'Security-Based Cooperation' (e.g., people should be involved with the immigration process to reduce conflict; and, job and economic security are important factors if people are to support the immigration process).

Factor 3   'Social Disintegration' (e.g., immigration limits access to housing, services, and jobs, which leads to intergroup conflict).

Factor 4   'Functional Conflict' (e.g., immigration has a positive influence on people's ability to solve their problems and be creative in addressing their needs).

Factor 5   'Religious Leadership' (e.g., religious leaders have an influence on improving intergroup relations toward immigration).

Factor 6   'Interpersonal Communication' (e.g., communication is important in promoting good intergroup relations about immigration).

Factor 7   'Media Impact' (e.g., information about immigration through the media is helpful and a positive influence in terms of people's attitudes and understanding toward immigration).

The seven factors have an eigenvalue greater than 1.0, and explain 63% of the variance.

Table 1.
Dimensions of intergroup conflict and factor analysis, Varimax Rotation

| ITEM | | FACTORS | | | | | | |
|---|---|---|---|---|---|---|---|---|
| | | 1 | 2 | 3 | 4 | 5 | 6 | 7 |
| 1 | Soviet immigration is crippling the country's ability to meet the needs of its citizens. | .40 | .14 | .45 | -.12 | -.07 | -.08 | -.05 |
| 2 | The government is making an effort to help immigrants. | .44 | -.03 | -.14 | .09 | .00 | -.11 | .34 |
| 3 | A lack of openness and trust exists between the government and the people over Soviet immigration. | .10 | .02 | .46 | -.01 | -.00 | .00 | -.13 |
| 4 | Information (e.g., newspapers, television, etc.) on why people need to help Soviet immigrants is good. | .08 | .05 | .07 | .05 | .12 | -.05 | .73 |
| 5 | Information (e.g., newspapers, television, etc.) about the importance of Soviet immigration is poor. | -.04 | .03 | .00 | .06 | .17 | -.05 | -.69 |

Table 1 (cont'd)

| ITEM | | FACTORS | | | | | | |
|---|---|---|---|---|---|---|---|---|
| | | 1 | 2 | 3 | 4 | 5 | 6 | 7 |
| 6 | Government assistance to Soviet immigrants comes at the expense of Israeli citizens. | .54 | -.03 | .36 | -.13 | -.05 | -.03 | -.06 |
| 7 | Soviet immigration will limit my ability to obtain a good paying job. | .66 | -.01 | .17 | -.00 | -.05 | .11 | -.02 |
| 8 | Soviet immigration should be limited. | .43 | -.41 | .30 | .03 | -.11 | -.06 | .16 |
| 9 | Soviet immigration will not affect my present job. | -.31 | .13 | .32 | .00 | .04 | -.08 | .03 |
| 10 | Soviet immigration will limit my ability to obtain a job with prestige. | .63 | -.10 | .21 | -.00 | .02 | -.05 | -.08 |
| 11 | Soviet immigration will affect my ability to obtain better housing. | .63 | .02 | .08 | -.10 | .04 | -.01 | .01 |
| 12 | Soviet immigration will limit my ability to improve my social status. | .57 | -.24 | .28 | -.01 | .03 | -.10 | -.11 |
| 13 | Soviet immigration will restrict my ability to receive public services (e.g., treatment, day care, etc.). | .30 | -.27 | .56 | -.11 | .07 | -.02 | .05 |
| 14 | Soviet immigration will cause conflict over available resources (job, housing, university acceptance, etc.) between Israeli citizens. | .38 | .22 | .39 | -.29 | -.12 | .08 | -.07 |
| 15 | Limited resources, as a result of Soviet immigration, will lead to violent, destructive, or irrational behavior among people. | .22 | -.00 | .59 | -.21 | -.07 | .12 | .08 |
| 16 | Conflict with Soviet immigrants cannot be avoided. | .20 | -.16 | .57 | -.14 | -.05 | -.02 | .17 |
| 17 | People need to accept the fact that there will be conflict with Israeli citizens and Soviet immigrants. | .20 | -.12 | .33 | -.02 | -.08 | .07 | .18 |
| 18 | Soviet immigration is important to the future of Israel. | -.32 | .55 | -.15 | .14 | .13 | .01 | -.08 |

Table 1 (cont'd)

| ITEM | | FACTORS | | | | | | |
|---|---|---|---|---|---|---|---|---|
| | | 1 | 2 | 3 | 4 | 5 | 6 | 7 |
| 19 | The Soviet immigration is causing people to be more creative in addressing society's problems. | .04 | .15 | -.00 | .63 | -.15 | -.03 | -.05 |
| 20 | Soviet immigration has a positive influence on how this country deals with its citizens. | -.04 | -.08 | -.17 | .70 | .06 | .04 | -.00 |
| 21 | Soviet immigration has helped to promote ways of meeting the needs of all people in this country. | -.22 | -.07 | -.14 | .56 | .18 | -.00 | -.11 |
| 22 | Conflict over Soviet immigration is an obstacle to the performance of Israeli citizens. | .35 | -.22 | .50 | .05 | -.10 | .05 | -.01 |
| 23 | Soviet immigration is obstructing peace between Arabs and Jews in Israel. | .37 | -.36 | .29 | .15 | -.13 | .00 | .14 |
| 24 | Soviet immigration will promote attempts by by government to improve the quality of Israeli citizens' lives. | -.01 | .04 | -.13 | .63 | .09 | .07 | -.01 |
| 25 | My family and friends believe Soviet immigration is a threat to their ability to succeed in life. | .56 | -.21 | .28 | -.00 | -.01 | -.06 | .09 |
| 26 | My family has a role in helping with the absorption of Soviet immigrants. | -.45 | .17 | -.00 | .20 | .16 | .10 | -.08 |
| 27 | Teachers have a role in reducing conflict and promoting people's understanding of Soviet immigration. | -.25 | .45 | -.00 | .05 | .35 | .30 | .07 |
| 28 | Religious leaders have a role in reducing conflict and promoting Soviet immigration. | -.05 | .14 | -.03 | .13 | .84 | .12 | -.01 |
| 29 | Religious leaders have the ability to improve people's attitude toward Soviet immigrants. | -.06 | .08 | -.08 | .12 | .84 | .09 | -.03 |

Table 1 (cont'd)

| ITEM | | FACTORS | | | | | | |
|---|---|---|---|---|---|---|---|---|
| | | 1 | 2 | 3 | 4 | 5 | 6 | 7 |
| 30 | Poor communication between Soviet immigrants and veteran Israeli citizens causes conflict. | .07 | .07 | .05 | -.00 | .12 | .68 | -.02 |
| 31 | If people could communicate better with each other, differences over Soviet immigration would be eliminated. | -.07 | .09 | -.09 | .02 | .14 | .67 | .07 |
| 32 | Too much communication in the media about Soviet immigration is a reason for conflict between Israeli citizens and new immigrants. | .44 | -.01 | .25 | -.03 | .01 | .13 | .14 |
| 33 | There is misunderstanding about Soviet immigration because of poor communication among citizens. | .09 | .01 | .09 | .14 | -.05 | .66 | -.04 |
| 34 | The more people are involved with Soviet immigration the more conflict between citizens will be reduced. | -.18 | .52 | .09 | .22 | .03 | .39 | .02 |
| 35 | If people were more secure in their jobs there would be less conflict between citizens and Soviet immigrants. | .06 | .67 | .02 | .00 | .07 | -.06 | .03 |
| 36 | If people were more secure in their economic situation there would be less conflict between citizens and Soviet immigrants. | .10 | .72 | .02 | -.05 | .06 | .01 | .13 |
| 37 | Conflict exists between Israeli citizens and Soviet immigrants because Soviet immigrants are receiving too many rewards and benefits. | .51 | .11 | .21 | -.01 | -.07 | .04 | .06 |
| 38 | I deserve at least the same benefits being received by a new immigrant because I am a citizen of Israel. | .65 | -.09 | .14 | -.03 | -.13 | -.02 | .08 |
| 39 | I am competing with Soviet immigrants for a job, housing, and/or a place at the university. | .61 | -.06 | .03 | -.11 | .03 | .10 | .04 |

Table 1 (cont'd)

| ITEM | | FACTORS | | | | | | |
|---|---|---|---|---|---|---|---|---|
| | | 1 | 2 | 3 | 4 | 5 | 6 | 7 |
| 40 | Good relationships between citizens and Soviet immigrants will promote cooperation. | -.16 | .60 | -.09 | .25 | -.02 | .17 | -.04 |
| 41 | Conflict with Soviet immigrants will be avoided by staying away from them and letting them solve their own problems. | .29 | -.43 | .33 | .10 | .11 | -.17 | .15 |
| 42 | If people put the needs of Soviet immigrants above their own, absorption will be successful. | -.19 | .17 | .10 | .40 | .13 | .08 | .18 |
| 43 | If Soviet immigrants give up expectations related to a better quality of life, conflict with Israelis will be reduced. | .17 | .19 | .32 | .22 | .14 | .11 | -.04 |
| 44 | Soviet immigration has caused the country to stop being apathetic. | -.05 | .08 | .09 | .50 | .09 | .14 | .34 |
| Eigenvalue | | 8.2 | 3.4 | 2.5 | 1.6 | 1.5 | 1.4 | 1.3 |

Table 2 contains the means and standard deviations of the intergroup conflict dimensions.

## Table 2.
### Means and Standard Deviations of the intergroup conflict dimensions (N=606)

| Dimensions | Mean | S.D. |
|---|---|---|
| 1. Dysfunctional Conflict | 36.83 | 9.38 |
| 2. Security-Based Cooperation | 24.51 | 4.29 |
| 3. Social Disintegration | 22.37 | 5.56 |
| 4. Functional Conflict | 16.05 | 4.56 |
| 5. Religious Leadership | 5.89 | 2.54 |
| 6. Interpersonal Communication | 9.73 | 2.54 |
| 7. Media Impact | 6.01 | 1.42 |

## Reliability

Kerlinger (1973) defined reliability as the 'accuracy or precision of the measuring instrument' (p. 443), which is enhanced by: 1) writing unambiguous items that individuals will not interpret differently; 2) including a sufficient number of items of equal kinds of quality; 3) writing clear and standard instructions; and 4) administering the instrument under standard and well-controlled conditions.

A summary of the factors, the number of items, the means, and Alpha (If Item Deleted) for the factor analysis of the intergroup conflict questionnaire is presented in Table 3. The Alpha reliability for the derived factors was acceptable.

### Table 3.
### Means and internal consistencies of intergroup conflict dimensions (N=606)

| Dimensions | No. of Items | Reliability Means | Alpha |
|---|---|---|---|
| 1. Dysfunctional Conflict | 13 | 2.14 | .86 |
| 2. Security-Based Cooperation | 7 | 3.75 | .75 |
| 3. Social Disintegration | 7 | 3.20 | .76 |
| 4. Functional Conflict | 6 | 2.63 | .66 |
| 5. Religious Leadership | 2 | 2.95 | .84 |
| 6. Interpersonal Communication | 3 | 3.24 | .55 |
| 7. Media Impact | 2 | 3.27 | .54 |

## Results

Table 4 contains a general comparison of the attitudes of all Jews and Arabs toward Soviet immigration. It reveals that Jews differ from Arabs significantly on 6 of the 7 dimensions: a) dysfunctional conflict; b) security-based cooperation; c) social disintegration; d) functional conflict; e) religious leadership; and f) media impact. Jews, in general, tend to have a more positive view of Soviet immigration than Arabs, believing that it is important to the future of the country, and that it can play a positive, creative role in society, so long as their economic security is not threatened by it (security-based cooperation and functional conflict dimensions). Jews also tend to believe, more strongly than Arabs, that religious leadership and the media have a positive role to play in improving the attitudes of people toward immigration and generating broader public support and cooperation (religious leadership and media impact dimensions).

Israeli Arabs tend to have a more negative view of Soviet immigration than Jews, in the sense that it will negatively affect their ability to secure better jobs, educational opportunities, housing and living standards. Arabs want the same benefits being given to the new immigrants, and tend to believe more strongly that immigration is likely to cause conflict because of the scarcity of resources, and thus should be limited (dysfunctional conflict and social disintegration dimensions).

Table 4.
Means and standard deviation and t-value for the intergroup conflict dimensions comparing Jews to Arabs

| Dimensions | Jews | | Arabs | | | |
|---|---|---|---|---|---|---|
| | Mean | S.D. | Mean | S.D. | t-Value | p |
| 1. Dysfunctional Conflict | 35.08 | 8.86 | 45.05 | 7.43 | -11.03 | .00 |
| 2. Security-Based Cooperation | 25.26 | 3.80 | 21.60 | 4.70 | 8.65 | .00 |
| 3. Social Disintegration | 21.49 | 5.30 | 26.15 | 4.90 | -8.60 | .00 |
| 4. Functional Conflict | 16.26 | 4.62 | 14.96 | 3.95 | 2.70 | .01 |
| 5. Religious Leadership | 6.04 | 2.43 | 4.96 | 2.26 | 4.36 | .00 |
| 6. Interpersonal Communication | 9.78 | 2.56 | 9.39 | 2.30 | 1.51 | .13 |
| 7. Media Impact | 6.04 | 1.45 | 5.80 | 1.36 | 1.60 | .01 |

Table 5, which compares Arabs to low-income Jews in Beer-Sheva, reveals significant differences on only 2 factors (dysfunctional conflict and security-based cooperation) which is fewer than between Arabs and Jews in general, and even fewer than between low- and high-income Jewish groups. As in the comparison to Jews in general, Arabs tend to believe that immigration will negatively affect their lives and ability to cooperate with others more so than low-income Jews (dysfunctional conflict dimension); while low income Jews are more likely than Arabs to believe that people's cooperation with and involvement in the absorption process can reduce conflict, as long as their job and economic security is not threatened (security-based cooperation). Unlike the general comparison between Jews and Arabs, the attitudes of low-income Jews and Arabs regarding the negative impact of immigration (i.e., in terms of access to housing, jobs and services, and its overall potential to lead to social conflict) are very similar (social disintegration). Also, Arabs and low-income Jews do not tend to believe that immigration has a positive, creative role in society (functional conflict).

**Table 5.**

**Means and standard deviation and t-value for the intergroup conflict dimensions comparing Arabs and low-income, urban Jews**

| Dimensions | Jews | | Arabs | | t-Value | p |
|---|---|---|---|---|---|---|
| | Mean | S.D. | Mean | S.D. | | |
| 1. Dysfunctional Conflict | 45.05 | 7.39 | 40.81 | 8.5 | 3.54 | .00 |
| 2. Security-Based Cooperation | 21.68 | 4.68 | 25.30 | 3.03 | -5.79 | .00 |
| 3. Social Disintegration | 26.09 | 4.83 | 26.04 | 5.04 | .07 | .94 |
| 4. Functional Conflict | 15.01 | 3.91 | 14.46 | 4.57 | .86 | .39 |
| 5. Religious Leadership | 4.95 | 2.25 | 5.46 | 1.99 | -1.57 | .12 |
| 6. Interpersonal Communication | 9.43 | 2.25 | 9.33 | 1.91 | .30 | .77 |
| 7. Media Impact | 5.83 | 1.35 | 6.20 | 1.13 | -1.90 | .06 |

Figure 1 graphically displays the scores of the Arabs, low-income Jews, middle/high-income Jews and kibbutz members on the intergroup conflict dimensions. In terms of three of the four most prominent dimensions (dysfunctional conflict, social disintegration, and functional conflict), attitudes tend to be closely related to socio-economic status.

Table 6, which compares Jews of low-income status in Beer-Sheva (primarily of Asian-African origin) and suburban Jews of the middle- and upper-classes (primarily of European-American origin), shows that these two groups differ significantly on 4 dimensions: a) dysfunctional conflict; b) security-based cooperation; c) social disintegration; and, d) functional conflict. People of low-income status tend to have a more negative view of Soviet immigration than those of middle- and high-income status in the sense that immigration impairs their ability to secure better jobs, housing and quality of life. Low-income people believe: they should receive the same benefits being given to the new immigrants; immigration should be limited; and that immigration is likely to cause conflict because of the scarcity of resources (social disintegration and dysfunctional conflict dimensions). Those from the upper middle- and high-income community are more likely to believe that immigration can play a positive, creative role, and that it is important to the future of the country. They also

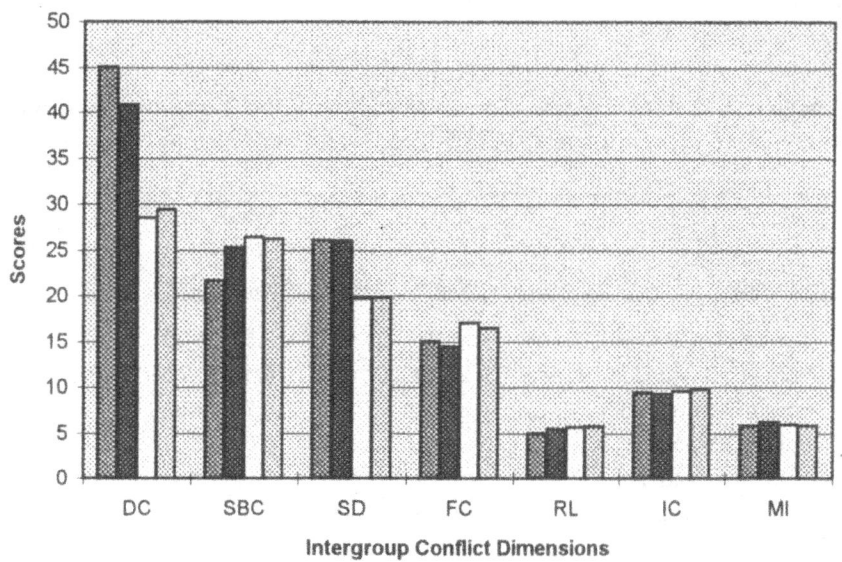

DC = Dysfunctional Conflict
SBC = Security-Based Cooperation
SD = Social Disintegration
FC = Functional Conflict
RL = Religious Leadership
IC = Interpersonal Communication
MI = Media Impact

■ Arabs
■ Low-income Jews
□ High-Income Jews
■ Kibbutz Members

Figure 1.
Intergroup conflict dimension scores of four subgroups

believe more strongly that good relations between citizens and immigrants will promote cooperation and limit conflict, insofar as there are good economic conditions and sufficient job security (functional conflict and security-based cooperation dimensions).

Table 6.

**Means and standard deviation and t-value for the intergroup conflict dimensions comparing Jews of low-income and high-income communities**

| Dimensions | Low-Income (N=69) Mean | S.D. | High-Income (N=70) Mean | S.D. | t-Value | p |
|---|---|---|---|---|---|---|
| 1. Dysfunctional Conflict | 40.81 | 8.54 | 28.53 | 8.43 | 8.40 | .00 |
| 2. Security-Based Cooperation | 25.30 | 2.03 | 26.41 | 3.40 | -2.01 | .05 |
| 3. Social Disintegration | 26.04 | 5.04 | 19.74 | 4.82 | 7.51 | .00 |
| 4. Functional Conflict | 14.46 | 4.57 | 17.09 | 5.05 | -3.18 | .00 |
| 5. Religious Leadership | 5.46 | 1.99 | 5.67 | 2.64 | -0.52 | .60 |
| 6. Interpersonal Communication | 9.33 | 1.91 | 9.61 | 2.98 | -0.65 | .52 |
| 7. Media Impact | 6.20 | 1.13 | 5.91 | 1.37 | 1.35 | .18 |

Table 7, which compares low-income Jewish residents of Beer-Sheva (primarily of Asian-African origin) and kibbutz members (primarily of European-American origin), shows these two groups differ significantly on 4 dimensions: a) dysfunctional conflict; b) social disintegration; c) functional conflict; and, d) media impact. Low-income residents of Beer-Sheva tend to have a more negative view of Soviet immigration than kibbutz members in the sense that it impairs their ability to secure better jobs, housing, and quality of life. They want the same benefits being given to the new immigrants, and more strongly believe that immigration should be limited, or it is likely to cause conflict because of the scarcity of resources (social disintegration and dysfunctional conflict dimension). Kibbutz members are more likely to believe that immigration can play a positive, creative role, and that it is important to the future of the country as long as jobs and economic stability remain secure (security-based cooperation and functional conflict dimensions). Low income Jews believe more strongly that the media can have a role in reducing conflict by improving the attitudes of people toward new immigrants (media impact dimension).

Table 7.

Means and standard deviation and t-value for the intergroup conflict dimensions comparing kibbutz members and low-income, urban Jews

| Dimensions | Kibbutz Members (N=66) | | Low-Income Jews (N=69) | | t-Value | p |
|---|---|---|---|---|---|---|
| | Mean | S.D. | Mean | S.D. | | |
| 1. Dysfunctional Conflict | 29.45 | 7.02 | 40.81 | 8.54 | -8.34 | .00 |
| 2. Security-Based Cooperation | 26.24 | 3.13 | 25.30 | 3.03 | 1.77 | .08 |
| 3. Social Disintegration | 19.76 | 3.91 | 26.04 | 5.04 | -7.91 | .00 |
| 4. Functional Conflict | 16.51 | 3.59 | 14.46 | 4.57 | 2.87 | .01 |
| 5. Religious Leadership | 5.71 | 2.39 | 5.46 | 1.99 | 0.66 | .51 |
| 6. Interpersonal Communication | 9.82 | 2.42 | 9.33 | 1.91 | 1.28 | .20 |
| 7. Media Impact | 5.79 | 1.33 | 6.20 | 1.13 | -1.95 | .05 |

A comparison was made between Jewish residents of the upper middle/high-income suburban community and those of the kibbutzim, both of whom are predominantly of European-American origin. These two groups did not differ significantly on any of the intergroup conflict dimensions, both having a consistently more positive view of immigration than the Arabs and the Jewish residents of a low-income neighborhood in Beer-Sheva (see Figure 1).

Discussion

This study reveals that the ethnicity and socio-economic status of Israeli citizens tend to be associated with their attitudes toward the impact of Soviet immigration on intergroup conflict. As expected, Jews tend to have a more positive attitude to Soviet immigration than Arabs. The immigration system in Israel is based on the 'Law of Return', which applies only to Jews, giving them the right to immigrate to Israel and receive citizenship automatically (Adler and Kahana, 1972). Thus, immigration [*aliyah*] is a central concept in the Zionist ideology, and commands a broad Jewish national consensus (Levine, 1983; Avineri, 1981). As Portes and Borocz (1989, p. 619) postulated, 'members of ethnic diasporas who join nation-states formed by their co-nationals, as in the case of Russian Jews emigrating to Israel', would be expected to receive sympathetic support from the public.

The study findings reveal that Arabs (compared to Jews) have a more negative view of the impact of Soviet immigration *vis-à-vis* their security, opportunities and place in society. This, again, is not surprising, since Arabs are at the bottom of the socio-economic stratum of Israeli society; therefore, they are the most concerned about the impact of immigration on the availability of scarce resources (Al-Haj, 1992; Semyonov and Lewin-Epstein, 1987). The Arab economy is primarily based on wage-labor in the Jewish sector, since there is no industrial or any other economic base in the Arab sector. Their economic vulnerability is increased by the fact that they have very limited access to the national opportunity structure (Al-Haj, 1992; Lustick, 1980). During the absorption of the Soviet immigrants in the early 1990s, statements by Israeli officials about using 'Hebrew labor' (i.e. new Jewish immigrants) to replace Arab employees further increased the Arabs' awareness of the threat Soviet immigration posed to their economic status (Al-Haj, 1992). This state of insecurity applied to professionals as well as to those with skilled and unskilled occupations. According to Al-Haj (1992, p. 96):

> . . . Soviet immigration is expected to negatively affect Arabs in high-rank positions. It is feared that some Arab physicians working in Israeli hospitals and official health services may be eased out to make room for Russian Jewish doctors. It will also be very difficult for Arab university graduates to compete with the newcomers for professional jobs. Even before this influx of immigrants the access enjoyed by Arab academics to such jobs was limited.

The findings show differences within the ranks of the Jewish population, based on socio-economic/ethnic status. Interestingly, the attitudes of low-income Jews in Beer-Sheva (who are primarily of Asian-African background) toward Soviet immigration and intergroup conflict, were closer to the attitudes of Arabs than they were to the attitudes of Jews from the middle/high-income suburban community and the kibbutzim. In particular, low-income Jews and Arabs tend to view immigration as an event that will impair their socio-economic status, opportunities, and quality of life; as well as limit social cohesion in the country. Low-income Jews, more than middle- and high-income Jews view immigration as a dysfunctional or negative condition. From an ethnic perspective, low-income Jews in this study, who are predominantly of African-Asian origin, perceive the Soviet immigrants (who are of the dominant European orientation) as recipients of services, benefits and other opportunities that they, as long-term citizens, have not received. Thus, competition for scarce resources becomes an intervening variable which negatively impacts their support for an unlimited immigration policy. As Goldscheider (1992, p. 10) predicted,

> It is likely that the descendants of previous waves of immigrants, particularly disadvantaged populations of non-European origins, will have negative reaction to these newcomers and to the government subsidies they will receive. . . . Although commitment to Jewish nationalism, Zionism, is among the determinants of immigration to Israel, ideological factors always operate in social-economic-political contexts.

On the other hand, residents of the middle/high-income suburban community and the kibbutzim, who form a relatively high status, economically stable group in Israeli society, consider immigration to be a functional event — one that has a positive influence on the ability of people to solve their own problems, overcome apathy, promote creativity, and contribute to the future success of the country. As long as they do not feel that it jeopardizes their job security or quality of life, they support unlimited immigration.

Israeli society is a complex configuration of multiple groups and interests that often come into conflict because of the deep-rooted, socio-economic stratification. It is not surprising, therefore, that immigration is viewed by particular segments of society as exacerbating this stratification, and thus, providing another source of intergroup conflict.

In a period marked by economic and social scarcities, Israel wants to retain its commitment to absorb large numbers of immigrants. Immigration is seen as a source of social conflict particularly by the segments of society that have traditionally formed the underclasses (i.e., Asian-African Jews and Arabs), in which low socio-economic status, limited opportunities, and high rates of unemployment and underemployment are the norm. Few constructive inroads for improving social cohesion and reducing social conflict can be expected unless major policies and programs addressing the needs of the underclasses are implemented in the fundamental areas of education, employment, housing, quality of life, and full integration into the opportunity structures of the country.

## References

Adler, H. and Kahana, R. (1972), 'The State Structure and Institutions', in Eisenstadt, S. and Kahana, R. (eds.), *Israel: A Society in Formation*

— *A Socio-Logical Analysis of Resources*, Magnes Press: Jerusalem, pp. 169-74. [Hebrew]

Alder, I. and Hodge, R. (1983), 'Ethnicity and the Process of Status Attainment', *Israel Social Science Research*, Vol. 1, No. 2, pp. 5-23.

Avineri, S. (1981), *The Making of Modern Zionism: The Intellectual Origins of the Jewish State*, Basic Books: New York.

Al-Haj, M. (1992), 'Soviet Immigration as Viewed by Jews and Arabs: Divided Attitudes in a Divided Country', in Goldscheider, C. (ed.), *Population and Social Change in Israel*, Westview Press: Boulder, CO, pp. 89-108

Barnard, C. (1962), *The Functions of the Executive*. Harvard University Press: Cambridge, MA.

Burns, T. (1961), 'Micropolitics: Mechanisms of Organizational Change', *Administrative Science Quarterly*, Vol. 6, pp. 257-81.

Coser, L. (1956), *The Functions of Social Conflict*, Routledge & Kegan Paul: New York.

Curtis, M. (1973), 'Utopia and the Kibbutz', in Curtis, M. and Chertoff, S. (eds.), *Israel Social Structure and Change*, Transaction: New Brunswick, NJ.

Dahrendorf, R. (1958), 'Toward a Theory of Social Conflict', *Journal of Conflict Resolution*, Vol. 2, pp. 170-83.

Goldscheider, C. (1992), 'Demographic Transformations in Israel: Emerging Themes in Comparative Context', in Goldscheider, C. (ed.), *Population and Social Change in Israel*, Westview Press: Boulder, CO, pp. 1-38

Grossman, D. (1993), *Sleeping on a Wire: Conversations with Palestinians in Israel*, Farrar, Straus and Giroux: New York.

Halper, J. (1985), 'The Absorption of Ethiopian Immigrants: A Return to the Fifties', in Ashkenazi, M. and Weingrod, A. (eds.), *Ethiopian Jews and Israel*, Special Issue of *Israel Social Science Research*, Vol. 3, Nos. 1&2, pp. 112-39. [also published as a book by Transaction: New Brunswick, NJ, 1987]

Kerlinger, R. (1973), *Foundations of Behavioral Research*, 2nd Edn., Holt, Rinehardt and Winston: New York.

Landau, J. (1993), *The Arab Minority in Israel, 1967-1991: Political Aspects*, Am Oved Publishers: Tel Aviv. [Hebrew]

Levine, E. (1983), 'Confronting the Aliyah Option', in Levine, E. (ed.), *Diaspora, Exile and the Jewish Condition*, Jason Aronson: New York, pp. 283-93

Lewin-Epstein, N. and Semyonov, M. (1986), 'Ethnic Group Mobility in the Israeli Labor Market', *American Sociological Review*, Vol. 51, pp. 342-51.

Lustick, I. (1980), *Arabs in the Jewish State: Israel's Control of a National Minority*, University of Texas: Austin, TX.

Matras, N., Noam, S. and Bar-Chaim, S. (1984), *Israeli Students and Bagrut Results: Studying Types, Army Service and Employment*, Brookdale Institute: Jerusalem.

Morgan, G. (1986), *Images of Organization*, Sage: Newbury Park, CA.

Nie, N., Haadlai, H., Jenkins, J., Steinbrenner, K. and Bent, D. (1975), *Statistical Package for the Social Sciences*, McGraw-Hill: New York.

Peres, Y. (1971), 'Ethnic Relations in Israel', *American Journal of Sociology*, Vol. 76, pp. 1031-41.

Perrow, C. (1986), *Complex Organizations: A Critical Essay*, 3rd Edn., Random House: New York.

Portes, A. and Borocz, J. (1989), 'Contemporary Immigration: Theoretical Perspectives on its Determinants and Modes of Incorporation', *International Migration Review*, Vol. 23, pp. 606-30.

Rekhess, E. (1993), *The Arab Minority in Israel: Between Communism and Arab Nationalism, 1965-1991*, HaKibbutz HaMeuhad: Tel-Aviv. [Hebrew]

Remba, O. (1973) 'Income Inequality in Israel: Ethnic Aspects', in Curtis, M. and Chertoff, S. (eds.), *Israel Social Structure and Change*, Transaction: New Brunswick, NJ.

Robbins, S. (1974), *Managing Organizational Conflict: A Nontraditional Approach*, Prentice-Hall: Englewood Cliffs, NJ.

Robbins, S. (1989), *Organizational Behavior*, Prentice-Hall: Englewood Cliffs, NJ.

Rosenbaum-Tamari, J. and Dimian, N. (1991), 'The Two Waves of Immigration: The Soviet Immigrants in the 1970s and the Onset of the 1990s', a paper presented at the Annual meeting of the Israeli Sociological Association, April 1991, Tel-Aviv.

Selzer, M. (1965), *The Outcasts of Israel: Communal Tensions in the Jewish State*, The Council of the Sephardi Community: Jerusalem.

Semyonov, M. and Lewin-Epstein, N. (1987), *Hewers of Wood and Drawers of Water*, ILR Press: New York.

Semyonov, M. and Tyree, A. (1981), 'Community Segregation and the Costs of Ethnic Subordination', *Social Forces*, Vol. 59, pp. 649-86.

Shavit, Y. (1984), 'Tracking and Ethnicity in Israeli Secondary Education', *American Sociological Review*, Vol. 49, pp. 210-21.

Smooha, S. (1984), *The Orientation and Politicization of the Arab*

*Minority in Israel*, Monograph Series on the Middle East, No. 2, Institute of Middle Eastern Studies, Haifa University: Haifa.

Smooha, S. (1976), 'Ethnic Stratification and Allegiance in Israel: Where Do Oriental Jews Belong?' *Il Politico*, Vol. 41, pp. 635-51.

Smooha, S. (1978), *Israel: Pluralism and Conflict*, Routledge and Kegan Paul: London.

Swirski, S. (1981), *Orientals and Ashkenazis in Israel: The Ethnic Division of Labor*, Makhberot LeMekhkor Ulebikoret: Haifa. [Hebrew]

Swirski, S. (1990), *Education in Israel: Schooling for Inequality*, Brirot: Tel-Aviv. [Hebrew]

Tessler, M. (1980), 'Arabs in Israel', in *Asia*, American Universities Field Staff Report, No. 1.

van den Berghe, P. (1978), *Race and Racism, 2nd Edn.*, John Wiley: New York.

Weber, M. (1968), *Economy and Society: An Outline of Interpretive Sociology*, Bedminster: New York.

# 7 Immigrant women as child care providers

*Julia Wrigley*

The increasing number of households in which both parents work, or where a single parent works, has led to a resurgent demand for in-home child care workers. When parents hire a nanny or babysitter, they must pay the entire wage of another person. It is only possible for one household to support a full-time adult worker where there is substantial economic inequality. There must be a pool of employers able to afford another person's sustenance, whether the parents provide payment entirely in cash or partially in kind. The pool of parents able to afford in-home child care grows when there is a large supply of low-wage workers available. In the United States, these conditions occur most strikingly in cities that serve as ports-of-entry for immigrants. Dark-skinned women pushing baby strollers containing blond babies are a common sight in wealthy districts of cities such as New York and Los Angeles.

Both historically and today, servant populations have been drawn mainly from migrant groups, whether internal migrants from rural to urban regions within a country, or immigrants from another country (Tilly and Scott, 1978; Chaney and Castro, 1989). Non-migrant workers have typically done domestic work only when they have suffered severe political repression and exclusion from more desirable jobs, as with African-American women in the American South (Palmer, 1989). Job gains won by African-Americans have partially freed them from domestic employment, while the increasing flow of Third World immigrants to the United States has made them the prime source of domestic workers. In any given city, the ethnic/national mix of domestic workers depends on the pattern of migration. In Los Angeles, most in-home caregivers are from Mexico or Central America. In New York, the market is more diverse, with women from the West Indies and the Dominican Republic filling the bulk of domestic slots.

In this article, I explore the role of immigrant women as in-home child care workers in the United States, focusing on how they are affected by the internal stratification of the market for children's caregivers. Although immigrant women from Third World countries do the bulk of domestic child care work, they are not the only workers in this market. They compete with others, including foreign *au pairs* (educated young women, generally from Western Europe, who work for a year or more to gain cultural experience), domestic *au pairs* (young women, almost always white, who are recruited from Midwestern or semi-rural states to work on the east or west coast), college students, and, at the upper end of the market, with 'professional' caregivers, such as the classic English nanny. These workers occupy different niches of the domestic child care market. In selecting a caregiver, parents choose among types of workers, as well as among individual candidates.

In a market with no barriers to entry (except, to some extent, sex, with many parents reluctant or unwilling to consider a male caregiver), parents, who for the most part are middle-class and well-educated, choose among workers who have different degrees of cultural distance from themselves. Based on interviews with employers and employees in Los Angeles, I suggest that the market for domestic child care workers is internally stratified, with the stratification turning on workers' perceived possession of what Pierre Bourdieu calls 'cultural capital' (1973). Those workers who project themselves as having the most cultural capital — that is, the most familiarity with modes of speech and behavior valued by their middle-class employers — command the highest wage and the best working conditions in the child care market. Immigrant women from Third World countries generally must do the most work for the least money in the domestic child care market: they are perceived as having the least cultural capital, whatever their level of individual caregiving skill or commitment.

The importance of cultural capital in the internal stratification of the market for in-home caregivers should not be overstated, since almost all caregivers receive relatively low wages and have few job protections. Some workers do better than others, however, and their different prospects and experiences shed light on broader processes of stratification in American society. In particular, the payoff for cultural capital in this market illustrates the far-reaching 'educationalization' of the society (see Collins, 1979). Parents are not only hiring an employee, but are hiring a daily substitute for themselves. Those parents with sufficient resources to hire an in-home caregiver tend to be well-educated, and their definition of 'quality' child care is bound up with a class-specific notion of how parents (or their substitutes) should talk to and engage young children. This leads some employing parents to place priority on finding caregivers who share what they define as key elements of their child-rearing style, including their interest in fostering their young children's verbal skills and intellectual development.

The importance of cultural capital in the market for in-home child care workers shows that educational demands permeate even the informal sector of the economy. Their importance is obvious in the formal sector, where workers have specified tasks and rights. In this sector, hiring is bureaucratized and educational credentials affect workers' eligibility for jobs, their wages, and their chances for promotion. In the informal sector, hiring remains personalized and workers can be fired arbitrarily. Typically, educational credentials are not relevant to workers' initial hiring and there is no career ladder to climb (Piore, 1980).

Those immigrant workers with low levels of education and limited English skills usually enter the informal or underground economy, since they lack the ability to compete in the formal market. This is particularly the case for undocumented immigrants. These workers constitute what Castells and Portes (1989) call downgraded labor. Those with some capital can exploit their own labor and that of their families to start and run small businesses; those without the capital to follow this route generally do low-wage factory work or enter service employment (Waldinger, 1986). Work in private households usually attracts those with the fewest options. The continuing importance of garment sweatshops in the regional economies of Los Angeles, New York, and Miami means that many undocumented women workers are able to secure factory jobs (Fernandez-Kelly and Garcia, 1989). Contrary to popular impression, substantially more female Mexican immigrants to Los Angeles work in factories than in private homes as domestics. Although it is not entirely clear why some women end up in factories and some in private households, evidence suggests that domestic work ranks below sweatshop work in terms of desirability. A higher proportion of those doing domestic work than of those doing factory work are undocumented. Private household workers earn lower wages than factory workers, and employment histories of workers show that many women begin as domestic workers when they first come to the country, but then switch to factory employment as they become more acclimatized and independent. Married women, or those with children present, find factory work more compatible with their own family lives and child-rearing (Pessar, 1987; Foner, 1987).

Aside from jobs where workers engage in specifically illegal activities, such as selling drugs (Stepick, 1989), there is probably no more informal part of the informal economy than domestic work. Even undocumented workers employed in small, fly-by-night garment sweatshops are generally paid by check and have some taxes taken out of their wages (Fernandez-Kelly and Garcia, 1989). Workers in private households are much more likely to be paid in cash and very few have any waged connection to the social welfare system; that is, very seldom are taxes paid on their behalf by employers or deducted from their pay. They are truly within the underground economy, their numbers unknown, their ranks filled largely by the undocumented, and their work almost entirely separated from the formal structure of social welfare benefits and payments found in the mainstream economy. Domestic workers generally operate without written contracts, without provisions for sick pay or vacation time, and without health insurance or pensions. They also must accept a kind of personalized service, akin to master-servant relations, reminiscent of an earlier era (Palmer, 1989). Even in this informal, personalized labor market, however, education has an indirect effect, with cultural capital, rather than degrees or diplomas, carrying weight in employers' hiring decisions and in their treatment of workers once hired. In this article, I explore that impact and what it tells us about the stratification faced by immigrant women from Third World countries in the child care market.

## Method

The present article rests on data drawn from an ongoing study of social class and child care (Wrigley, 1989; 1990), which considers relations between parents and in-home caregivers, both historically and in the contemporary United States. In one part of the project, together with two research assistants, Dolores Trevizo and Benita Roth, I conducted interviews with employing parents and caregivers in the Los Angeles area. We focused on two neighborhoods, one a middle-class area of Santa Monica and the other a much wealthier neighborhood just east of the campus of the University of California at Los Angeles (UCLA). By interviewing intensively in two neighborhoods, we hoped to form a picture of employment relations and their complexities.

Because of the informal nature of domestic employment, there is no good means of ascertaining how many people work in private homes looking after children or of compiling a list of workers or employers from whom we could draw a sample. Many workers are undocumented and are concerned about taking any actions that might draw the attention of immigration authorities. With these constraints, we operated by finding employers through neighborhood contacts. Those interviewed generally provided names of others, and this created a snowball sample. Dolores Trevizo, who did the interviews with Latina caregivers, found them by several means, including approaching them in parks, getting their names from employers, or locating them through her own personal contacts. Almost all of these interviews were conducted in Spanish. In some cases we were able to interview employee/employer pairs, although we interviewed them separately. We also interviewed the owners and managers of domestic employment agencies in the Los Angeles area, as a way of getting an overview of the market for private household workers.

**Parents' hiring choices**

Many parents are novice consumers of child care services and have little sense of how to make their way around the child care market. They make some initial decision about what type of caregiver they think they want, but interviews showed that this was a matter on which parents often changed their minds with experience. Initial high expectations tended to fade with experience, as parents discovered that women doing low-paid, low-status work often did not conform to their dream image of enthusiastic, self-activating employees who would lift all their child care and housekeeping burdens. Employers' beliefs about what they could demand from employees varied with the workers' social characteristics or cultural capital. Those parents who opted for workers with high levels of cultural capital generally had to pay more and accept less work than those opting for workers with lower levels of cultural capital. While formal educational credentials are seldom proffered or required in the child care market, workers' cultural capital is assessed by their general level of education, their nationality (with some national origins carrying more cultural prestige than others), their level of English fluency, and more subtle indicators of where they stand in the social scale, such as their speaking style, dress, and demeanor.

When hiring, the employers' first task is to decide what type of caregiver they want, since search mechanisms differ for workers from different backgrounds. The internal differentiation of the market is reflected in different means of finding foreign *au pairs*, immigrant women, and domestic *au pairs*. Most hiring is done through informal contacts, but the networks for different types of employees (e.g., *au pairs* or immigrants) seldom overlap. To access appropriate networks, parents must ask friends or acquaintances who have specific experience with the type of caregiver they want to hire. One pair of corporate lawyers, for example, tapped into a network of Swedish *au pairs* developed by colleagues in their firm. Others in the market for immigrant women ask friends or relatives, who often suggest women recommended by their own caregivers. Some parents lack access to such networks, or do not want to rely on them, so advertise in newspapers, choosing different publications depending on what kind of caregivers they are seeking.

Domestic employment agencies typically specialize in one sector of the market for child care workers. This type of internal differentiation is typical of labor markets in the informal sector, where characteristics such as ethnicity or age, or in this case, ethnicity and educational level, become dividing lines between market segments (Castells and Portes, 1989). Several agencies in the greater Los Angeles area service the small market for domestic American *au pairs*. These agencies emphasize the advantages of hiring American workers, projecting images of fresh-faced farm girls eager to pitch in for families. Others specialize in foreign *au pairs*, but most agencies match employers with immigrant women. Even within this sector, there is considerable stratification. Some agencies serve the low end of the market, operating out of back offices in obscure locations, while others have expensive premises on prestigious streets. The elite agencies attract wealthy parents from Los Angeles' corporate and show business communities. The most upscale agencies provide a full range of domestic help, including chauffeurs, housekeeping couples, cooks (of several different grades of skill), and maids, as well as nannies. This degree of employee specialization is not found among agencies serving less wealthy populations; for these agencies, the only real division among their employees concerns those who do child care and those who do cleaning. Even this division usually blurs at the lower ends of the market, since parents want to hire one person who will take care of all their needs.

Elite agencies cater to employers who want something akin to the servants of old. They have the money to pay domestic workers and houses big enough to provide living space for them. Elite agencies refuse to handle workers who do not speak English well, cutting off the largest segment of the immigrant labor pool. While owners of domestic employment agencies were understandably loath to discuss the legal status of the workers they have placed, they intimated that realistically they had to handle undocumented workers. The low-end agencies make no bones about this. They mainly place women with limited proficiency in English and they offer no guarantees; if employers do not like the employee once she is hired, no second chances are allowed. These agencies cater to parents who want full-time caregivers but either cannot or do not want to spend much money. They also make no attempt to assess the adequacy of the working or living conditions the workers will face at the hands of their employers.

These varying agencies can find market niches because there is employer demand for each type of child care worker. Some parents hold quite specific (and often irrational) prejudices about the caregivers' nationalities. One mother reported in an interview that she favored Salvadorans but would reject women from Guatemala. Another said that she had specifically chosen to hire a West Indian woman rather than a Central American immigrant because she thought the West Indian would be firmer with her twins. Owners of employment agencies report some parents are not explicit about their likes and dislikes, but will, for example, consistently reject black applicants. Some agencies proselytize for their type of child care worker, particularly if they serve a more obscure corner of the market. In Los Angeles, unlike New York, it is not common to recruit young women from the American midwest, so an agency that pioneered in this market subtly and not-so-subtly extolled the advantages of 'All-American' caregivers in its advertising.

In general, the wealthiest parents we interviewed hired immigrant women who were well-acculturated and had relatively high-level qualifications (that is, they spoke English well, could drive, and had experience and good references). Some chose to hire UCLA students or other employees whom they viewed as being more culturally similar to themselves than immigrant women, but in the wealthy area of Los Angeles where we interviewed, we found few *au pairs* or students and many long-term immigrant workers. The parents had the resources to provide relatively good wages and good living conditions. They also had sufficient money to retain caregivers even after their children reached school age; unlike parents who strain to pay for caregivers, and who dispense with them as soon as their children are old enough for preschool or kindergarten, these parents had the means to create long-term domestic employment relations of a sort traditional among the upper class. As *au pairs* generally work for only a year before returning to their home countries or going to college, they have less appeal than immigrant workers for parents who envision many years of household child care service.

In wealthy enclaves, fewer mothers of young children go out to work than in more middle-class areas. These families have sufficient money for mothers to stay home if they wish, but they can also afford to hire domestic child care help, which frees them to have a social life and engage in volunteer activities. In the neighborhood where we conducted interviews, for example, many of the mothers were very active around the local schools. As the mothers did not work, the parents did not view the caregivers as maternal substitutes so much as assistants (however extensive their hours or tasks in reality). We found that when mothers stay home, parents tended to be less concerned about caregivers' educational levels than when both parents are out of the house all day. These wealthy families could also afford to hire a range of household employees, including cleaning women, leaving the caregivers free to focus on the children. Moreover, the abundance of resources meant that parents could easily provide many types of enriching experiences for their young children, such as enrolling them in high-status preschools. This extra enrichment reduced the sense that their children's daily experience was bounded by what the caregiver provided. These parents, in short, had the means to hire workers with high levels of cultural capital, but most, rather than maximizing on this dimension, chose workers from the top of the immigrant market who would stay for the long term. They structured their households so that they could still feel confident that they would successfully pass on their cultural advantages to their children.

Parents with fewer resources have to make more trade-offs in the child care market. In the more middle-class area where we interviewed, we found parents who were acutely conscious of these trade-offs. One working mother of three young children reviewed her history of searching for the perfect caregiver, one with 'a certain level of education, who takes initiative, is somewhat of a hustler, who can drive, who has a card [allowing her to work legally], and who is acculturated.' She recognized the difficulties of the search:

> There is a point where that person is no longer interested in this kind of work. I mean obviously. They can work as a clerk or a secretary, a teachers' aide. Make more money, not put in the hours. This job has long hours, and it's not a lot of money. I think we're up against that boundary line. That's why I think I settle with Consuela. She's not the best candidate, but the best might be $500 a week, or somebody who's doing another factory job or something.

## Cultural capital and the workers' ability to specialize

The trade-offs employers make can be seen in regard to house cleaning. Those workers with the highest status and the most perceived cultural capital generally do the least house cleaning while on the job. They are able to avoid house cleaning in favor of child care. It should be noted that many domestic workers prefer house cleaning to child care (Trevizo, 1990). They make more money per hour, have more autonomy, and do not experience the crushing sense of responsibility that can burden child care workers. They almost always have multiple employers and so are less economically dependent than caregivers who work for one family. While house cleaning can be considered a desired option when choosing between different types of domestic labor, those working as caregivers usually want to avoid being burdened with both housework and child care. Among caregivers, status distinctions affect how much housework they do in addition to their child care duties. Parents view high-status caregivers' work with children as sufficiently valuable that they do not load them with extra duties. The British nanny provides the classic example. Only one such nanny has appeared in the interviews done so far. The nanny, a woman in her fifties imported from England, did no housework except that directly related to the care of the child (e.g., she prepared the child's meals and organized the child's clothes). Similarly, an interview with the owner of a domestic employment agency serving New York City's most elite families confirmed that nannies are not expected to do any housework. He commented that the families served by the agency had such long traditions of hiring nannies that they fully understood the restrictions on assigning nannies housework. In this narrow stratum of the child care market, most parents are not novice employers.

Traditionally, upper-class parents created hierarchies of servants in which those most culturally similar to the parents had the most access to the children. On a miniature scale, some Los Angeles employers do the same. Those with high-status caregivers with perceived cultural capital often hire lower-status workers to do cleaning and cooking. In the household with the British nanny, a Central American immigrant woman cleaned, and the employers, both corporate lawyers, were considering hiring another employee to do the family's grocery shopping. Another dual-career professional family hired three domestic workers, with the most trusted of the three supervising the other two. Those workers with the least status have little means of repelling parents' demands for household labor. Some engage in types of personal service, such as serving parents at meals, at one time almost extinct in middle-class households.

When parents shift from one category of employee to another, they sometimes readjust their expectations to fit the new worker's status. As one example, another pair of corporate lawyers hired a Salvadoran immigrant to look after their young son. Although generally satisfied with her work, they decided to fire her after several years because they thought she was becoming too economically dependent on them (she borrowed money), and they were also disturbed by her frequent use of the family car. They hired an older white American woman. They were pleased with her, but found they could not ask her to do the grocery shopping, as they had asked her predecessor, because the new caregiver complained that the shopping made her too tired. She only did child care, while her predecessor had done far more housework. In another, more complex example of a household hierarchy, a pair of doctors hired two caregivers so they could have near-complete child care coverage (the parents both worked long hours and one of their two young children was severely retarded). One of the caregivers was more culturally similar to the parents than the other. When both were present, the higher-status caregiver did the child care and the second worker did the housework. Only when the second worker was alone did she do the child care.

Sometimes parents decide not to hire a particular worker because they recognize that status considerations will make it impossible for them to get desired housework from her. One Los Angeles mother reported that a highly-qualified older woman answered a classified ad she placed for a child care worker. The woman wanted $550 a week, however, and would not do any cleaning. The mother told her the cost was excessive, noting that 'It's just really hard to find everything in one person'. The highly qualified caregiver might have been too costly for her in any case, but the applicant's refusal to do housework greatly increased her 'true' price, as the parents felt they would have had to also hire a cleaning woman.

Those parents who seek and hire child care workers with high levels of perceived cultural capital make their child-centered expectations clear in how they describe what they want the workers to do. One mother said the caregiver's job was to 'engage the child in life'. She had hired a variety of caregivers, including one who had received some academic training in child development at UCLA and another who was a relatively well-educated German *au pair*. Another mother said that she chose to hire college students because she wanted people who could speak English, who could read to the kids, and who would really interact with them. She recruited from UCLA because, she said, 'the people who go to that school are intelligent, they have these skills'. Some employers with these types of expectations hire immigrant women as child care workers, but more often, people who speak in these terms look for college students or *au pairs*. They then protect the caregivers' time by not asking that too much housework be done.

Particularly in dealing with immigrant women with little power in the child care market, parents can quickly let their roles as employers supersede their parental roles. The very act of becoming an employer seems to create a strong desire not to be 'taken' and to make sure that the caregiver truly works for her money. Some caregivers report that parents spy on them at the parks, closely inspect their housekeeping, and fret over how much they eat. The parents have become bosses in relationships with few formal rules or boundaries. Parents define their desires as 'needs' in explaining why they hired caregivers, and they can quickly become angry and frustrated if they see caregivers as not helping them with their needs. Even if they initially feel uncomfortable having others work for them, most soon adjust. As one said, 'Hey, it's an easy thing to adapt to'.

Domestic workers know that parents develop high expectations regarding house cleaning. Some parents genuinely want their caregivers to focus on the children, but immigrant women, usually obliged to do both housework and child care, don't always believe this. One mother commented that no matter how many times she told her caregiver the housework was the last thing to worry about, it remained the caregiver's priority. Those parents who are most anxious that their children receive focused attention from caregivers structure situations where caregivers do not have dual responsibilities, often by creating worker hierarchies. Interviews with those running domestic employment agencies suggest that those with money for just one employee are probably the most inclined to hire an all-purpose house cleaner/caregiver who lacks the economic and social power to define her job.

## Immigrant caregivers and parents' social obligations

When parents hire caregivers whom they perceive as culturally similar to themselves, they acquire some of the social obligations due to peers. When parents hire peers or semi-peers, they must spend time with the caregiver as well as with their children. Those parents who are separated from their children's caregivers by social class do not usually express any sense of social obligation to the caregiver. Immigrant women from Third World countries fall at the bottom of the status hierarchy and few parents treat them as anything close to status equals. New parents who are just beginning their careers as employers sometimes treat their first caregiver as a quasi-family member, even if she differs radically from them in social class, but often report that they learn this is a mistake. They seldom repeat the same behavior with later caregivers.

The ritual of meals helps define who is included within a household or family relationship and who is not. *Au pairs* expect to eat with the families where they work. Parents must be willing to incorporate them into the family framework, and if they are not willing to do so, they must opt out of the *au pair* market. Some parents find the burden of sharing meals with *au pairs* to be so heavy that they decide to switch to hiring Central American immigrant women instead. They then expect these women to eat by themselves.

Many parents with immigrant Latina caregivers do not include them in meals. They quickly see the advantages of having a caregiver supervise children's meals, leaving them free to have adult conversation at their own dinner table. A Latina caregiver reports that when the family eats, she usually takes the youngest child into the living room and eats with him there, leaving the parents to have their meal in peace. Another fed the children in the playroom and then served the employers their dinner. A woman from Mexico described her nightly meal: she prepared dinner for two young boys, and then, 'While they were eating, I too would have to eat, you know, rapidly in the kitchen. By the time they finished, I had to pick up the dishes, wash them'. This employer provided very little food for her; when she bought her own food, the employer ate it at will, saying that it was her refrigerator.

Employers pick up informal lore about the social treatment of caregivers from each other. One employer said that she originally planned to have her children's caregiver eat with the family, but her sister-in-law warned her against it. On reflection, she decided it would be too hard to disinvite the caregiver later. Another woman commented that her husband had 'grown up with maids and nannies and live-ins, so he's comfortable with people who work for him, and I'm not'. She wanted to make the caregiver feel like part of the family, but her husband said, 'they're not part of the family, they work for us'. People who never grew up with class boundaries in their households are instructed by those who did and are acclimatized to excluding the women who work for them from social interactions. Others decide it is simply more practical and efficient to keep caregivers' at arms length. One mother commented that she was close only to her first caregiver: 'I think what happened over time is the relationships with the caregivers have been more distant'. With her first caregiver, she had learned about her life and her family. When new caregivers came, the mother no longer wanted to invest the time to chat with them. She just wanted them to get the job done and confined herself to giving them instructions when necessary. Some parents find social interaction with caregivers so distasteful that they deliberately choose caregivers they feel can be ignored. At the extreme, this can mean making a point of hiring caregivers who do not speak English. One mother from the middle-income neighborhood where we interviewed explained the advantages of hiring non-English speaking caregivers. Since her Latina caregiver did not speak English, the mother could talk on the telephone without being overheard. She had fired a previous caregiver who she thought spoke English only too well:

> I don't want to have anybody around that I feel like is invading my privacy or doesn't know how to get lost. I had somebody here for a few days, I'd be doing something and she'd just sit herself down and sort of start chatting with me, you know. She spoke perfect English.

This mother does not work, so she is home a good deal and retains primacy in her relations with her children. She wants a caregiver who will ease her life but she does not feel she is looking for a mother-substitute. As her children are not highly dependent on the caregiver, it makes it easier for her to put her own interest in privacy above their presumed interest in being able to communicate with their caregiver. This mother emphasized that her caregiver was 'not a nanny. She is a housekeeper'. This mother had rejected the idea of hiring an *au pair* because of the social obligations it would entail. The reality is that educated young women will not do domestic work except on a short-term basis and on conditions that put them a social step above hard-pressed immigrant women who often must accept whatever they can get. The difference is seen not only in the amount and kind of work done in the household, and in the social obligations the parents acquire toward the caregiver, but in parents' fears about workers' dependency. Low-paid immigrants working in sweatshops or private households may turn to their employers for assistance when faced with crises. Immigrant entrepreneurs in the garment industry try to maintain the goodwill of even poorly-paid workers by serving as intermediaries in the workers' dealings with the larger world (Waldinger, 1986, p. 159). Most provide short-term loans for rent and help workers with legal problems. Similarly, immigrant domestic workers who live on the margin sometimes approach their employers for help in paying medical bills or traveling to see sick family members in their home countries.

In sheltered middle class residential havens, most employers have had few personal encounters with the harsh underside of American society. They find this world indirectly brought into their homes when they hire caregivers who live in conditions of hardship. Many employers are impervious to the difficulties of their employees' lives, but crises sometimes bring home to them the lack of social services in the United States. Without health insurance for themselves or their families, caregivers can be overwhelmed by medical bills. Having hired a caregiver to ease their burdens, many employers, initially sympathetic, become impatient when they feel their caregivers have too many problems. They fear the potential economic dependency of a woman living on the edge. Sometimes they help the caregivers, by, for example, paying for a trip to El Salvador, but they then expect gratitude and become angry and disappointed if they don't think they get it.

One employer described a 19-year-old Mexican immigrant who worked for her as having an 'attitude problem'. The employer complained that the caregiver felt things were due her and declared that, 'I really felt I was very good to her. I did a lot of extra things for her'. The employer helped the caregiver get a social security card and amnesty. She said, 'I did a lot of those kinds of things and drove her those places during the time when she was working for me, but I was servicing her'. The employer became deeply displeased when she felt the caregiver did not recognize how well she had been treated. This story was not atypical.

Money issues can cause great trouble between caregivers and employers. Some caregivers turn to their employers for loans or ask their help in dealing with demanding creditors. Employers soon get weary of obliging. One employer took a caregiver to court when she failed to pay a phone bill. Her battle to secure the money had a gender aspect of its own: her husband told her that if she could recover the money, she could spend it as she chose rather than putting it into the general household account. This spurred her efforts to recover the money, which became a personal crusade. A lawyer described negotiating a formal payback arrangement for her caregiver after she had gotten in over her head with a $1200 furniture purchase from a discount furniture company. The employers paid the company and then deducted a specified amount from each of the caregiver's paychecks. When the caregiver's problems continued, the employer fired her. Another employer said of her caregiver, 'For a while we were loaning her money all the time if she asked. We put an end to that, because it was obvious if we didn't there was no end to it. You know, she would pay it back, but it was just more work of keeping books, and that's not what she's here for'. The caregiver had wanted money to help bring her brother into the country. This employer said that with future caregivers, she would avoid learning about their lives so as not to be drawn into their problems. Employers pass on informal lore to each other, and one common bit of advice concerns the need to keep from involvement with caregivers' lives or personal concerns.

On their side, caregivers sometimes ask employers for loans because they see no alternative, but they recognize the dependence this brings. One Guatemalan woman reported that she and her husband worked doing housekeeping and child care for a couple. When her husband became ill and required major surgery, the employers paid. To repay this debt, the Guatemalan couple worked seven-day weeks, the husband, still convalescent, taxing his strength so he could work off the loan.

Employers feared a different kind of dependency from young women who came from something closer to their own social class or general background. They feared the psychic collapse of these women rather than their economic or practical needs. One employer saw these women as draining her emotionally.

> Well, they come up and whine about their love life and complain and I feel like an older sister or mother when I have to listen to them... When they're younger they're very weak, they're depressed about this, you know, just things that are normal for younger girls.

Other employers said much the same thing, including one who commented that when she hired an 18-year-old, 'It was like having another adolescent'. Another contrasted the different types of problems she saw with immigrant women and *au pairs*. Her children's caregiver, a Salvadoran immigrant, did not come 'problem free. She's got a lot of problems and lot of things that come into our household'. The caregiver was often sick, had money problems, and was troubled by her family's needs in El Salvador. The situation, the employer concluded, was hardly better with *au pairs*, who wanted to be shown around the city and get involved with local life and who became a responsibility for the parents.

For a few employers, the emotional problems presented by *au pairs*, whether domestic or European, went beyond neediness. Several had hired young women who had breakdowns or other serious problems and had to be shipped back home. These truly traumatic events sometimes led the employers to forget about seeking educated young women and to place a higher value on finding stable and mature women, generally immigrants.

## Social class and childrearing values

Parents have different ways of trying to secure what they consider quality care, itself often a class-specific concept (Heath, 1983; Kohn, 1983). They can try to hire caregivers who share their basic values and cultural style. This tends to be expensive and to embroil them in the complexities of dealing with young people who have their own social worlds, emotional demands, and sense of entitlement. Further, such caregivers tend to do little or no housework. Some parents aggressively pursue this option, believing it offers by far the best chance for securing quality care. These parents are critical of the care they see immigrant women providing. A Santa Monica mother said she felt she had made the right choice when she hired UCLA students.

> From what I've seen I think that I have the best deal as far as the person who lives with us. The people that I've seen, you know I see other child care givers all the time. I see them picking up the kids at school. I see how they are with the kids. I know that Tom, he's not perfect in every way, and I know that he has a personality, and when the kids see him they're happy. He's happy. They talk, and that's a lot better than seeing these other women, they don't speak much English, they don't speak to the kids at all. There's no interaction between them . . . I'd rather not have anybody than have this kind of a robot person just doing it because they need the money.

Economists have pointed to the costs of search processes, whether the cost to workers of searching for jobs or employers of seeking workers. Parents find searching for caregivers time-consuming and often frustrating. In the case of immigrant workers, parents' face particular hiring difficulties because of the social gulf between themselves and the applicants. They have little means of evaluating workers who do not present formal credentials and who often speak little English. Under these circumstances, the true vetting of employees often happens after they are hired. From their side, employees can form initial impressions of employers, but, working as they do in a highly personalized environment where much depends on the personality of the parents (and, to some extent, of the children), they also can be faced with unpleasant surprises soon after starting work. Many working relationships last only a few days or weeks, with parents rapidly hiring and firing a succession of workers and some workers quickly deciding to search for better conditions elsewhere. On other occasions, however, parents and caregivers decide to make the best of what may be an uneasy relationship and not to incur the cost of further search.

It is generally the mothers who undertake the search for caregivers and they who are most reluctant to initiate new searches. Their husbands may become exasperated with particular workers and urge their wives to fire them and look for new applicants, but wives can become quite wary, knowing how difficult the process can be. As one mother said,

> I just settled [with a particular woman], I mean my husband wasn't happy about the decision. I said, 'John, I am so tired. This has been the worst six to eight months, years, I don't know how long it was [when she was running through a sequence of caregivers]. It was just the worst period of time. She's not optimal, but I want to stay with her for now.'

When parents are tired of searching but not entirely satisfied with the caregivers they have hired, they may try to change the way caregivers do their jobs. They invest in the cost of training the worker, despite the informal nature of the work relationship and uncertainty about how long it will last. This 'retraining' effort can involve them in considerable difficulties, since it involves essentially the imposition of their own child-rearing values and ideas on caregivers who do not necessarily share them. Parents generally have more power over Central American immigrant women than they do over short-term *au pairs*. Their power over the caregiver is maximized when the caregivers have few resources, when racial discrimination keeps the caregiver locked into the bottom of the labor market, and when parents do not see the caregivers as having any particular claim to child-rearing expertise. In such situations, parents typically feel they have a right to have their child-rearing ideas followed. They tell the caregiver what they want done, and when there are specific disagreements, they expect their wishes will be followed.

One doctor reported that her caregiver, an older Filipina woman, had what she considered old-fashioned ideas about the need to sterilize baby bottles. She told her to stop sterilizing them and the woman obeyed her directions. She also had a disagreement with the caregiver on a more complex matter. The caregiver expressed disapproval of one child by increasing the attention and affection she gave the other, until the parents made their disapproval clear. The parents also sensed that the children were watching too much television; the husband spoke to the caregiver and got her to change. In all of these instances, the parents assumed their wishes would prevail and the caregiver did in fact accede to their requests.

Parents with elaborate child-rearing ideologies can find that caregivers are unable or unwilling to fully adopt their practices. One couple, where both parents were psychologists, implemented a full-fledged behavioral modification program to control the behavior of one of their children, a daughter, who was quite difficult. Their caregiver, an immigrant from Mexico, tried to follow the program as outlined by the parents, but could not do so successfully. Without telling her, the parents advertised for a new caregiver and interviewed applicants at a friend's house. The caregiver was not dismayed to be replaced, however, at least according to the parents, since she recognized that she and the child did not have a successful relationship.

Other parents try to influence the caregivers' child-rearing style by outlining specific schedules and requirements for the caregivers to follow. To keep children from watching too much television, parents often insist that caregivers take children to the park for hours each day. In some cases, caregivers spend the bulk of the morning and the afternoon at local playgrounds. The ritual of the parks is an intrinsic part of the caregiving experience for most workers. Here, however, there are also individual variation and employer idiosyncrasy. A mother refused to allow her caregiver to go to the park at all, afraid that she would compare wage rates with other caregivers. Other employers set up other schedule requirements. One mother told the caregiver (in this case a student) that the children were to read every afternoon for a specified half-hour period. Others have specific rules about television watching and what kinds of food their children can eat.

Caregivers usually acquiesce when the parents draw up rules and requirements. They are often painfully aware, however, that their own child-rearing experiences and values have little interest for the parents. The immigrant women often have children of their own. In interviews, several reported being separated from their children, sometimes because some or all of their children had remained in Mexico or Central America, sometimes because they had to leave their children with relatives elsewhere in the United States because they were working long hours or living in employers' houses. Their situations are difficult, and on a daily basis the women bear considerable emotional and practical hardship. It is striking that their employers seem almost wholly unaware of this aspect of their employees' lives (except when it intrudes on the caregivers' ability to do the job). Communication between parents and caregivers is often sufficiently minimal that parents have little interest in the caregivers' own ideas, focusing on them only when they see a specific problem.

For the most part, caregivers seem to accept the parents' right to set the basic terms of the child care arrangement. They try to conform with parents' wishes. As one caregiver, a Mexican immigrant, said:

> We just go in the homes, take care of their children and we have to follow their rules because you can't change the rules. This is what they expect in their household and you have to go by it.

Some are critical of the parents' child-rearing style, thinking the parents are indifferent or lax. They are dismayed by the values they see, but feel they must keep their thoughts to themselves. Others admire what they see as the strengths of the parents' mode of child-rearing. Beatrice, quoted above, was highly reflective about the child-rearing differences she observed. She commented that the parents did not do manual labor, so they did not come home tired.

> I think that has a lot to do with it, since the parents didn't come home tired from doing manual labor, they didn't come home dragging themselves. So they would come home able to give their children all their time, tenderness. That is a nice way, because one would start cooking and the other would play with the children. So when one sees this and sees these rules, you realize that is why these children are raised differently, because they have almost 100 percent of the attention.

She also observed that the parents had the luxury of coming home to a clean house, which allowed them to concentrate on their children. In her view, the parents closely controlled the children's environment and tried to make it instructive:

> They have the same values, but we let the children watch whatever they want, and not them. We let them eat candy, not them. We let them not take naps, not them. They buy them lots of instructive toys. When my kids were little, I didn't do this. I would buy them the toys that they wanted. They, from the moment the child can see, can think, can move, the parents buy instructive toys.

Parents have other strategies for trying to secure what they consider appropriate care, even when they are absent on a daily basis and their caregivers' basic child-rearing style may differ from theirs. Nearly all the parents enrolled children older than two or three to some form of preschool. The caregiver would take the children to and from the schools, which offered trained teachers. Some parents also made a point of trying to supply key elements of middle-class care themselves. They read to the children at night and saw themselves (and the children's preschools) as providing desirable forms of stimulation. Other parents switched caregivers as their children got older and became more verbal. Many believe that babies need loving physical care, but older children need more stimulating companionship. This leads some to fire non-English-speaking caregivers once their children learn to talk. In one case, a mother commented on her view that her Guatemalan caregiver did well with her baby but not with her two older children:

> She's really great with Robert. She takes really good care of him physically. That's one thing we found with a lot of housekeepers, especially from Central America, or people who've just come to this country. They like the babies. They don't have to worry about any psychological interaction, about how they should handle this. They don't have to be sophisticated that way. Babies love everybody, and they'll go to anybody. So they really enjoy the babies much more. And a lot of them, one problem we've had is that they like to walk around all day carrying the baby. That's all they do. So she's good with him, and the older boys are not here during the day. When they're here, I'm here.

This mother did not think her caregiver provided enough stimulation for the older boys, but did not define this as a major problem, since she herself was on the scene when they were home. She would not, however, have been willing to leave the older boys with the caregiver on a daily basis. She evolved her own method of dealing with what she perceived as the caregiver's limitations, a perception that at root involved different child-rearing modes and values.

**Conclusion**

Immigrant women make up the bulk of domestic workers. They do low-paid, off-the-books work in private households, with few or no benefits and no job security. While cleaning women usually have multiple employers, among whom they rotate on weekly or semi-weekly schedules, child care workers typically work for only one household. This creates in modern households something close to the master/servant relations of previous generations. Despite this modern recreation of an old form, even this most informal part of the informal economy has been altered by the spread of educational values through the society. Middle-class parents, in particular, very much want their children to receive stimulation as well as physical care.

The child care market has distinctive features, in that most parents are highly emotionally invested in their children's care and in some sense are searching for a substitute for themselves. They are also, however, searching for an employee and are motivated by more typical goals of finding low-cost help. The parent/employer roles do not always coexist easily. Further, there can be confusion or conflict over the worker's role in looking after the mechanics of the household (and thus, indirectly, the parents themselves) versus the worker's role in caring for the child or children. Parents' choices between different types of caregivers, such as *au pairs* or immigrant women, are intimately bound up in the economics and emotional dynamics of households.

Parents' wide-ranging expectations set the stage for conflicts between what caregivers can deliver and what parents expect. These conflicts are particularly acute for Third World immigrant women, such as Central American immigrants, because they lack the social power and cultural capital to protect themselves from across-the-board demands for child care and housekeeping work. Faced with employers' expectations that they will entertain, instruct, and talk with their young children, they also feel, realistically, that they will be judged on the cleanliness and order of the house. Those who work for wealthy employers can sometimes escape conflicting demands, since their employers hire specialized workers to clean and to look after children. Those workers in less prosperous households, who have to shoulder the whole child care and house cleaning burden, have a more daunting task. This is particularly the case because parents have their own ideas about how their children should be treated, and often their child-rearing styles do not come naturally to women who grew up in radically different circumstances. The social gulf between parents and Third World immigrant caregivers manifests itself in different styles of child-rearing, but parents often have little insight into the lives and values of those they hire to manage their homes and children. To keep their jobs, caregivers suppress their own child-rearing views, but this does not always occur smoothly or consistently.

The internal stratification of the domestic child care market becomes fully evident only when analyzing the differential treatment of caregivers with different levels of perceived cultural capital. Those with cultural credentials that 'travel', such as educational credentials or the ability to project familiarity with middle-class home life and verbal styles, fare better than those immigrants who enter domestic work as the first step in a long process of cultural adaptation and economic establishment in their new country. The detachment of household work from the mainstream and from formal credentialling mechanisms makes it more striking that there is a payoff for education. The occupation accepts virtually all comers, but they are differentially treated and rewarded, within the bounds of a generally low-paid line of work.

The resurgence of domestic employment has led some parents to create strategies for trying to transmit their educational advantages to their children, even while enjoying the kind of personalized service that is only available in highly unequal societies. Some strategies turn on parents' efforts to find culturally similar caregivers and others turn on parents' abilities to exercise power over caregivers, most of whom are immigrants from Third World countries. Most parents, however, do not escape social dilemmas arising from their dual roles as parents and employers. For the immigrant caregivers, the dilemmas are still more acute, since they find themselves in low-wage employment that embodies contradiction: virtually anyone is deemed qualified to do the work, but caregivers occupy culturally sensitive positions at the heart of family relations. Responsible for children's daily care and socialization, many experience daily reminders that their own culture is not considered suitable for transmission. Some of these dilemmas are as old as employer/servant relations, and some are newly arisen in an education-conscious society. Both sets of dilemmas, old and new, result from the social inequality which underlies these child care situations and which therefore elude resolution.

## References

Bourdieu, P. (1973), 'Cultural Reproduction and Social Reproduction', in Brown, R. (ed.), *Knowledge, Education, and Cultural Change*, Tavistock: London, pp. 71-112.

Castells, M. and Portes, A. (1989), 'World Underneath: The Origins, Dynamics, and Effects of the Informal Economy', in Portes, A., Castells, M. and Benton, L.A. (eds.), *The Informal Economy: Studies in Advanced and Less Developed Countries*, The Johns Hopkins University Press: Baltimore, MD, pp. 11-37.

Chaney, E.M. and Garcia Castro, M. (eds.) (1989), *Muchachas No More: Domestic Workers in Latin America and the Caribbean*. Bibliography by M.L. Smith, Temple University Press: Philadelphia, PA.

Collins, R. (1979), *The Credential Society: An Historical Sociology of*

*Education and Stratification*, Academic Press: New York.

Fernandez-Kelly, M.P. and Garcia, A.M. (1989), 'Hispanic Women and Homework: Women in the Informal Economy of Miami and Los Angeles', in Boris, E. and Daniels, C.R. (eds.), *Homework: Historical and Contemporary Perspectives on Paid Labor at Home*, University of Illinois Press: Urbana, IL, pp. 165-79.

Foner, N. (1987), 'The Jamaicans: Race and Ethnicity among Migrants in New York City', in Foner, N. (ed.), *New Immigrants in New York*, Columbia University Press: New York, pp. 195-217.

Heath, S. (1983), *Ways with Words: Language. Life and Work in Communities and Classrooms*, Cambridge University Press: New York.

Kohn, M. (1983), *Class and Conformity*, University of Chicago: Chicago, IL.

Palmer, P. (1989), *Domesticity and Dirt: Housewives and Domestic Servants in the United States, 1920-1989*, Temple University Press: Philadelphia, PA.

Pessar, P.R. (1987), 'The Dominicans: Women in the Household and the Garment Industry', in Foner, N. (ed.), *New Immigrants in New York*, Columbia University Press: New York, pp. 102-29.

Piore, M.J. (1980), 'The Technological Foundations of Dualism and Discontinuity', in Berger, S. and Piore, M. (eds.), *Dualism and Discontinuity in Industrial Society*, Cambridge University Press: Cambridge (UK).

Stepick, A. (1989), 'Miami's Two Informal Sectors', in Portes, A., Castells, M. and Benton, L.A. (eds.), *The Informal Economy: Studies in Advanced and Less Developed Countries*, The Johns Hopkins University Press: Baltimore, MD, pp. 111-31.

Tilly, L. and Scott, J. (1978), *Women, Work and Family*, Methuen: New York.

Trevizo, D. (1990), Latina 'Baby-Watchers' and the Commodification of Care, Master's Thesis, Department of Sociology, University of California at Los Angeles: Los Angeles, CA.

Waldinger, R. (1986), *Through the Eye of the Needle: Immigrants and Enterprise in New York's Garment Trades*, New York University Press: New York.

Wrigley, J. (1989), 'Do Young Children Need Intellectual Stimulation? Experts' Advice to Parents, 1900-1985', *History of Education Quarterly*, Vol. 29, pp. 41-75.

Wrigley, J. (1990), 'Children's caregivers and ideologies of parental inadequacy', in Abel, E.K. and Nelson, M.K. (eds.), *Circles of Care*, State University of New York Press: Albany, NY.

# 8 Korean and Filipino immigrant women in the Los Angeles labor market

*Hye-Kyung Lee and Stavros Karageorgis*

### Introduction

Women immigrants have undeservedly received less research attention than men. On the one hand, nearly one out of every two international migrants in the world is female; moreover, female immigrants to the United States, a major country of destination, have slightly outnumbered their male counterparts since 1930 (Houstoun, Kramer and Barrett, 1984; Zlotnik, 1990). On the other hand, most scholars have been interested in economically active migrants and have tended to assume that these were young males. Nevertheless, some women immigrants have shown significantly high labor-force participation rates in the destination country. In addition, the labor market behavior of women systematically differs from that of men. With these factors in mind, as well as the need to achieve a thorough understanding of international migration for policy and decision-making purposes, the experience of immigrant women must be examined explicitly. In this paper,[1] we focus specifically on Korean and Filipino women immigrants to the United States, and their labor market adjustment in the Los Angeles area, relative to that of other immigrant women.[2]

The Philippines and Korea rank second and third to Mexico as source countries for legal immigrants to the United States. In 1987, 72,351 Mexicans emigrated to the United States, along with 50,060 Filipinos and 35,849 Koreans (Arnold, Carino, Fawcett and Park, 1989, p. 815). Despite sharing similar pre-immigration backgrounds and motives for immigration, Korean and Filipino immigrants show different adjustment patterns.

The most important difference between these two groups is their level of involvement in small businesses. Korean immigrants are over-represented in self-employment; Filipino immigrants are under-represented. For example, about 32% of Korean immigrant men, and about 13% of Korean immigrant women, were self-employed in the Los Angeles labor market in 1980, as compared to only about 5% and 2% of Filipino immigrant men and women. By examining the labor force participation and earnings of these two Asian immigrant groups of women, this paper sheds light on inter-group differences in female self-employment and, correlatively, on those between the immigrant groups overall.

*Previous research on immigrant women*

An extensive body of literature deals with the socio-economic adjustment of immigrants, reflecting the interest of both policy-makers and academic researchers. Relevant research has identified *assimilation*, *labor market segmentation*, and *immigrant self-employment* as crucial factors affecting the socio-economic well-being and advancement of immigrants.

The degree and rate of assimilation characterizing an immigrant group and its members have been the core explanatory variables of 'assimilation theory'. Gordon (1964) distinguished between economic, social and cultural assimilation, and argued that immigrants' socio-economic well-being and advancement developed hand-in-hand with their level of attainment of the above dimensions of assimilation, culminating in full immersion in the Anglo-American mainstream.

More recently, Chiswick (1978, 1980, 1984) has revived the same theme, emphasizing the effects of assimilation on labor market behavior and the earnings of immigrants. According to him, immigrants experience some initial downward mobility due to the low transferability of their human capital in the new country and their lack of work-related information about the new labor market. The socio-economic attainment of immigrants in the destination country, however, improves over time, finally reaching parity with that of the native-born. Studies of the labor-market participation and earnings of immigrant women (Evans, 1984; Long, 1980; Ortiz and Cooney, 1984; Reimers, 1985; Wong and Hirschman, 1983) have supported this view, showing that assimilation, exemplified by, for example, enhanced proficiency in English and a lengthier residence in the United States, improves immigrant women's socio-economic adjustment and advancement.

Assimilation theory and its predictions have, in the long run, reflected quite accurately the experience of European immigrants to the U.S. However, researchers have also found persistent difficulties for female and non-European immigrants (and natives) in attaining the levels and rates of socio-economic advancement predicted by assimilation theory (Beck, Horan and Tolbert II, 1978; Bonacich, 1972, 1976, 1979; Doeringer and Piore, 1971; Gordon, 1972; Piore, 1975, 1977). These 'segmentation' researchers claim that certain groups of immigrants tend to systematically concentrate in the secondary sector of the economy and labor market, regardless of their human capital and their levels of assimilation. This sector is characterized by small-to-medium-sized business firms, low barriers to entry, very price-elastic demand conditions, small profit margins and, therefore, precarious jobs, low wages, poor working conditions, etc.

Since the socio-economic profile of the secondary sector is persistently flatter than that of the primary sector, the above immigrant (and gender and native ethnic) groups tend to escape the predicted 'assimilation-cum-socio-economic-mobility' path of assimilation theory. Regarding immigrant women specifically, several researchers (Almquist and Wehre-Einhorn, 1978; Boyd, 1984; Sullivan, 1984; Tienda, Jensen and Bach, 1984), have noted their 'doubly disadvantaged' status. Immigrant women are both female and foreign-born. According to these studies, immigrant women, either because they are 'resource disadvantaged' or because they are 'labor-market disadvantaged' (Light and Rosenstein, 1995), enter an already male-female and native-foreign-born segregated labor market in which women and immigrants occupy low-prestige and low-income positions.

Finally, different immigrant groups' rates of involvement, and success in self-employment—i.e., the degree of their effective 'entrepreneurial capacity' (Light and Karageorgis, 1994)—have been seen as important in explaining inter-group differences in socio-economic well-being, and mobility. The rate at which different ethnic groups are able to open and operate businesses has long been seen as an important component of the degree of immigrant social and economic mobility in the United States (Goldscheider and Kobrin, 1980; Light, 1972; Model, 1985; Waldinger, Aldrich, Ward et al., 1990).

Research on differential immigrant group concentration and success in self-employment has identified labor market disadvantage, ethnic resources, class resources, and ecological processes in the destination countries as crucial explanatory factors (Evans, 1989; Kim, Hurh and

Fernandez, 1989; Light and Bonacich, 1988; Waldinger, 1989; Yoon, 1991). Although the extent of economic mobility among the immigrant self-employed varies, self-employment has generally permitted some immigrant groups to overcome labor market disadvantages, often without assimilating to the extent that assimilation theory would predict (for extensive references, see Light and Karageorgis, 1994). Little research has, nevertheless, focused specifically on how the level of involvement and success in self-employment on the part of immigrant women may have affected both their own, and their immigrant group's overall socio-economic well-being and advancement.

*Korean and Filipino immigrant women in the United States*

The Immigration Act of 1965 changed the major sources of immigration to the United States. Since then, Asia, and in particular the Philippines and Korea, has become the major sending area. About half a million (449,000) Filipinos and about 300,000 Koreans were admitted to the United States as legal immigrants between 1965 and 1980. Thereafter, more than 40,000 Filipino and 30,000 Korean immigrants have legally entered the United States each year (USINS, 1965-87).

Although young, single males predominated among the earlier waves of Korean and Filipino immigration, more recently immigration of entire families has been more typical. Accordingly, more than half of recent arrivals from these two countries have been women. Although the percentage of females from both countries is similar, the form of female immigration differs.

The majority of Korean women were housewives or women without occupation outside the home, immigrating only as 'tied-movers' to their head of family, whereas many Filipino women were occupational immigrants. For instance, 90% or more of Korean women aged 20 years and over were housewives and/or women without occupations during the 1970s, while only half of Filipino female immigrants were women without occupations in 1970, although in 1979 the percentage increased to 72%.[3]

The two different types of female immigration may be explained by differences in the status and economic achievement of women in Korea and the Philippines. Women in the Philippines have demonstrated higher educational and economic levels of achievement than have women in Korea. In the Philippines, the number of women in post-secondary education equaled or exceeded that of men during the 1960s and 1970s; in Korea, on the other hand, women reached only about 40% of men's enrollment during the same decades (NBS, 1982, pp. 114-5; NSDB, 1976; UNESCO, 1970, pp. 62-5).

Despite similar labor force participation rates of women in the two countries, their occupational distribution pattern has been different. For example, only about 4% of all Korean working women are professionals, compared to 10% of Filipino working women. If we compare the percentage distribution of individuals by gender across broad occupational categories, we find that only one-third of all Korean professionals between 1976 and 1983 were female, whereas over 60% of Filipino professionals were female.

The predominance of Filipino women in professional occupations is particularly characteristic of the health professions. Except for physicians, among whom the number of females almost equals that of males, other health-related professionals in the Philippines (such as pharmacists, medical technologists, nurses, institutional food professionals, etc.) are predominantly female (Pido, 1986, p. 77). In fact, many Filipino professional women entered the United States under the occupational preference section of its immigration law. Therefore, immigration among Filipino women was more highly selective in terms of human capital and professional occupation than it was for Korean women.

### Data, sample and variables

Data for this paper were derived from the Public Use Microdata Samples of the 1980 U.S. Census of Population (U.S. Bureau of the Census, 1983).[4] In order to increase the number of Korean and Filipino cases, the 5% (A sample) and the 1% (C sample) were merged into a 6% sample.

In this paper we compare Korean, Filipino, other-minority, white-immigrant, and native-born white women with respect to labor force participation and earnings. Korean and Filipino immigrant women are the major groups for analysis, and white and other-minority women are reference groups. The racial/ethnic designation is the respondent's self-identification (Korean, Filipino, white, and other). The white groups in this paper refer only to European-origin whites. All others belong to the other-minority category which includes Hispanics, blacks, and other Asians. The variables used in the analysis appear in Table 1.

## Table 1.
## Variables used in the analysis

| Dependent | Variables |
|---|---|
| WORK | Dummy variable, 1 for a woman who worked in the labor market in 1979, 0 for otherwise |
| INCOME | Natural logarithm of income from all sources, 1979 |

| Independent | Variables |
|---|---|

*Human Capital and Current Employment Characteristics*

| | |
|---|---|
| YRSED | Years of schooling |
| YRSED' | YRSED'= (YRSED — 11.4),$^2$ 11.4=b/2 where b is the slope of the bivariate regression of YRSED$^2$ on YRSED |
| EXP | Potential labor market experience, EXP=AGE — YRSED — 6 |
| EXP' | EXP' = (EXP — 22.6)$^2$, 22.6=b/2 where b is the slope of the bivariate regression of EXP$^2$ on EXP |
| WORK75 | Dummy variable for work history in 1975: 1 for those who worked in 1975, 0 otherwise |
| HOURS | Natural logarithm of hours worked, 1979 |
| WEEKS | Natural logarithm of weeks worked, 1979 |

*Marital Status and Female-Specific Variables*

| | |
|---|---|
| MARRIED | Dummy variable for marital status |
|   SNG* | 1 for those never married, 0 for otherwise |
|   MSP | 1 for those married with spouse present, 0 for otherwise |
|   WDS | 1 for those widowed, divorced, or separated, 0 otherwise |
| NUMCH | number of children ever born to a woman |
| KIDSAGE | Age composition of children |
|   NO-CH* | 1 for those having no children in the household, 0 otherwise |
|   CH<6 | 1 for those having children under age 6, 0 otherwise |
|   CH6-17 | 1 for those having children aged 6 to 17, 0 otherwise |
|   CH0-17 | 1 for those having children aged 0 to 17, 0 otherwise |
| YRSMAR | Years since her first marriage |

*Assimilation Variables*

| | |
|---|---|
| IMMIGR | Period of immigration |
|   IMM65- | 1 for those immigrated prior to 1965, 0 otherwise |
|   IMM65-69 | 1 for those immigrated during 1965-69, 0 otherwise |

Table 1 (cont'd)

| Independent | Variables |
|---|---|
| IMM70-74 | 1 for those immigrated during 1970-74, 0 otherwise |
| IMM75-79* | 1 for those immigrated during 1975-79, 0 otherwise |
| ENGLISH | Dummy variable for English ability |
| ENGonly | 1 for those who are monolingual in English, 0 otherwise |
| ENGvwell | 1 for those speak English 'very well', 0 otherwise |
| ENGwell | 1 for those speak English 'well', 0 otherwise |
| ENGnot* | 1 for those speak English 'not well' or 'not at all', 0 otherwise |
| CITIZEN | Dummy variable for U.S. citizenship |
|  | 1 for those with citizenship, 0 otherwise |
| *Class of Worker* |  |
| CLASS | Dummy variable for a class of worker |
| CLsal* | 1 for a salary worker, 0 otherwise |
| CLgvt | 1 for a government worker, 0 otherwise |
| CLself | 1 for a self-employed, 0 otherwise |
| CLeoc | 1 for a employee of own corporation, 0 otherwise |
| *Labor Market Segmentation* |  |
| SECTOR** | Segment of labor market |
| PRIM | 1 for those industries of the primary sector, 0 otherwise |
| MIXED | 1 for those industries of the mixed sector, 0 otherwise |
| SECON* | 1 for those industries of secondary sector, 0 otherwise |
| *Ethnicity Variable* |  |
| ETHNICITY | Dummy variable for ethnicity |
| KOREAN | 1 for Korean immigrants, 0 otherwise |
| FILIPINO | 1 for Filipino immigrants, 0 otherwise |
| OTHER | 1 for Other minority immigrant women, 0 otherwise |
| WHITE* | 1 for white immigrant women, 0 otherwise |

\* This will be the omitted category in the logit regression analysis.
\*\* See note 7 for our operationalization of sectors

For analysis of labor force participation, we included all adult females aged 20 to 64 who were not in school. For analysis of earnings, the study population was limited to women aged 20 to 64 in 1980, who were not in school, worked at least one week in 1979, and reported an occupation and a positive income. The Los Angeles Metropolitan area (Los Angeles,

Orange, Riverside, San Bernardino, and Ventura Counties), where about one fifth of Koreans (21.8%) and Filipinos (16.1%) in the U.S. reside, was the geographic site selected for our study.

## Overview

The background characteristics of the five groups are shown in Table 2. Korean and Filipino women were of about the same average age (37 years old) as the native-born white women, while foreign-born whites were somewhat older than the other four groups. Filipino immigrant female workers had the highest average level of education; the other-minority women the lowest. An average Filipino immigrant woman had at least three years of college education, whereas an average other-minority immigrant woman had less than a high school education. All other female workers had, on average, at least one year of college education.

While a similar proportion of Korean and Filipino immigrant women were married with their spouse present, the proportion of single Filipino women was twice that of the Korean women. Moreover, while all groups averaged less than two children, other-minority immigrant women had, on average, slightly more than two children.

The two outstanding differences between Korean and Filipino women were in their English proficiency, and class-of-worker categories. Almost half of Korean female workers reported that their English was poor, while only 3% of their Filipino counterparts did so. Whereas 13% of Korean women were self-employed or worked as employees of their own corporations, only about 2% of Filipino immigrant women were so employed.

**Table 2.**
**Characteristics of 20-64 year-old female workers, L.A., 1980**

|       | Korean | Filipino | Other  | FB-White | NB-White |
|-------|--------|----------|--------|----------|----------|
| N     | 775    | 1,544    | 6,280  | 4,725    | 5,788    |
| AGE   | 36.5   | 36.6     | 34.7   | 42.8     | 38.5     |
|       | <9.4>  | <9.5>    | <10.6> | <11.9>   | <12.6>   |
| YRSED | 12.8   | 14.8     | 9.1    | 12.8     | 13.1     |
|       | <3.3>  | <3.2>    | <4.6>  | <2.8>    | <2.3>    |
| EXP   | 17.7   | 15.8     | 19.5   | 24.1     | 19.4     |

Table 2(cont'd)

|  | Korean | Filipino | Other | FB-White | NB-White |
|---|---|---|---|---|---|
|  | <10.4> | <10.3> | <11.8> | <12.5> | <13.1> |
| WORK75 | 64.4 | 79.3 | 63.2 | 76.2 | 72.7 |
| MARRIED |  |  |  |  |  |
| SNG | 11.2 | 21.2 | 21.4 | 12.3 | 17.7 |
| MSP | 76.4 | 70.0 | 62.7 | 63.6 | 57.2 |
| WDS | 12.4 | 8.7 | 15.9 | 24.0 | 25.1 |
| NUMCH | 1.7 | 1.7 | 2.1 | 1.6 | 1.6 |
|  | <1.6> | <1.9> | <2.1> | <1.5> | <1.6> |
| KIDSAGE |  |  |  |  |  |
| NO-CH | 35.7 | 42.4 | 36.0 | 63.1 | 61.5 |
| CH<6 | 12.9 | 18.4 | 19.5 | 6.3 | 8.9 |
| CH6-17 | 40.9 | 26.3 | 27.9 | 27.2 | 25.3 |
| CH0-17 | 10.5 | 12.9 | 16.6 | 3.4 | 4.2 |
| YRSMAR | 15.4 | 16.6 | 17.1 | 22.6 | 21.2 |
|  | <10.6> | <12.9> | <12.1> | <12.4> | <12.5> |
| IMMIGR |  |  |  |  |  |
| IMM65- | 6.6 | 9.7 | 24.5 | 70.9 | N/A |
| IMM65-69 | 9.3 | 20.5 | 19.0 | 12.3 | N/A |
| IMM70-74 | 35.5 | 36.3 | 29.6 | 6.5 | N/A |
| IMM75-79 | 48.6 | 33.6 | 26.8 | 10.3 | N/A |
| ENGLISH |  |  |  |  |  |
| ENGonly | 4.5 | 5.2 | 5.4 | 57.0 | 96.5 |
| ENGvwell | 15.4 | 61.3 | 22.1 | 28.6 | 3.1 |
| ENGwell | 35.0 | 30.8 | 25.2 | 11.4 | .2 |
| ENGnot | 45.2 | 2.7 | 47.3 | 3.0 | .2 |
| CITIZEN | 31.5 | 40.2 | 23.8 | 55.7 | N/A |
| CLASS |  |  |  |  |  |
| CLsal | 81.8 | 83.2 | 88.3 | 80.4 | 79.0 |
| CLgvt | 5.2 | 14.8 | 8.1 | 11.4 | 15.3 |
| CLself | 11.2 | 1.6 | 3.0 | 6.4 | 4.9 |
| CLeoc | 1.8 | .5 | .6 | 1.8 | .9 |

Standard deviations are given in < > brackets.

*Labor force participation*

Table 2 also presents the percentage of working women; i.e., those who reported their occupation and industry, worked at least one week in 1979, and had a positive income in 1979. Filipino women show the highest labor force participation rate among our categories. About four out of every five Filipino immigrant women were in the Los Angeles labor market in 1979. Korean women, on the other hand, had the same labor force participation rate as white immigrant women, but less than Filipino women.

In order to examine human capital and assimilation effects on labor force participation, we conducted a logit regression of labor force participation for each ethnic group (see Table 3). Among female immigrants in general, age, education, and marital status affected labor force participation: younger, more educated, single women had higher odds of being in the paid labor force. Marital status, however, had no significant effect for either Korean or Filipino women: both worked outside the home as much as their single counterparts.

Two assimilation variables—period of immigration and English proficiency—influenced the labor participation of immigrant women in general. Among all immigrant women, except for Koreans, recent arrivals participated less frequently in the labor market than earlier arrivals. Neither period of immigration nor English proficiency affected the participation of Korean women. This surprising result probably reflects the role of the Korean ethnic economy in the Los Angeles labor market (Light and Bonacich, 1988). This ethnic economy, composed of Korean entrepreneurs and their co-ethnic employees, (see Light and Karageorgis, 1994) has been shown to offer so many employment opportunities to Koreans that even Korean immigrant women with serious language problems were as likely to find work as their longer-resident and more English-proficient counterparts. This result is consistent with Ong's (1985) finding for Chinese immigrant women in San Francisco, confirming that assimilation is less important for immigrant women who arrive to find a well-developed ethnic economy in which to work.

Table 3.
Logit regression of women's labor force participation, L.A., 1980

|  | Korean | Filipino | Other | FB-White | NB-White |
|---|---|---|---|---|---|
| ALL WOMEN | | | | | |
| a | 5.496 | 5.647 | 5.538 | 5.770 | 5.738 |
| AGE | -.010* | -.025** | -.011** | -.023** | -.026** |
| YRSED | .019* | .055** | .016** | .045** | .087** |
| MSP | -.178 | .014 | -.293** | -.464** | -.364** |
| WDS | -.054 | -.101 | -.069 | .003 | .131* |

Table 3 (con't)

|  | Korean | Filipino | Other | FB-White | NB-White |
|---|---|---|---|---|---|
| NUMCH | -.034 | -.018 | -.035** | -.037** | -.020* |
| CH<6 | -.435** | -.298** | -.348** | -.523** | -.633** |
| CH6-17 | .149 | -.079 | -.011 | -.083 | -.070* |
| CH0-17 | -.194 | -.319** | -.326** | -.676** | -.728** |
| IMM65- | .006 | .309* | .163** | .228** | |
| IMM65-69 | .060 | .524** | .332** | .213** | |
| IMM70-74 | .076 | .402** | .343** | .301** | |
| ENGonly | -.181 | -.091 | .068 | .288** | |
| ENGvwell | .033 | .290* | .201** | .215* | |
| ENGwell | .059 | .137 | .044 | .183 | |
| CITIZEN | .247** | .169 | .058 | .046 | |
| Prsn $x^2$ | 1299 | 1894 | 4482 | 3834 | 8814 |
| P | .338 | .599 | .436 | .369 | .501 |
| **MARRIED WOMEN** | | | | | |
| a | 5.374 | 5.477 | 5.646 | 5.281 | 5.235 |
| AGE | .004 | -.018* | -.016* | -.013 | -.038** |
| YRSED | -.011 | .088** | .031* | .038* | .155** |
| NUMCH | -.073* | -.002 | -.022 | -.044 | .078 |
| CH<6 | -.205 | .121 | -.805** | -.387 | -.832** |
| CH6-17 | .379** | .053 | -.124 | -.076 | -.189 |
| CH0-17 | .129 | -.096 | -.680** | -.879** | -1.147** |
| IMM65- | -.308 | .081 | .142 | .097 | |
| IMM65-69 | .068 | .271 | .393* | .085 | |
| IMM70-74 | .014 | .130 | .543** | .327 | |
| ENGonly | -.411 | -.867* | -.176 | .334 | |
| ENGvwell | .207 | -.001 | .124 | .160 | |
| ENGwell | .146 | -.129 | -.204 | .171 | |
| CITIZEN | .290* | .345** | .328* | .215* | |
| Hincome | -.00001** | -.00001** | -.00001 | -.00001** | -.00002** |
| Hself-emp | -.259** | -.560** | -.173 | -.363** | -.015 |
| HnotWK | -.210 | -.054 | -.577** | -.258 | -.201 |
| Prsn $x^2$ | 836 | 965 | 419 | 538 | 511 |
| P | .373 | .289 | .211 | .253 | .071 |

a   All human capital, female-specific and assimilation variables are held constant. The parameter reported is the antilog of the regression coefficient minus one. When multiplied by 100, it gives the percent difference in earnings.
\*   Statistically significant at the .05 level of significance
\*\*  Statistically significant at the .01 level of significance

More than two-thirds of immigrant women in our sample were married with spouse present. Their labor force participation, unlike that of single women, is potentially influenced by factors associated with their spouses. To ascertain the influence of such factors, and to distinguish them from those of assimilation, we introduced husband's income from all sources at 1979 into our analysis. The results appear in the lower half of Table 3.

Age, education, and the presence of children of any age affected immigrant wives' labor force participation in the expected direction: youth, increased levels of education, and childlessness increased the odds that an immigrant wife would be participating in the labor force. However, age and education did not affect labor force participation of Korean immigrant wives. In addition, their children's ages did not lower probability of immigrant wives' labor force participation for either group. Furthermore, our finding that having only school-age children (ages 6-17) increased the odds for Korean wives' participation in the labor market, suggests (given the Korean traditional gender division of household labor) that Korean school-age children presumably help with family chores and child-care, thus freeing their mothers to work outside the home.

Finally, period of immigration, and English proficiency had no significant effects for almost all immigrant wives of either group, although they did influence immigrant single women's labor force participation. This result suggests that married immigrant women participate in the labor market regardless of their level of assimilation, while immigrant single women are more likely to work outside the home the more assimilated they are.

Table 3 also reveals the effects of husbands' characteristics on their wives' participation in the labor force. The higher a husband's earnings, the lower the likelihood that his wife worked, regardless of ethnicity. Also, having a self-employed husband lowered an immigrant wife's probability of labor force participation as market-remunerated labor.

To examine the precise effect that self-employment of the husband had on his wife's engagement in paid work, we examined several characteristics of Korean and Filipino immigrant couples (see Table 4). We found that 129 Korean, as opposed to only two Filipino, immigrant wives of self-employed men reported their occupation and industry without classifying themselves as either paid or unpaid employees. This discrepancy represents, we argue, unreported immigrant wives' labor force participation. In the Korean case, the addition of the 'discrepant' 129 wives in the 'unpaid family worker' category would push the proportion of unpaid family workers among Korean immigrant wives to almost 20%!

Table 4.
Some characteristics of Korean and Filipino immigrant couples[a]

|  | Korean Couples | | Filipino Couples | |
|---|---|---|---|---|
| N | 840 | (100.0%) | 958 | (100.0%) |
| *WIVES* | | | | |
| Mean Age | 37.0 | <8.7> | 38.3 | <9.2> |
| Mean Education | 13.2 | <3.3> | 15.0 | <3.0> |
| Paid Worker[b] | 517 | (61.5) | 835 | (87.2) |
| Report Occupation & Industry | 646 | (76.9) | 857 | (89.5) |
| Potential Unpaid Family Workers | 129 | (15.4) | 2 | (0.2) |
| Unpaid Family Worker | 33 | (3.9) | 6 | (0.6) |
| *HUSBANDS* | | | | |
| Mean Age | 40.7 | <8.8> | 39.7 | <9.4> |
| Mean Education | 14.7 | <3.4> | 14.9 | <3.0> |
| Mean Income in $ | 16,485 | <14,945> | 15,946 | <10,079> |
| *SELF-EMPLOYED WIVES* | | | | |
| Total | 134 | (100.0%) | 26 | (100.0%) |
| With self-employed husband | 98 | (73.1%) | 6 | (23.1%) |
| *SELF-EMPLOYED HUSBANDS* | | | | |
| Total | 285 | (100.0%) | 41 | (100.0%) |
| With self-employed wife | 98 | (34.4%) | 6 | (14.6%) |
| With wife as unpaid labor | 162 | (56.8%) | 8 | (19.5%) |
| *BOTH WIFE & HUSBAND SELF-EMPLOYED* | | | | |
| Total | 98 | (100.0%) | 6 | N/A |
| Pearson correlation | .354 | | .155 | |
| Work in same industry | 60 | (61.2%) | 0 | N/A |

Percentages are in ( ) parentheses and standard deviations are in < > brackets.
[a] Foreign-born co-ethnic husbands and wives.
[b] Those who reported their industry and occupation, worked at least one week in 1979, and had a positive income in 1979.
N/A: Numbers not available due to small number of cases (N<10).

The wider discrepancy among Korean as opposed to Filipino wives may reflect differences in gender relations and ideology. Although Korean wives actually work in family-owned small businesses, they tend to identify themselves as housewives, not as unpaid family workers. This factor overlays the inherent difficulty that family members, who have both family-business and household responsibilities, face in properly distinguishing between hours or weeks worked for the family-owned business(es) from those worked for the household itself, and in accurately measuring their individual contribution to family income. Therefore, we surmise that Korean wives tended not to report their hours or weeks worked in 1979, or their individual incomes, even though they did report their occupation and industry.

Among Korean immigrant couples, therefore, the husband's self-employment increased the probability of his wife's engagement in unpaid' family work, a finding consistent with those seen in case studies of Korean immigrant businesses, which report heavy reliance on family labor, especially that of wives (Light and Bonacich, 1988; Yoon, 1991, p. 313). A Korean husband's self-employment is highly correlated with his wife's self-employment. Furthermore, among Korean couples with both spouses self-employed, the majority were composed of spouses self-employed in the same, precisely-defined industry, suggesting that they worked as partners. Self-employed Korean immigrant husbands, therefore, utilized their wives labor as partners (21%), or unpaid family workers (57%).

*Earnings attainment*

Table 5 presents mean annual earnings and mean hourly wages. An interesting finding is that the earnings gap between ethnic women is less than that between ethnic men (see Lee, 1988, Table 5.1). For example, the annual earnings gap between whites and all other ethnic men was between about $6,000 and $10,000, whereas it was only between about $1,500 to $3,500 for women. Furthermore, Filipino immigrant women earned slightly more than white women. This came at the cost of longer working hours: while Filipino women annually earned more than white women, their hourly wages were lower. Similarly, Korean women earned slightly less than whites, but their hourly wages were far lower. Korean and Filipino immigrant women, therefore, worked more weeks and longer hours than did white women, but they earned less per hour.

In order to examine the relative importance of human capital, assimilation and self-employment variables for immigrant women's earnings attainment, we performed a regression analysis for each ethnic group on the natural logarithm of annual earnings (to correct for skewness in the distribution of annual earnings) on various established indicators. The results appear in the lower part of Table 5. Returns to human capital (i.e., education and work experience), especially education, are lowest among Korean and Filipino women, indicating a labor market disadvantage (Light and Rosenstein, 1995).

Contrary to our expectations, marital status and the presence of children did not lower the earnings of Korean and Filipino women. Indeed, having more children, and having only school age children, increased the earnings of Korean women. Thus, Korean immigrant mothers who have children of school age do not only have a higher likelihood of participation in the labor force, but they are also better remunerated when they do so.

Table 5 also demonstrates a systematic assimilation effect. The longer immigrants had stayed in the United States, the more they tended to earn, controlling for all other theoretically important variables.[5] The assimilation effect on earnings attainment, however, was less systematic for Korean immigrant women. Indeed, Korean immigrant women with a serious English language problem earned as much as co-ethnic women fluent in English, other things being equal. This result may be attributed to the beneficial effects of the Korean ethnic economy in Los Angeles (Light and Karageorgis, 1994).

In order to examine the effect of self-employment on earnings, we included two variants of self-employment in our analysis. One was unincorporated self-employment, the other was as employee of one's own corporation. The effects on earnings of both variants were positive and statistically significant for all immigrant minority men (Korean, Filipino and other-minority group) in the Los Angeles labor market; they all earned significantly more than their co-ethnic salaried workers (see also Lee, 1988). However, the results for immigrant women were more complex.

First, there were marked differences between unincorporated self-employed, and employees of their own corporation. Women employees of their own corporation earned more than salaried women, while unincorporated self-employed women earned less than salaried women. This is particularly the case for the two white groups. Second, regardless of the types of self-employment, Filipino self-employed women earned much less than their co-ethnic salaried worker counterparts.

## Table 5.
## Mean annual earnings, mean hourly wages, and coefficients of model of income attainment of female workers

|  | Mean Annual Earnings In Dollars | | | | |
| --- | --- | --- | --- | --- | --- |
|  | Korean | Filipino | Other Min | FB-White | NB-White |
| Income | 9,246 | 11,751 | 7,201 | 10,848 | 10,734 |

|  | Mean Hourly Wages In Dollars | | | | |
| --- | --- | --- | --- | --- | --- |
|  | Korean | Filipino | Other Min | FB-White | NB-White |
| Income | 6.65 | 7.54 | 6.26 | 9.37 | 9.37 |

|  | Coefficients of Income Attainment | | | | |
| --- | --- | --- | --- | --- | --- |
|  | Korean | Filipino | Other Min | FB-White | NB-White |
| a | 3.413 | 4.243 | 3.560 | 3.214 | 2.666 |
| YRSED | .029** | .027** | .046** | .049** | .057** |
| YRSED´ | .003* | .006 | .003** | .004** | .004** |
| EXP | -.017* | -.004 | .001 | .006** | .013** |
| EXP´ | -.00001 | -.0005** | -.0002** | -.0003** | -.0003** |
| WORK75 | .133* | .191** | .060** | .222** | .222** |
| HOURS | .351** | .269** | .380** | .504** | .634** |
| WEEKS | .939** | .947** | .829** | .792** | .841** |
| MSP | .152 | -.056 | .003 | -.121* | -.158** |
| WDS | .279 | -.056 | .067 | .10 | .110 |
| NUMCH | .051* | -.005 | -.011* | -.024** | -.034** |
| CH<6 | .085 | .036 | .007 | -.028 | -.045 |
| CH6-17 | .148* | -.033 | .018 | -.076** | -.007 |
| CH0-17 | -.001 | -.004 | .020 | -.094 | -.025 |
| YRSMAR | .007 | .0005 | .0004 | .002 | -.002 |
| IMM65- | -.027 | .282** | .194** | .062 |  |
| IMM65-69 | .216* | .253** | .166** | .139** |  |
| IMM70-74 | .144* | .205** | .067** | .060 |  |
| ENGonly | .181 | -.384** | .068 | .172** |  |
| ENGvwell | .040 | -.304** | .071** | .152* |  |
| ENGwell | .0003 | -.319** | .054* | .143* |  |

Table 5 (cont'd)

| | Coefficients of Income Attainment | | | | |
|---|---|---|---|---|---|
| | Korean | Filipino | Other Min | FB-White | NB-White |
| CITIZEN | .123 | .047 | .108** | .048* | |
| Cgvt | -.122 | .022 | -.060 | -.048 | .040 |
| Cself | .090 | -.370** | .067 | -.100* | -.219** |
| Ceoc | .194 | -.187 | .277* | .201** | .294** |
| $R^2$ | .5187 | .5428 | .4733 | .5057 | .5500 |

a  All human capital, female-specific and assimilation variables are held constant. The parameter reported is the antilog of the regression coefficient minus one. When multiplied by 100, it gives the percent difference in earnings.
\*   Statistically significant at the 0.05 level of significance
\*\*  Statistically significant at the 0.01 level of significance

To examine the segmented labor market effect, we 'dummy coded' industrial sector variables and added them to our regression model as controls (see Table 6).[6] The percentage distribution of workers across the sectors shows that native-born white women were over-represented in the primary sector, while Korean, Filipino, and other-minority women were concentrated in the secondary sector (56.5%, 47.2% and 60.3%, respectively). The percentage of Filipino women working in the secondary sector exceeded that of white women, regardless of nativity.

The percentage distribution across sectors by 'class of worker' generally confirmed the representativeness of the overall distribution. The important exception was the government class of worker, for which the sectoral percentage distribution differs from the overall distribution. Except for Filipino women, women government employees in the categories of our sample were significantly more concentrated in the primary sector than their co-ethnics in the other classes of worker. Moreover, government employees were also significantly over-represented in the primary sector as compared to the other two sectors. To the extent that primary sector employment—which for this study means being employed in an industry where over 73% of the employees are white (see note 6)—does indeed confer the benefits segmented labor market theorists argue it does, these findings suggest that women government employees, except for Filipinos, fared better than their co-ethnics in the private sector by being over-represented in the primary sector.

## Table 6.
### Percent distribution of sectors and returns to the primary and mixed sectors relative to the secondary sector, L.A., 1980

| | Percentage Distribution | | | | |
|---|---|---|---|---|---|
| | Korean | Filipino | Other Min | FB-White | NB-White |
| *All Workers* | | | | | |
| PRIM | 22.8 | 31.5 | 22.2 | 43.2 | 49.8 |
| MIXED | 20.6 | 21.3 | 17.5 | 25.8 | 24.9 |
| SECON | 56.5 | 47.2 | 60.3 | 31.0 | 25.3 |
| *Self-Employed* | | | | | |
| PRIM | 21.8 | 45.2 | 22.5 | 42.1 | 53.3 |
| MIXED | 26.7 | 29.0 | 26.7 | 30.6 | 27.7 |
| SECON | 51.5 | 25.8 | 50.8 | 27.3 | 19.0 |
| *Salaried* | | | | | |
| PRIM | 21.8 | 30.5 | 20.0 | 39.9 | 45.8 |
| MIXED | 19.9 | 21.3 | 17.5 | 27.0 | 27.1 |
| SECON | 58.4 | 48.1 | 62.6 | 33.1 | 27.1 |
| *Government* | | | | | |
| PRIM | 42.5 | 34.9 | 51.6 | 67.2 | 68.7 |
| MIXED | 17.5 | 20.1 | 16.5 | 13.9 | 12.9 |
| SECON | 40.0 | 45.0 | 31.9 | 18.9 | 18.4 |
| | Coefficients of Income Attainment | | | | |
| | Korean | Filipino | Other Min | FB-White | NB-White |
| *All Workers* | | | | | |
| PRIM | -.026 | -.087** | .090** | .110** | .082** |
| MIXED | .044 | -.178** | .050* | .004 | .039 |
| *Self-Employed* | | | | | |
| PRIM | -.309 | .848 | -.039 | .066 | -.155 |
| MIXED | .423 | .520 | -.084 | .044 | -.086 |
| *Salaried* | | | | | |
| PRIM | .026 | -.087* | .139** | .153** | .134** |
| MIXED | .028 | -.166** | .059* | .008 | .071* |
| *Government* | | | | | |
| PRIM | -.158 | -.234** | -.057 | -.060 | -.070 |
| MIXED | -.055 | -.313** | .023 | .033 | -.162* |

\* Statistically significant at the .05 level of significance
\*\* Statistically significant at the .01 level of significance

Inspection of the regression coefficients for being employed in the mixed and primary sectors revealed that the sectoral effect varied by class of worker and ethnicity. To the extent that our operationalization of sectors/segments, according to their composition in terms of majority-minority race/ethnicity of their labor force, validly reflects that posited by segmented labor market theories, we expected those coefficients to be positive and significant, reflecting a net advantage in earnings attainment resulting from being employed in the primary and mixed as opposed to the secondary sector.

In fact, the sectoral effect was more systematic and significant for salaried workers than for the self-employed, and more systematic for other immigrant women and whites than for Korean and Filipino women. The sectoral effect was insignificant for Korean women, a finding possibly attributable to their extensive participation in the Korean ethnic economy. The sectoral effect among Filipino women salaried workers, on the other hand, was in the opposite direction from that hypothesized by the segmented labor market theories. Filipino women in the primary sector earned significantly less than those in the secondary sector!

The above result is explicable on the basis of the definition of each sector (see note 6) and the high qualifications of many immigrant Filipino women, especially in the health professions. In the overwhelmingly white (over 73% of the labor force) primary sector, and the Los Angeles ethnically representative mixed sector, Filipino women pay a price for their minority ethnicity status; in the over 47% minority secondary sector, on the contrary, well-qualified Filipino women received superior returns on their human capital than in the other sectors. This is strongly and significantly the case especially among government employees: Filipino women government employees, who worked with predominantly minority co-workers, were relatively 'privileged', compared to those working within ethnically balanced, and predominantly white work forces. In short, Filipino women seemed to have had a comparative advantage in the secondary sector of the Los Angeles labor market, especially when they worked for the government.

Finally, in order to examine how well Korean and Filipino immigrant women adjusted in the Los Angeles labor market relative to their white immigrant peers, we examined the relative earnings differentials, as presented in Table 7. Unlike the previous results, which were based upon separate regressions for each ethnic group, the results in Table 7 are based on a pooled sample of immigrant women, dummy coded for Korean, Filipino, other-minority, and white ethnicity. White immigrant women were the omitted reference group for this regression analysis.

### Table 7.
### Earnings differences for immigrant female workers relative to the white immigrant female workers, L.A., 1980

|  | Korean | Filipino | Other |
|---|---|---|---|
| *All Workers* | | | |
| OVERALL[a] | -.146 | .156 | -.387 |
| CONTROLLED[b] | .052 | .040 | -.078** |
| *Self-Employed* | | | |
| OVERALL | .143 | .068 | -.104 |
| CONTROLLED | .201 | -.227 | -.012 |
| *Salaried Employees* | | | |
| OVERALL | -.199 | .109 | -.420 |
| CONTROLLED | .035 | .044 | -.091** |
| *Government Employees* | | | |
| OVERALL | -.140 | .440 | -.229 |
| CONTROLLED | -.001 | .103 | -.021 |

[a] Differences in mean naturalized log annual earnings.
[b] All human capital, female-specific, and assimilation variables are held constant. The parameter reported is the antilog of the regression coefficient minus one. When multiplied by 100, it gives the percent difference in earnings.
** Statistically significant at the .01 level of significance.

The most interesting finding in Table 7 is that ethnicity generally made little difference for women's earnings, except for the other-minority immigrant women workers.[7] Once all human capital and assimilation variable effects had been controlled, Korean and Filipino female salaried workers earned as much as white immigrant women in the Los Angeles labor market. Their counterparts—immigrant Korean and Filipino male salaried workers—earned about 20% less than white immigrant salaried workers, net of all human capital and assimilation variables.

The earnings differentials of self-employed women, however, should be noted carefully. Although the coefficients are not significant due to the small number of cases, the sign of the coefficients confirms what we found in Table 6: self-employment does not offer better earnings to Filipinos, but it does to Korean women. Korean self-employed women earn as much as, or even more than, self-employed white women.

The finding that there were fewer ethnic differences in earnings for immigrant women than there were for immigrant men may reflect a 'floor' effect. A floor effect is operative when earnings cannot go any lower than a particular level. The Los Angeles labor market presumably already imposed a heavy enough penalty on all women because of their gender, so that little room remained for further ethnicity-based penalties on earnings.

## Conclusions

In this paper, we examined the labor force participation and earnings attainment of Korean and Filipino immigrant women in relation to white majority (immigrant and native), and other-minority immigrant women. First, we found that the impact of assimilation on women's labor force participation depended on their marital status and ethnicity. On the one hand, married women tended to work outside the home less than single women, regardless of their degree of assimilation; single women were more likely to work the more assimilated they were.

On the other hand, the assimilation effect was not important for Korean women. Korean immigrant women's comparatively high labor supply in the market may be explained by the presence of a vibrant and extensive Korean ethnic economy in Los Angeles. Presumably, the Korean ethnic economy offers so many employment opportunities to Korean ethnics that recent Korean immigrant women, even those with a serious language problem, are as likely to be in the labor market as their longer-resident and more English-proficient counterparts.

As far as Filipino immigrant women are concerned, their exceptionally high labor supply may be related to the high-skill selectivity of Filipino female immigration, especially those from the health-related professions. Additionally, regarding the effect of assimilation on earnings attainment, we found that the assimilation effect was weaker for Korean than other groups of women in our study cohort.

Second, we found that the labor market segmentation effect, by majority-minority labor force composition, varied by class of worker and ethnicity. The sectoral effect on earnings was larger for salaried workers than for the self-employed, and it was more systematic for the other-minority immigrants and whites than for Korean and Filipino women. Once again, the unimportance of the sectoral effect for Korean women may be due to their high participation in their own ethnic economy.

Furthermore, we found the reverse of the expected sectoral effect among Filipino (private and public sector) salaried workers. Those in the primary and mixed sectors earned less than their counterparts in the secondary sector. This result suggests that the highly-skilled Filipino immigrant women may have had a comparative advantage working in the secondary sectors of the Los Angeles labor market (i.e., in industries in which over 73% of the labor force was of minority race/ethnicity).

Third, we found that, although female self-employment was generally quite unusual, self-employment was, nonetheless, quite advantageous for Korean women. Korean self-employed women earned as much as, or even more than, their co-ethnic salaried women and white immigrant self-employed women. The high concentration of Korean men and women in self-employment seems to be related to their relative success in self-employment. Korean immigrants showed the highest rate of self-employment among the groups studied: 32% of Korean men, 33% of Korean women, 34% of Korean husbands, and 16% of Korean wives were self-employed. Furthermore, up to 20% of Korean wives worked as unpaid family workers in family-owned businesses. We suggest that the role of self-employment in immigrant adaptation, general socio-economic mobility and in particular ethnic groups should be analyzed in the context of the immigrant family, its socio-cultural and economic priorities and, consequently, its adaptation strategies.

As far as Filipino immigrant women are concerned, their relatively low rates of self-employment, and their rather dismal fortunes therein, seem to reflect the fact that Filipino women's access to good jobs in the mainstream economy leaves them with little incentive to engage in small businesses. Due to their fluency in English, their high human capital, and their concentration in relatively well-paid professional occupations, Filipino immigrant women show the highest labor force participation in the Los Angeles labor market, with yearly earnings exceeding those of native-born white women. In the Filipino women's case, success and concentration in wage and salary employment in the general labor market makes self-employment less attractive.[8]

Finally, we found that there were fewer ethnic differences in female earnings than in male earnings. This picture of relative earnings equality, especially among female salaried workers, was one of 'shared misery' rather than 'shared economic success'. The reference group's (white immigrant women) earnings were so much lower, compared to those of men, that they constituted an earnings 'floor'. Women's earnings were low enough, it seems, to afford those of immigrant and minority status a dubious protection against further ethnicity-based earnings penalties.

**Notes**

1. Most of the original research and data analysis for this paper derives from the principal author's doctoral dissertation, especially Chapters 6-8 (Lee, 1988).
2. The selection of these two immigrant groups is justified by the fact that the preponderance of female immigrants is more substantial for Koreans and Filipinos as compared both to all immigrants and to all Asian immigrants. For example, about 60% of both Korean and Filipino immigrants during the 1970s were female, whereas only slightly over 50% of either all immigrants or of all Asian immigrants were female.
3. Over 70% of Korean immigrants and about 55% of Filipino immigrants during the 1970s belonged to the aggregated category which includes wives, children, and persons without occupations (U.S. INS, 1970-79, Table 8). To estimate the number of adult women without occupation, we subtracted the number of children (male and female below 20 years old) from this aggregated category, assuming that most adult male immigrants reported their occupation to the INS. The adjusted proportions of housewives and/or women without occupation are 90.5% in 1970 and 94.3% in 1979 for Korean immigrant women, and 51.9% and 72.2% for Filipino immigrant women.
4. The Public Use Microdata Samples (PUMS) from the 1980 Census contain individual- and household-level information from the 'long-form' questionnaires distributed to a sample of the population enumerated in the Census. The Census Bureau provided the 5% and 1% samples for the United States.
5. The inclusion of both period of immigration and English fluency variables in the model causes a multi-colinearity problem for Filipino immigrant women.
6. Following Portes and Bach (1985, p. 218), we used ethnicity as a criterion for operationalizing the labor market segments: the primary sector is a white majority labor market, and the secondary sector is a minority labor market. Dividing the population of the Los Angeles Metropolitan area labor market into whites and non-whites, we first examined the proportion of each of the two groups in each of the industries classified at the detailed three-digit industrial code level of the U.S. Census. We then compared the proportions of these two groups in each three-digit level industry to the overall proportions of total white (about 63%) and non-white (about 37%) population in all

industries. Following this, we classified industries into three categories: (1) industries where the labor force was disproportionately white (more than 73%) were defined as the primary sector, (2) industries where the labor force was disproportionately non-white (more than 47%) were defined as the secondary sector, and (3) industries where the labor force reflected the ethnic composition of the Los Angeles Metropolitan area (from 53 to 73% white and from 27 to 37% non-white) were defined as the mixed sector. This procedure produced 84 primary, 85 secondary, and 62 mixed industries, for a total of 231 industries.

7 By itself, of course, the statistical significance and negative sign of the ethnicity coefficient for the earnings attainment of 'other immigrant' women is not particularly instructive, given the great breadth of the category.

8 An ethnic group's successful penetration of the general labor market does not by itself imply the dynamic shrinking of its ethnic economy, either in terms of number of co-ethnics therein employed or of their earnings, as seems to be the case among Filipinos. Efficient, and successful, ethnic economies may utilize the 'representatives' of the ethnic group in the general labor market to create more demand at higher prices for the ethnic economy's products, secure cheaper and more abundant raw material and capital sources, locate trustworthy and solvent non-co-ethnic partners etc., and to generally improve the image and social standing of the ethnic group in general, and its ethnic economy in particular.

# References

Almquist, E.M. and Wehre-Einhorn, J.L. (1978), 'The Doubly Disadvantaged: Minority Women in the Labor Force', in Stromberg, A.H. and Harkess, S. (eds.), *Women Working*. Mayfield Publishing Company, pp. 63-88.

Arnold, F., Carino, B.V., Fawcett, J.T. and Park, I.H. (1989), 'Estimating the Immigration Multiplier: An Analysis of Recent Korean and Filipino Immigration to the United States', *International Migration Review*, Vol. 23, pp. 813-38.

Beck, E.M., Horan, P.M. and Tolbert II, C.M. (1978), 'Stratification in a Dual Economy: A Sectoral Model of Earnings Determination', *American Sociological Review*, Vol. 43, pp. 704-20.

Bonacich, E. (1972), 'A Theory of Ethnic Antagonism: The Split Labor

Market', *American Sociological Review*, Vol. 37, pp. 547-59.

Bonacich, E. (1976), 'Advanced Capitalism and Black/White Race Relations in the United States: A Split Labor Market Interpretation', *American Sociological Review*, Vol. 41, pp. 34-51.

Bonacich, E. (1979), 'The Past, Present, and Future of Split Labor Market Theory', *Research in Race and Ethnic Relations*, Vol. 1, pp. 17-64.

Boyd, M. (1984), 'At a Disadvantage: The Occupational Attainments of Foreign-Born Women in Canada', *International Migration Review*, Vol. 18, pp. 1091-119.

Chiswick, B.R. (1978), 'The Effect of Americanization on the Earnings of Foreign-Born Men', *Journal of Political Economy*, Vol. 86, pp. 897-921.

Chiswick, B.R. (1980), 'Immigrant Earnings Pattern by Sex, Race, and Ethnic Grouping', *Monthly Labor Review*, Vol. 103, pp. 22-5.

Chiswick, B.R. (1984), 'Human Capital and the Labor Market Adjustment of Immigrants: Testing Alternative Hypotheses', Discussion Paper, No. 7 (March), Migration and Development Program, Harvard University: Cambridge, MA.

Doeringer, P.B. and Piore, M.J. (1971), *Internal Labor Markets and Manpower Analysis*, Lexington Books: Lexington, MA.

Evans, M.D.R. (1984), 'Immigrant Women in Australia: Resources, Family, and Work', *International Migration Review*, Vol. 18, pp. 1063-90.

Evans, M.D.R. (1989), 'Immigrant Entrepreneurship: Effects of Ethnic Market Size And Isolated Labor Pool', *American Sociological Review*, Vol. 54, pp. 950-62.

Goldscheider, C. and Kobrin, F. (1980), 'Ethnic Continuity and the Process of Self-Employment', *Ethnicity*, Vol. 7, pp. 256-78.

Gordon, D.M. (1972), *Theories of Poverty and Underemployment*, Lexington Books: Lexington, MA.

Gordon, M. (1964), *Assimilation in American Life*, Oxford: New York.

Houstoun, M.F., Kramer, R.G. and Barrett, J.M. (1984), 'Female Predominance of Immigration to the United States since 1930: A First Look', *International Migration Review*, Vol. 18, pp. 908-63.

Kim, K.C., Hurh, W.M. and Fernandez, M. (1989), 'Intra-Group Differences in Business Participation: Three Asian Immigrant Groups', *International Migration Review*, Vol. 23, pp. 73-95.

Lee, H-K. (1988), Socioeconomic Attainment of Recent Korean and Filipino Immigrant Men and Women in the Los Angeles Metropolitan Area, 1980, Ph.D. Dissertation, University of California-Los Angeles: Los Angeles, CA.

Light, I. (1972), *Ethnic Enterprise in America*, University of California

Press: Berkeley, CA.
Light, I. and Bonacich, E. (1988) *Immigrant Entrepreneurs: Koreans in Los Angeles 1965-1982*, University of California Press: Berkeley, CA.
Light, I. and Karageorgis, S.N. (1994), 'The Ethnic Economy', in Smelser, N. and Swedberg, R. (eds.), *Handbook of Economic Sociology*, Princeton University and Russell Sage Foundation: Princeton, Ch. 26.
Light, I. and Rosenstein, C. (1995), *Race, Ethnicity and Entrepreneurship in Urban America*, Aldine de Gruyter: Hawthorne, NY.
Long, J.E. (1980), 'The Effect of Americanization on Earnings: Some Evidence for Women', *Journal of Political Economy*, Vol. 88, pp. 620-9.
Model, S. (1985), 'A Comparative Perspective on the Ethnic Enclave: Blacks, Italians, and Jews in New York City', *International Migration Review*, Vol. 19, pp. 64-81.
National Bureau of Statistics (NBS) (1982), *Social Indicators in Korea*, Economic Planning Board, Republic of Korea: Seoul.
National Science Development Board (NSDB) (1976), Enrollment in Higher Education by Level (All Schools) and by Discipline, unpublished data, National Science Development Board: Bicuta, Rizal, Philippines.
Ong, P. (1985), 'Does Assimilation Matter? Labor Participation Among Chinese Immigrant Wives', unpublished manuscript, University of California at Los Angeles: Los Angeles, CA.
Ortiz, V. and Cooney, R. (1984), 'Sex Role Attitudes and Labor Force Participation among Young Hispanic Females and Non-Hispanic White Females', *Social Science Quarterly*, Vol. 65, pp. 392-400.
Pedraza, S. (1991), 'Women and Migration: The Social Consequences of Gender', *Annual Review of Sociology*, Vol. 17, pp. 303-25.
Pido, A.J.A. (1986), *The Filipinos in America: Macro/Micro Dimensions of Immigration and Integration*, Center for Migration Studies: New York.
Piore, M. (1975),'Notes for a Theory of Labor Market Stratification', in R. Edwards, Reich, M. and Gordon, D. (eds.), *Labor Market Segmentation*, D.C. Heath: Lexington, MA, pp. 125-50.
Piore, M. (1977), 'The Dual Labor Market: Theory and Implications', in *Problems in Political Economy: An Urban Perspective*, D.C. Heath: Lexington, MA, pp. 93-96.
Portes, A. and Bach, R.L. (1985), *Latin Journey: Cuban and Mexican Immigrants in the United States*, University of California Press: Los Angeles, CA.
Reimers, C.W. (1985), 'Cultural Differences in Labor Force Participation among Married Women', *The American Economic Review*, Vol. 75, pp. 251-5.

Sullivan, T. (1984), 'The Occupational Prestige of Women Immigrants: A Comparison of Cubans and Mexicans', *International Migration Review*, Vol. 18, pp. 1045-62.

Tienda, M., Jensen, L. and Bach, R.L. (1984), 'Immigration, Gender and the Process of Occupational Change in the U.S., 1970-1980', *International Migration Review*, Vol. 18, pp. 1021-44.

UNESCO (1970), *National Science Policy and Organization of Research in the Philippines*, Science Policy Studies and Documents, No. 22, United Nations Educational, Scientific and Cultural Organization: Paris.

U.S. Bureau of the Census (1983) *Census of Population and Housing, 1980: Public-Use Microdata Samples*, Technical Documentation, US Immigration and Naturalized Service (USINS): Washington, DC.

U.S. Bureau of the Census (1965), *Statistical Yearbook of the Immigration and Naturalization*, US Immigration and Naturalized Service (USINS): Washington, DC.

U.S. Bureau of the Census (1987), *Service*, US Immigration and Naturalized Service (USINS): Washington, DC.

Waldinger, R. (1989), 'Structural Opportunity or Ethnic Advantage? Immigrant Business Development in New York', *International Migration Review*, Vol. 23, pp. 48-72.

Waldinger, R., Aldrich, H., Ward, R. and Associates (1990), *Ethnic Entrepreneurs: Immigrant Business in Industrial Societies*, Sage Publications: Newbury Park, CA.

Wong, M.G. and Hirschman, C. (1983), 'Labor Force Participation and Socioeconomic Attainment of Asian-American Women', *Sociological Perspectives*, Vol. 26, pp. 423-46.

Yoon, I.-J. (1991), 'The Changing Significance of Ethnic and Class Resources in Immigrant Businesses: The Case of Korean Immigrant Businesses in Chicago', *International Migration Review*, Vol. 25, pp. 303-32.

Zlotnik, H. (1990), 'Conference Report: International Migration Policies and the Status of Female Migrants', *International Migration Review*, Vol. 24, pp. 372-81.

# 9 We don't want no goddamn black refugees! The politics of Haitian refugees in Florida

*Alex Stepick and Tareena Joubert*

In 1977, President Carter's Immigration and Naturalization Service (INS) Commissioner, Leonel Castillo, the first ethnic minority person to hold that position, reversed an oppressive policy toward Haitian refugees who had been arrving in southern Florida. Rather than having them jailed, he agreed to release without bond Haitians who had been detained in local jails and to issue them work authorizations while their asylum hearings were pending.

INS staff in Miami and others in southern Florida immediately objected to both the release from detention and the issuance of work authorizations. The INS Commissioner was called into the office of one of Florida's leading Congressman. From behind his desk, the Congressman leaned toward the INS Commissioner. Wagging his finger, he shouted, 'We don't want anymore goddamn black refugees in Florida!' The INS returned to a policy of denying legal rights to Haitians who wanted to claim political asylum. Commissioner Castillo's temporary policy reversal was a small blip in a remarkably consistent, resolute policy to deter Haitian refugees from coming to the U.S. and to convince those who made it to return home.

Gunnery Sgt. Earns Rinvil was the chief translator for the thousands of Haitian refugees housed at the U.S. Naval Base in Guantanamo, Cuba in 1994. He often worked 18-hour days that left him exhausted, frustrated, and hoarse. When he began to translate Janet Civil's story about a field full of burning people, he suddenly was no longer tough. 'She said she can't stand to look at people's heads getting chopped off and getting burned', Rinvil translated after wiping away the tears. Ms. Civi's story was hardly uniquely gruesome or fearful (Winfield, 1994).

I am 17 years old. My mother and father are both dead. Our home was used as a voting bureau during the 1990 elections and so after the coup, in 1992, the military came to our home and shot my father. I saw him killed before my very eyes. Right after that my mother and I went into hiding but we went to two different places. The military found my mother and beat her so bad that a few days later she died in the hospital. . . . My older brother died at sea, when he was attempting to escape Haiti. . . . I am afraid to go back to Haiti. All my family has been killed. I have a relative in New York. Please let me go there (Herbert, 1995).

This terrified teenager had sponsors ready and able to provide him with a new life in the United States. Instead, the U.S. government forcibly repatriated him to Haiti. One girl, who had insisted that her father was dead, was returned to Haiti when authorities at Guantanamo insisted even more strongly that he was alive and perfectly capable of caring for her. They sent her back to Haiti where she discovered that he was, in fact, dead.

Quartermaster's Mate First Class Kathy Hoyt, a 14-year veteran of the Coast Guard, admitted, 'I feel real sad. When they see us, they'll change into their best clothes'. Hoyt added that she tries to avoid looking into the Haitians' eyes. The Coasties, as they call themselves, were charged with intercepting boats of potential Haitian refugees before they entered U.S. waters, a task that they have had since President Ronald Reagan first instituted the interdiction policy, as it was officially known, in 1981. In 1993, as thousands of Haitians fled Haiti's military dictatorship, the U.S. Coast Guard abandoned all drug interdiction activities in the Caribbean to focus on keeping Haitians from reaching U.S. shores.

In 1994, waves of Haitian and Cuban boat people fled their homelands for the U.S. More than 20,000 Haitians and 30,000 Cubans ended up in custody at the Guantanamo U.S. Naval Base on the eastern tip of Cuba. The U.S. government allowed virtually all the Cubans into the U.S. It forcibly returned to Haiti almost all of Guantanamo's Haitian refugees. For those Cubans not immediately paroled into the U.S. the government released a list of names of all Cuban refugees detained. The names of Haitian refugees detained were not released. Among Guantanamo's Haitian refugees were 356 children who arrived there unaccompanied by any adult. Most had witnessed Haiti's paramilitary forces murder close family members. Some barely escaped Haiti with their own lives. The U.S. government fought to send these children back to Haiti.

## Resolute racism, foreign policy and local concerns

This dual standard toward Haitian and Cuban refugees is hardly novel. To the contrary, the U.S. has exercised a remarkably consistent and resolute policy to deny Haitian asylum seekers entry to the U.S. Throughout the 1970s and 1980s, Haitian asylum seekers in the United States had the highest rate of rejection of claims of any national group. Until 1994, only for Haitians did the U.S. maintain permanent Coast Guard patrols in Haitian waters to intercept potential Haitian refugees fleeing their homeland (Stepick, 1982, p. 144).

Some have attributed this apparent discrimination against Haitians to racism and others to U.S. Cold War foreign policy designed to support friendly, non-communist regimes. Both explanations are partially true, but the prime motivation is considerably more narrow. While racism and Cold War politics played a role in U.S. policy toward Haitian asylum seekers, local politics in the state of Florida, the destination of most Haitian asylum seekers, fundamentally inspired the U.S. policy. The real goal of U.S. policy towards Haitian asylum seekers has been to alleviate Floridians' fears that allegedly poor, black refugees would overwhelm Florida's beaches. Since Lyndon Johnson was President and through President Clinton, the U.S. federal government has consistently and resolutely rejected Haitian refugees because of Floridian anti-Haitian prejudice. Explored in the following are the evolution of that policy and the at least tempo-rary resolution that came with the initiation of democracy in Haiti after the election of, first, Jean Bertrand Aristide as President and then his successor Rene Preval.

*Early humanitarian immigrants*

U.S. policy toward Haitian immigrants had not always been so harsh. During President Kennedy's term in the early 1960s, the U.S. actively responded to the extremely repressive and vicious regime of Haitian President Francois Duvalier. In 1961, U.S. Ambassador Newbegin was recalled to Washington after Duvalier was fraudulently reelected by a margin of 1,320,780 to 0. The CIA and the Special Operations Branch of the State Department armed and supported several exile invasions aimed at overthrowing Duvalier. In 1963, after Haiti's military forcibly occupied the Dominican Embassy in Port-au-Prince, the Kennedy administration cut off economic and military aid, suspended diplomatic relations for a month, and evacuated all American citizens from Haiti. The U.S. did not resume economic aid to Haiti until after Francois

Duvalier's death nearly ten years later.

During this period, the U.S. actively encouraged Haitians to immigrate. U.S. consular officers readily approved non-immigrant Haitian visas and virtually all of these immigrants arrived in the U.S. legally via airplane. Many subsequently overstayed their visas, but the U.S. Immigration and Naturalization Service (INS) did not pursue their cases. In contrast to later policies toward Haitians who arrived by boat in South Florida, the U.S. government allowed these Haitians to remain in the U.S. (Loescher and Scanlan, 1984, p. 319).

*The cold war restrictions*

After the death of President Kennedy, however, Cold War concerns took precedence and the U.S. ignored Duvalier's human rights violations. Nevertheless, the brief period of welcome extended to Haitians during the Kennedy administration served to establish a significant Haitian exile community in the U.S., primarily in New York, although significant numbers also headed for Paris, Montreal, Chicago, and Boston (Buchanan, 1979a, 1979b, 1980, 1983, 1984; Dejean, 1980; Fouron 1985; Glick, 1975, Glick, DeWind, Brutus et al., 1987; Glick and Fouron, 1990; Keely et.al., 1978; Laguerre, 1984; Saint-Louis, 1988; Souffrant, 1974; Woldemikael, 1989). Through the 1980s, some estimates put the New York Haitian community at between 150,000 and 300,000. Despite the size of the Haitian community in New York City and the fact that a substantial number appeared to be in the country illegally, neither public opinion nor the U.S. government defined this immigration as a political problem nor did Haitians receive much public attention. The public and the government, however, have always defined Haitians in Florida as a problem.

In September 1963, the first Haitian boat people arrived on South Florida's shores. After having been taken into custody by the INS, they claimed political asylum. INS denied their request and returned them to Haiti (Subcommittee on Immigration, Citizenship, and International Law, 1976). No more boat people were detected for another 10 years.

During the Nixon administration of the late 1960s through the mid-1970s, the U.S. consul in Haiti allegedly made it more difficult for Haitians to migrate both permanently and temporarily to the U.S. Permanent immigrants had to demonstrate that they had a job awaiting them in the U.S. (Yamada, 1984). For temporary migrants, the U.S. consul reportedly began asking for stronger proof of the visa applicant's intention to return to Haiti (Dominguez, 1975).

Deterring permanent legal migration increased unregulated immigration by boats. Between 1972 and 1977, an estimated 3,500 Haitians arrived on the shores of southern Florida. They founded a migration network and the flow increased geometrically over the next few years, with over 1,800 Haitians arriving in 1978, 2,500 in 1979, and over 25,000 in 1980. By 1980, the flow had become big business, with smugglers virtually advertising in Haiti. Haitian government officials not only viewed the flow as a type of safety valve, but many also benefitted from kickbacks received from the smugglers (Stepick, 1986).

In contrast to those who had migrated to the U.S. earlier and by airplane, boat arrivals in southern Florida, though they total less than one-fifth the number in New York, have been the object of much publicity, legal disputes, and policy debate. Since 1972, national political authorities, goaded by local political groups in southern Florida, have attempted both to deter Haitian immigration and to deport those Haitians already in Florida. Members of south Florida's political elite, including Democratic Party members, elected officials, and some exiled Cubans, believed that the boat people disrupted the community and drained public resources (Miller, 1984, Stepick, 1982, 1986).

Negative stereotypes of poor blacks fleeing the western hemisphere's poorest country motivated Floridians' concerns. They presumed the Haitian 'boat people' to be uneducated, unskilled, rural peasants who were likely to be disease-ridden. Although these stereotypes were subsequently disproved (Portes and Stepick, 1985, 1987; Portes, Stepick and Truelove, 1986; Stepick and Portes, 1986), they still moved south Florida leaders to appeal to their local Congressmen, who apparently pressured the INS into a response. The INS thereafter began to expend a far greater effort in controlling the flow of Haitians (Stepick, 1982). Haitians in Miami then became viewed as a problem of tremendous potential impact. Top INS and Justice Department officials feared that a humanitarian policy toward Haitians might produce a flood of Jamaican and other Latin American migrants who would use asylum procedures as a mechanism for gaining entry to the U.S. (Noto, 1978; Gullage, 1978).

A top INS official decided that, rather than releasing Haitians and providing them with work permits, the 'most practical deterrent to this problem [the Haitian claims for asylum] was expulsion from the United States' (Crewdson, 1980). Officials in the Justice Department and the INS then designed the 'Haitian Program' which had two principal thrusts: to deny Haitians in detention access to lawyers and to prejudge as undeserving any Haitian claims for asylum (Lawyers Committee, 1978; Loescher and Scanlon, 1984; Stepick, 1982, Zucker, 1983). Haitians quickly numbered among those with the highest rejection rate of political asylum applications.

Ironically, the anti-Haitian initiatives did not entirely succeed because of the victims' own defenselessness. The plight of Haitian asylum seekers elicited public compassion and the concern of churches and philanthropic organizations. In Miami, African American churches, the media, the liberal branch of Florida's Democratic party, along with the established Haitian community, all spoke against the U.S. policy and in favor of the Haitian refugees. At the national level, church groups, primarily the National Council of Churches, followed by public interest lawyers, national African American groups (particularly the Congressional Black Caucus), and other civil rights organizations, unions, and eventually state and local officials with a fiscal interest in legalizing the Haitians' status, repeatedly sought to assist the Haitians in their efforts to combat the federal government (Yamada, 1984).

Haitian advocates filed court cases challenging every aspect of the federal government's policy (Haitian Refugee Center v. Civiletti, 1980, Sannon v. United States, 1980). The cases had two fundamental thrusts: that U.S. asylum policy violated the rights of the Haitian asylum applicants, and that the government had unfairly prejudged the Haitians' claims for political asylum. While the Haitian plaintiffs sought no relief with respect to the substance of their asylum applications, they did seek an opportunity for a fair and nondiscriminatory reprocessing of their claims (Haitian Refugee Center v. Civiletti 1980; Jean v. Nelson 1984, 1985; Louis v. Nelson 1983; Sannon v. United States 1980).

*Cubans versus Haitians — The 1980 crisis*

What most affected Haitian policy, however, only coincidentally involved Haitians. In 1980, the Third World laid claim to Miami. The in-flow of Haitians coming by boat peaked right at the time of the Cuban flotilla from the port of Mariel. Within a few months, Miami's Cuban community ferried 125,000 of their compatriots across the straits to Florida. While the Cuban and Haitian boat flows differed in most respects, they fused as one in the public mind. The coincidence of the two flows underscored the glaring disparities in the receptions accorded to each group. No government official ever attempted to summarily deport a Mariel refugee; U.S. Coast Guard cutters towed and escorted boats carrying Cubans to Key West, not back to Cuba. No matter how much the media disparaged Mariel entrants, they were still Cuban and thus effectively insulated from the fate awaiting the boats from Haiti.

The U.S. government's justification for the differential treatment hinged on the distinction between 'political' refugees and 'economic' migrants. The argument did not wash. Clearly many Mariel refugees had left in search of better opportunities, while many Haitians had experienced genuine persecution. The Miami District Court repeatedly heard testimony like that of Mr. Solivece Romet:

> Held by the Tonton Macoutes for four days during which he was forced to stand in a 2 by 3 foot cell. Beaten repeatedly as a consequence of which he showed deep scars in his skull and developed a speech impediment. After escaping to Florida in a sailboat, he was detained by the Immigration and Naturalization Service. INS was trying to deport him on the grounds that he was an economic immigrant (Silva, 1980).

In fact, the difference between the Cubans and Haitians streaming into Miami had less to do with individual motivations than with the country they left behind (communist versus right-wing), the community that received them (politically powerful Cubans versus politically invisible Haitians), and their color (overwhelmingly white Cubans versus black Haitians). This last realization mobilized the black political establishment in defense of the Haitians. 'If we can take in the refugees of other countries, we can take in the refugees of Haiti', declared Andrew Young, then the U.S. Ambassador to the United Nations, in a March visit to Miami (Grimm and Bartlett, 1980). On April 19, 1980 Jesse Jackson led a march of one thousand people to a hotel in Miami where the government was holding sixty Haitian women and children who had arrived by boat the preceding week. In Washington, the Congressional Black Caucus led the political battle. U.S. representatives Shirley Chisholm, Walter Fauntroy, and Mickey Leland all argued on the Haitians' behalf in personal meetings with the Attorney General, the Secretary of State, and the President. Shortly thereafter, Senator Edward Kennedy attacked U.S. policy as racially biased and demanded to know if Haitians would be treated the same as Cubans (Sawyer, 1980).

Faced with this combined offensive, the government relented. Lower federal courts found that the INS had indeed violated Haitians' rights and ordered INS to reprocess Haitian asylum claims. President Carter assigned the processing of Haitian and Cubans to a new administrative entity — the Cuban-Haitian Task Force, which promised equal treatment for Cubans and Haitians. While this meant fewer benefits for Cubans, it was a dramatic step forward for Haitians.

The victories were hardly total or final, however. The courts never accorded the Haitians a legal immigration status. Instead, they only forced the federal government to reprocess Haitian asylum claims. Carter's designation of the Cuban-Haitian Task Force temporarily avoided the question, at least for those Haitians who arrived while the Mariel boatlift continued. But Mariel ended in the Fall of 1980, leaving Haitians again to fend for themselves. Soon they faced the same discriminatory polices as before. The federal courts of appeal subsequently reversed many of the victories the Haitians had achieved in the district federal courts.

*Interdiction and repatriation*

In January 1981, Ronald Reagan assumed the Presidency. During the transition period between Reagan's November 1980 election and January 1981 inauguration, the south Florida Republican Party and Congressional delegation pressured for strong measures to curb the flow of Haitian boat people.

The Reagan administration readily complied with a multi-prong attack directed solely at Haitians: detention of new arrivals, interdiction and return of Haitians in boats at sea, and cooperation of the Haitian government in stopping the flow (Task Force, 1981). Sometime between the spring and summer of 1981, the INS changed its policy of regularly releasing Haitians to one of detention without parole, with a limited humanitarian exception. Editorials appeared in the major newspapers and numerous community groups spoke out against the policy demanding that the Haitians be released.

Haitian advocates again sought redress through the courts and again they achieved partial satisfaction. Cases that had been processed during the June speed-up were ordered reprocessed. At the end of June, 1982, The Organization of American States' Inter-American Human Rights Commission commenced an investigation of human rights violations in the detention of Haitians in the U.S. At the same time, the federal court ordered that Haitians then detained were to be released if counsel could be found for them (Louis v. Nelson 1983).

Almost two years later, however, the Federal Appeals Court ruled against the Haitians when they claimed that the U.S. had discriminated against the Haitians. More importantly, the Appeal Court maintained that, because they were in a special legal category called exclusion proceedings (which meant that the INS had stopped them before they crossed a U.S. border), the Haitians had no rights under the Constitution with respect to their applications for admission, parole, or political asylum in the United States. In short, the Federal Appeals Court asserted that the U.S. government could legally discriminate against Haitians.

In the meantime, the Reagan administration had begun initiating other strategies that would skirt the courts' review and drastically curtail the flow of Haitians to Florida's southern shores. On 23 September 1981, the U.S. and Haitian governments signed an agreement of cooperation concerning the interception of Haitian boats leaving Haiti (U.S. Department of State, 1981). President Reagan then signed an Executive Order that authorized a U.S. Coast Guard cutter to intercept boats found sailing in the straits between Haiti and the Bahamas that were suspected of transporting Haitians to the U.S. (Fuller, 1981; U.S. GAO, 1983). If such evidence were discovered, the boats and their passengers were to be towed back to Haiti. Refugee claims were to be adjudicated on board by a team consisting of State Department members, an INS representative, and a Creole interpreter.

The program cost approximately $30 million annually and for more than a decade the U.S. government deemed virtually no Haitians to have worthy asylum claims (U.S. Department of State, 1986). At the same time, the number of Haitians detected by INS and the Coast Guard who made it to Florida's southern shores dropped precipitously from slightly over 8,000 for 1981 to only 134 for 1982.

The federal government viewed the corrupt and repressive Haitian regime as the root cause of the Haitian refugee problem. Corruption and repression by friendly, right-wing regimes have seldom motivated the U.S. to push for a change in a foreign government. But in this case, thousands of Haitians were migrating to a southern U.S. state, Florida, and claiming political asylum. Florida had no need for low wage, unskilled labor. Thus, even though Duvalier was a staunch anti-communist and offered low-wage labor and tax holidays to U.S. businesses, the U.S. government sought changes. They first hoped for changes within the Duvalier government, but when these failed to materialize, the U.S. assisted in Duvalier's ouster, which came in February 1986, by giving Jean-Claude Duvalier passage to France aboard a U.S. military transport.[1]

*Repression, corruption and Haitian democracy*

After the official end of Duvalier rule, the Haitian masses rejoiced, for they believed democracy would finally come to their country. The flow of Haitians attempting to reach southern Florida noticeably slackened, although U.S. policy remained constant. A Coast Guard cutter still patrolled Haitian shores and any Haitian who made it to the U.S. had little chance of being granted asylum.

The end of Duvalier did not deliver Haitians from repression and corruption. Instead, what Haitians refer to as Duvalierism without Duvalier prevailed. From the time of the ousting of Duvalier in February 1986 until December 1990, Haiti experienced four military coups and a fraudulent election. With each government since the fall of Duvalier, violations of human rights, conditions of poverty, and government corruption remained integral elements of everyday life (Amnesty International, 1987). As conditions failed to improve, arrivals of Haitians seeking asylum climbed again and the U.S. maintained interest in changing the Haitian government. Unstable conditions caused several multinational corporations to withdraw. Relations with the United States government were rocky at best at this time and U.S. aid fell below the $50 million level during the late 1980s (*Washington Times*, 1991).

In December of 1990, Haitians elected as President, Jean Bertrand Aristide, a Catholic priest, giving him an overwhelming 67% of the vote. The electoral triumph of Aristide caused a substantial drop in the exodus of refugees from the country. Democracy and the associated decline in Haitian 'boat people' proved brief, however. The Haitians with power, the military and the business class, feared the leftist ideas suggested by the grass-roots priest-turned-president. On his first day in office, Aristide retired eight generals and the police chief of Port-au-Prince, the capital and largest city. Some wealthy Haitians offered as much as $5,000 apiece to soldiers and policemen for their participation in a coup. On 30 September 1991, after about 8 months in office, President Aristide was overthrown by the Haitian military. After the coup, corruption and human rights violations increased tremendously. The military beat, tortured, arrested without warrant, and murdered supporters of the ousted president (Amnesty International, 1992).

President Bush denounced the overthrow and demanded that Aristide be reinstated. The U.S. then led the Organization of American States (OAS) to establish an economical embargo against Haiti, hoping to convince the coup leaders to negotiate the return of Aristide. The results in Haiti were not what Bush had anticipated. Instead of the reinstallation of President Aristide, hundreds of Haitians began fleeing in small boats, most of them heading toward Florida again. An estimated 38,000 people fled Haiti during the first eight months following the coup. From 29 October 1991 to 12 February 1992, the United States Coast Guard spent $4.8 million, an average of $45,000 per day, intercepting, housing, and returning most Haitians to Haiti (*Haiti Insight*, 1992).

The U.S. government of the time confronted a dilemma. Their fundamental goal was to respond to the concerns of many south Floridians that the refugees would overwhelm them. At the same time, they opposed the human rights violations and repression in Haiti that occasioned the refugee surge. As an immediate solution, the U.S. turned Guantanamo Naval Base, at the eastern tip of Cuba, into a detention center where they housed Haitians until they could determine if they had a well-founded fear of persecution. Critics referred to Guantanamo as a 'Haitian concentration camp' and the Haitians as 'modern day lepers' (*Atlanta Journal and Constitution*, 1993). Jesse Jackson commented, 'It was wrong to lock out Jews in 1939 and condemn them to death and it is wrong to lock out the Haitians in 1993' (*Newsday*, 1993). The U.S. was nevertheless treating some Haitians better than they had before. Previously, the U.S. had determined that less than 5% of Haitians claiming political asylum had a well-founded fear of persecution, the fundamental criteria for asylum or refugee status. While actual conditions in Haiti had not changed much, U.S. resolve had. The acceptance rate of Haitian asylum claims jumped to approximately 30%, still far less than the 100% of Cubans accepted into the U.S., but far better than before.

The Guantanamo solution, however, proved insufficient. More and more Haitians abandoned their island. As government officials laboriously reviewed each individual's claim to asylum (as opposed to simply giving every claim the benefit of the doubt as historically was done for Cubans), the Guantanamo detention facility filled up. Either more Haitians had to be let in, other places found, or they had to be returned to Haiti. The U.S. found other countries unwilling to provide much cooperation. The solution, as it had been in the previous crises of the 1970s and 1980s was to repress the flow. By the 10th anniversary of the program, the day before the September 1991 coup, a total of 24,559 Haitians were reported to have been intercepted in international waters by the U.S. Coast Guard (Frelick, 1992). Of that number, federal authorities allowed only 28 to pursue asylum claims.

On 24 May 1992, from his Maine home, Bush issued the 'Kennebunkport Order', a measure that significantly strengthened Reagan's interdiction policy. Under the Kennebunkport Order, Haitians intercepted by the U.S. Coast Guard would no longer have the opportunity to plead their case to an on-board team from the State Department and the INS. Instead, all Haitian 'boat people' could be summarily and immediately returned to Haiti. The major difference between the Reagan order and that of Bush was that under the latter there was *no* chance for Haitians interdicted on the high seas to apply for political asylum; Haitians were immediately sent back to Port-au-Prince (Lennox, 1993). The policy worked, at least for awhile and in the sense that it kept a new influx of Haitians out of southern Florida.

While the massive boatlift of Cubans from Mariel was more than twelve years old, disparate treatment of Haitians and Cubans persisted. On 29 December 1992 a pilot of a Cuban commuter plane with 53 passengers diverted the plane from its domestic destination and headed for Miami. The co-pilot and security guard were tied up, gagged with handkerchiefs soaked in chloroform, and then handcuffed. Upon landing in Miami, these two plus three more flight crew members requested to be returned to Cuba. The others on board requested political asylum. After several hours, all were released. Authorities claimed the pilot's action did not constitute a hijacking because he was the pilot of the plane and had merely diverted its destination (*New York Times*, 1992)

On 18 February 1993, a former Haitian soldier, Woody Marc Edouard boarded a missionary plane for a Haitian internal flight. After firing a shot into the floor as a warning, Edouard convinced the pilot to proceed to Miami. Upon arrival in Miami, he surrendered to authorities, claiming that he was fleeing political persecution in Haiti. Rather than being released and hailed as a hero, the federal government accused him of air piracy, jailed him pending a trial, and threatened him with a 20 year sentence if convicted.

In 1994, the number fleeing Haiti escalated as terror in Haiti increased and the regime's unwillingness to reinstall the democratically-elected Aristide persisted. Then, just as had happened in 1980, Cubans, too, began departing for Miami in flimsy, unseaworthy boats. Florida leaders feared a replay of 1980 and they argued with the federal government to stop the flow. They succeeded in Haitianizing U.S. Cuban refugee policy. For the first time since Fidel Castro took power in 1959, the U.S. did not welcome Cuban refugees. Instead, the U.S. spent over $1 million a day to deflect over 30 thousand Cuban refugees to Guantanamo to await their fate beside the 15,000 Haitians there. The flow of Cubans gradually ebbed, but the U.S. still did not treat Cubans entirely the same as Haitians. Most Haitians were still returned to Haiti, but of the 30,000 Cubans, except for a few who clandestinely returned to Cuba, all eventually came to the U.S.

The most effective resolution of the Haitian refugee problem came in September 1994, when U.S. troops invaded Haiti, ousted the coup leaders, and paved the way for exiled President Aristide's return to Haiti. While Aristide's reassumption of the presidency did not instantaneously solve Haiti's problems, it provided sufficient hope to deter refugees. Haitian boat refugees dropped to virtually zero with Aristide in power. In 1996, Aristide stepped down as President as another democratically-elected President, René Preval, took over. For the first time in Haitian history, one democratically-elected President peacefully replaced another. At the same time, the uncontrolled flow of Haitians to the U.S. virtually ceased.

**Conclusions**

Local, state of Florida political forces have motivated the consistent, resolute policy against Haitian refugees. While U.S. racism and Cold War politics each have influenced this policy, at moments each of these faded. The Kennedy administration encouraged the immigration of Haitians, who are predominantly black. Both the Kennedy and Reagan administrations opposed the right-wing Haitian regime, both seeking the regime's overthrow in spite of its anti-Communist commitment. Reagan succeeded — Jean-Claude Duvalier abandoned Haiti for French exile, and Duvalier's ouster ultimately led to the democratic election of a left-leaning priest. But the Haitian military and its right-wing allies subsequently deposed him. Reagan, Bush, and then Clinton justified their own approaches to the problem in terms of support for Haitian democracy. At the same time, they, and previous U.S. presidents, did all they could to deny political asylum to Haitians fleeing Haiti's repression and corruption.

Why would U.S. presidents claim to oppose repression in Haiti while denying asylum to those fleeing that repression? The explanation of this paradox lies in the anti-Haitian prejudice of some of Florida's leaders and Florida's influence and power on the national scene. At least one important Florida political official was unabashedly racist. More generally, Floridians have expressed grave reservations over Haitians coming to their shores. Floridians exert pressure primarily behind closed doors, such as the Florida Congressman mentioned above who declaimed that Floridians did not want any more 'god damn, black refugees'. INS, a weak and beleagured bureaucracy, listens and responds because it cannot afford to alienate an important Congressman from an important state.

Publicly, Florida's citizens are more indirect. In 1980, Dade County Florida, the site of Miami, Florida's largest and most immigrant city, overwhelmingly passed an anti-bilingual, anti-multicultural referendum (Castro, 1992). The movement, led by white, working-class individuals, arose directly in response to the turmoil caused by the Mariel and Haitian inflows of 1980 and marked the beginning of anti-bilingual referenda throughout the U.S.

Public officials generally express their concerns in terms of the costs of hosting refugees. As soon as the federal court ordered HIV-positive Haitians released, Florida's Governor, Lawton Chiles, requested emergency federal funding for south Florida hospitals and other agencies. People in the Miami area remember all too well who paid the price of the Washington decision that permitted refuge in the U.S. for the 'Marielitos' of Cuba. Florida lawmakers are still fighting for federal reimbursement for the cost of food, shelter, education, and medical services for the 125,000 Cubans who came ashore during the Mariel boatlift in 1980. For Cuban refugees, those objections are likely to produce increased federal spending; but for Haitians, they reinforce the policy of deterrence. The federal government continues to favor Cubans because of the inertia of Cold War politics, because Cubans here have achieved their own political and economic influence, and because of the predominantly white color of their skin.

In contrast, whatever power Haitians have comes only from their own powerlessness. The federal government's repression of Haitian refugees has led human and civil rights interests to support the Haitian cause. Using the Federal Courts, they have succeeded sufficiently to forestall repeatedly efforts to deport Haitians. While repression always reemerged, enough Haitians were freed and permitted into the U.S. to allow the formation of a Haitian community in south Florida. Haitian advocates fought constant, difficult, and wearisome battles. Only with Jean Bertrand Aristide's assumption of the Presidency in Haiti did the refugee struggle decline. With democracy emerging in Haiti, the pressures to migrate from repression disappeared and were reduced to those associated with families across the seas.

**Note**

1 U.S. foreign policy and the pressure of Congressional and other groups did not directly produce Duvalier's downfall. They contributed to it only because of the presence of other equally important factors, the newfound militancy of the Church, the downturn in the Haitian economy, and the resurgence of a split in Haiti's elite. Nevertheless, the U.S. remained the most important external force precipitating the departure of Duvalier.

# References

Amnesty International (1987), *Haiti: Deaths in Detention, Torture and Inhumane Prison Conditions*, Amnesty International: New York.

Amnesty International (1992), 'Haiti', *Amnesty International Report, 1992*, Amnesty International: New York.

*Atlanta Journal and Constitution* (1993) 'A Simple Matter of Decency', 21 March.

Buchanan, S. (1979a), 'Haitian Women in New York City', *Migration Today*, Vol. 7, No. 4, pp. 19-25, 39.

Buchanan, S. (1979b), 'Language Identity: Haitians in New York City', *International Migration Review*, Vol. 13, No. 2, pp. 298-313.

Buchanan, S. (1980), Scattered Seeds: The Meaning of Migration for Haitians in New York City, Dissertation, New York University: New York.

Buchanan, S. (1983), 'The Cultural Meaning of Social Class for Haitians in New York City', *Ethnic Groups*, Vol. 5, pp. 7-30.

Buchanan, S. (1984), 'The Social Character of Religion in Rural Haiti', in Foster, G. and Valman, A. (eds.), *Haiti: Today and Tomorrow*, University Press of America: Lanham, MD, pp. 35-56.

Castro, M. (1992), 'The Politics of Language', in Grenier. G. and Stepick, A. (eds.), *Miami Now!* University Press of Florida: Gainesville, FL, pp. 109-132.

Crewdson, J., (1980), 'Ruling Nears in Haitians' Lawsuit Alleging U.S. Bias', *The New York Times*, 12 June, pp. A1, col. 4, D18, col. 1.

Dejean, P. (1980), *The Haitians in Quebec*, Ottawa, Canada: Tecumseh Press.

Dominguez, V. (1975), *From Neighbor to Stranger: The Dilemma of Caribbean Peoples in the United States*, Antilles Research Program, Yale University: New Haven, CT.

Fouron, G. (1985), Patterns of Adaptation of Haitian Immigrants of the 1970s in New York City, Ed.D. Dissertation, Columbia University: New York.

Frelick, B. (1992), *Report on the Americas Immigration*, U.S. Committee for Refugees: Washington, DC, Vol XXVI, 1 July, p. 2.

Fuller, J. (1981), 'Memorandum for the Cabinet: Immigration Issues', July 10, Office of Cabinet Administration, The White House: Washington, DC.

Glick, N. (1975), The Formation of a Haitian Ethnic Group, Ph.D. Dissertation, Columbia University: New York.

Glick-Schiller, N., DeWind, J., Brutus, M-L., Charles, C., Fouron, G. and

Thomas, A. (1987), 'All in the Same Boat? Unity and Diversity in Haitian Organizing in New York', In Sutton, C. and Chaney, E. (eds.), *Caribbean Life in New York City: Sociocultural Dimensions*, Center for Migration Studies: New York, pp. 182-201.

Glick-Schiller, N. and Fouron, G. (1990), '"Everywhere We Go We Are in Danger": Ti Manno and the Emergence of a Haitian Transnational Identity', *American Ethnologist*, Vol. 17, No. 2, pp. 329-347.

Grimm, F. and Bartlett, E. (1980), 'Political Heavyweights Bring Bout Here', *Miami Herald*, 9 March, pp. 1B, 7B.

Gullage, R. H. (1978), 'Memorandum from R. H. Gullage, Acting District Director, Miami Office, INS to all employees', 12 August 23.

*Haiti Insight* (1992), 'Interdiction: A Costly Operation', Haiti Insight, Vol 3, No. 7, p. 10.

Haitian Refugee Center v. Civiletti, (1980), 503 F. Supp 442 (S.D. Fla 1980) modified sub nom.

Haitian Refugee Center v. Smith (1982), 676 F.2d 1023 (5th Cir.).

Haitian Refugee Center (1983), Master Exhibit on Human Rights Violations, Repression, and the Persecution of Returnees in Haiti, Haitian Refugee Center: Miami, FL, October 1.

Herbert, B. (1995), 'In America; Guantanamo's Kids', *The New York Times*, 10 May, Section A, page 23.

Jean v. Nelson, (1984), 727 F. 2d. 957.

Jean v. Nelson, (1985), 105 S. Ct. 2992.

Keely, C. et.al. (1978), 'Profiles of Undocumented Aliens in New York City: Haitians and Dominicans', *Occasional Papers and Documentation, No. 5*, Center for Migration Studies: Staten Island, NY.

Laguerre, M. (1984), *American Odyssey: Haitians in New York City*, Cornell University Press: Ithaca, NY.

Lawyers Committee for International Human Rights, International Human Rights Law Group, and Washington Lawyers Committee for Civil Rights under Law, (1978), 'Report on Haitians in Miami', Lawyers Committee for Civil Rights under Law: Washington, DC.

Lennox, M. 1993), 'Refugees, Racism, and Reparations: A Critique of the United States' Haitian Immigration Policy', *Stanford Law Review*, Vol 45, pp. 687-724

Loescher, G. and Scanlan, J. (1984), 'U.S. Foreign Policy and Its Impact on Refugee Flow from Haiti', *New York Research Program in Inter-American Affairs*, Occasional Paper No. 42, New York University: New York.

Louis v. Nelson (1983), 570 F, Supp. 1364.

Lundahl, M. (1979), *Peasants and Poverty: A Study of Haiti*, Croom-

Helm: London.
Miller, J. (1984), *The Plight of Haitian Refugees*, Praeger, New York.
*The New York Times* (1992), 'Cuban Pilot Diverts Airliner to Florida; 48 Seek Asylum', 30 December.
*Newsday* (1993), 'Plea for Asylum: Jesse Jackson, 40 Others Arrested in Protest over Haitian Detainees', 16 March.
Noto, M. (1978), 'Memorandum from Mario T. Noto, Deputy Commissioner INS to Leonel Castillo, Commissioner, INS', August 25.
Portes, A., Stepick, A. and Truelove, C. (1986), 'Three Years Later: A Report of the Adaptation Process of (Mariel) Cuban and Haitian Refugees in South Florida', *Population Research and Policy Review*, Vol. 5, pp. 83-94.
Portes, A. and Stepick, A. (1985), 'Unwelcome Immigrants: The Labor Market Experiences of 1980 Cuban and Haitian Refugees in South Florida', *American Sociological Review*, Vol. 50, pp. 493-514.
Portes, A. and Stepick,A. (1987), 'Haitian Refugees in South Florida, 1983-1986', *Dialogue No. 77, Occasional Papers Series*, Latin American and Caribbean Center, Florida International University: Miami, FL.
Saint-Louis, L. (1988), Migration Evolves: The Political Economy of Network Process and Form in Haiti, The U.S. and Canada, Ph.D. Dissertation, Boston University: Boston, MA.
Sannon v. United States, (1980), No. 74-428 Civ-JLK (S.D. Fla).
Sawyer, K. (1980), 'Refugee Policy Draws Fire in Hearing', *Washington Post*, 13 May, p. A6.
Silva, J. (1980), 'Court Told of Living Death in Haitian Prison', *Miami News*, 9 April, p. 4A.
Souffrant, C. (1974), 'Les Haitiens aux Etats-Unies', *Population, Special Issue* No. 29.
Stepick, A. (1982), 'Haitian Boat People: A Study in the Conflicting Forces Shaping U.S. Immigration Policy', *Law and Contemporary Problems*, Vol 45, p. 165.
Stepick, A. (1986), *Haitian Refugees in the United States, Second Edn*, Rvzd., Minority Rights Group: New York (First Edition, 1982).
Stepick, A. and Portes,A. (1986), 'Flight into Despair: A Profile of Recent Haitian Refugees in South Florida', *International Migration Review*, Vol. 20, No. 2, pp. 329-250.
Subcommittee on Immigration, (1976), Citizenship, and International Law, 'Haitian Emigration', House Committee on the Judiciary, 94th Congress, 2nd session, committee print: Washington, DC.
Task Force on Immigration and Refugee Policy (1981), 'Issue Paper — Subject: What Policy Should the United States Adopt with Regard to

Foreign Persons Who Enter South Florida Without Visas?' No. 3 (26 June) (memorandum to President Reagan from task force established by him, 6 March 1981).

U.S. Code, (1980), Public Law No. 96-20, 94 Statute 102, reprinted in U.S. Code, *Congressional and Administrative News*: Washington, DC.

U.S. General Accounting Office (1983), 'GAO Report — Detention Policies Affecting Haitian Nationals', U.S. GAO: Washington, DC, 16 June.

U.S. Department of State (1986), 'U.S. Assistance to Haiti', Special Report No. 141, Bureau of Public Affairs, Washington, DC, February.

U.S. Department of State (1981), 'Migrants — Interdiction', Agreement between the United States of America and Haiti, effected by Exchange of Notes, Signed at Port-au-Prince, 23 September 1981. Treaties and Other International Acts Series, 10241, pursuant to PL 89-497, approved 8 July 1966 (80 Stat. 271; 1 U.S.C. 113).

*Washington Times* (1991), 'Leery of Socialism, U.S. Doubles Aid to Haiti', 8 February.

Winfield, N. (1994), 'Thousands of Haitians Can Tell Tales of Terror', *The Charleston Gazette*, 18 July, p. 2A.

Woldemikael, T. (1989), *Becoming Black American: Haitians and American Institutions in Evanston, Illinois*, AMS Press: New York.

Yamada, N. (1984), The Haitian Migration to South Florida, Bachelor of Arts Honors Essay, Harvard College: Cambridge, MA, November.

Zucker, N. (1983), 'The Haitians vs. the U.S.: The Courts as a Last Resort', *Annals of the American Academy of Political Science and Social Science*, Vol. 467, pp. 151-162.

# 10 Application of photography to immigration studies: Iranians and Yemenis in California

*Jonathan Friedlander, Mehdi Bozorgmehr, and Ron Kelley*

Case studies in California, of Yemenis and Iranians underscore two major movements of immigrants in the world today. The labor migration experience of Yemenis is common to millions of poor Middle-Eastern villagers attracted by the prospects of employment in the oil-rich states of the Gulf and in the industrialized West. Conversely, the Iranians represent one of the highest status immigrant groups to enter the United States in large numbers (Bozorgmehr and Sabagh, 1988). Occupationally, the Yemenis and Iranians are similar to many other immigrant groups in the United States. The Yemenis in California are part of a largely low-skilled agricultural and service-oriented labor force, which historically has been dominated by Latin American nationals. The Iranians on the other hand are similar to entrepreneurial and professional immigrant groups, most notably the earlier waves of Cuban exiles (Fagan, Brody and O'Leary, 1968) and Korean immigrant entrepreneurs (Light and Bonacich, 1988). Unlike the Cuban 'golden exiles', who were both well-to-do and welcomed to America (Portes, 1969), the Iranians have encountered a generally hostile reception in the United States. The overriding theme of displacement conceptually joins the markedly different experiences of the Yemenis and Iranians in a comparative framework. Similarly, it applies to Ethiopian and Russian immigrants in Israel (Photo 1).

Our intent is to encourage an understanding of photography and its application within specific social science disciplines and contexts. The methodological issues considered include the types of visual data recorded by the multiple photographers involved in the two projects, and the validity and reliability of photographic evidence *vis-à-vis* specific

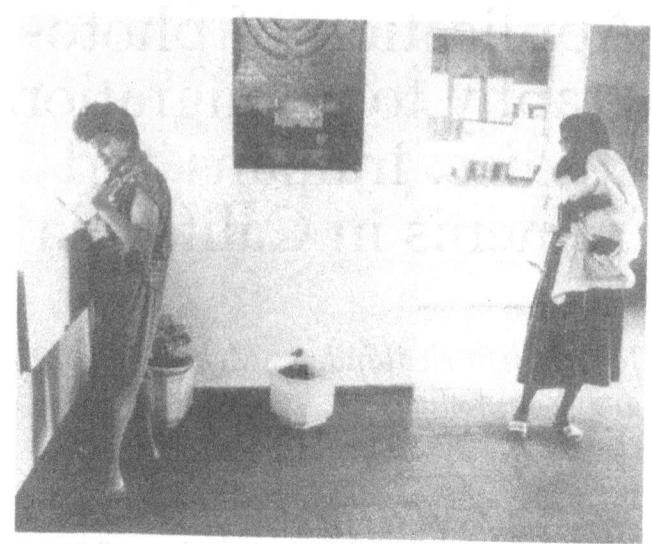

Photo 1: Russian and Ethiopian immigrant women in absorption center, Ashkelon, Israel [Photograph by Ron Kelley (original in color)]

research criteria applied in the social sciences: theory, access, reactivity, sampling, and representativeness. From the perspective of photographic criticism, exploration will be made of the nature of the medium and its value to social science research. Specific aspects of Yemeni and Iranian immigration, identity, and culture will also be illuminated in discussions of photographic content.

Photographers in the United States have long been interested in documenting immigration. Perhaps the best known photographer of this genre is Lewis Hine, who photographed immigrants on Ellis Island at the turn of the twentieth century. This humanistic tradition continued with Jacob Riis's poignant *How the Other Half Lives* (1970), which documented the tenements of New York inhabited by immigrants. In most of these photographs, the consequences of immigration are depicted as social problems: poverty, dilapidated housing, and shanty town settlements. Considering that immigration to the United States in the 1980s has reached a peak second only to the massive tide of the turn of the century (Jasso and Rosenzweig, 1990), it is not surprising that photographers are once again drawn to this subject. Regarding the refugee experience, Gold (1992) has studied and visually documented Vietnamese and Soviet Jewish political refugee communities in California. Specific to the issue of documented and undocumented migrant farm laborers in California, *In the Fields* (Light, Minick and Tansey, 1982) continues the tradition of 'concerned photography' rooted in the visual study of American society. Today's immigrants, however, are far more diverse than their predecessors. The new post-1965 immigration is comprised of a broader spectrum of social classes originating from a wider range of countries than the old immigration (Massey, 1981; Portes and Rumbaut, 1990). Among these new groups, one finds a myriad Middle-Eastern immigrants, including the subjects of this article — Yemeni labor migrants and 'high status' Iranian immigrants.

## Case studies of Yemenis and Iranians

### Yemeni labor migrants in California

The photography of Yemeni immigration, undertaken in both the sending and host countries, had sought to integrate the images in the context of a publication, with featured articles on the history and conse-quences of the migration in Yemen; the major Yemeni communities in Buffalo, New York, South Dearborn, Michigan, New York City, and the San Joaquin Valley, California; the emergent folklore of Yemeni immi-gration; and, Yemeni migration and settlement as documented and inter-preted by using the 1980 US Census and the US Immigration and Natu-ralization Service data (Sabagh and Bozorgmehr, 1988). It is noteworthy that while the census generates the most extensive data on the charac-teristics of foreign-born populations, 'data on the ethnicity of the popula-tion living in group quarters are only available for major groups such as Hispanics' (Sabagh and Bozorgmehr, 1988, pp. 144). Thus, the ethnic identity and size of the Yemeni and other relatively small minority populations are lost within the broad and indistinguishable 'Other' cate-gory. The volume also includes transcribed interviews with the workers and an interpretative essay on the photography. The project and its multilayered design, incorporating visual, textual, and oral evidence, materialized in the publication *Sojourners and Settlers* (Friedlander, 1988).

The classification 'sojourner' describes the status of some of the Yemenis who lived in California's San Joaquin Valley during the early part of the five-year span of the project (1981-86). Yemeni villagers began to arrive in the San Joaquin Valley in the early 1960s, initially as a small number of individuals and subsequently as a chain migration which swelled in the early 1970s to approximately 5,000 workers. By the end of the project in the mid-1980s, the status and size of the population had changed drastically as a growing number of individuals chose to settle, in some cases bringing their families from Yemen to California. At the same time, the total Yemeni farmworker population dwindled significantly as economic recessions, changing immigration laws in the United States, spiralling inflation in Yemen which depreciated the value of the wages earned abroad, and the increasing cost of transcontinental travel made sojourning impractical, forcing many workers to abandon farm labor or return to Yemen permanently.

The relatively small community of Yemeni farmworkers in California represents a microcosm of a phenomenon which has shaped the modern history of the former North Yemen (Yemen Arab Republic), which is now part of the unified Republic of Yemen. It is estimated that, during the 1970s 'era of affluence', one-quarter of the Yemeni adult male population was engaged in contract labor abroad, regionally and in the West (Swanson, 1988). Understandably, this enormous 'temporary' out-migration, which lasted almost thirty years has altered the course of Yemen's economy and traditional social order (Wenner, 1988). The 1991 Gulf War, which involved Yemen on the side of Iraq and resulted in the expulsion of the very large population of Yemenis from Saudi Arabia — paradoxically, their rival neighbor and benefactor — has put a halt for the time being to migration as a viable economic option for Yemenis.

The spectrum of the Yemeni immigrant experience is conveyed in *Sojourners and Settlers* by color images from Yemen and black-and-white photographs taken in the United States. This was not a deliberate attempt to portray the home country in the richness and variety of color and the host country, conversely, in terms of the limited dimensionality inherent in the black-and-white format. Rather, this juxtaposition emerged from the independent choices of the photographers. Such choices, however, were not arbitrary.

Color photography, which finds its application most readily in commercial circles, *National Geographic*-styled venues, and popular snapshot photography, employs the interplay of colors as an important element of the visual matrix. Color itself — even devoid of shape or content — is powerfully emotive. For the artist, color is one more element to be harnessed and orchestrated toward the photograph's expressive unity. The aesthetics of Western art typically hold that a quality image should manifest unity of structure and content toward a particular mood, point, or statement. This follows the old adage that the 'form' (the structural design of lines, shapes, hues, and color, if included) must be an extension of its conceptual content; i.e., the artist's intent. In traditional social science circles, of course, such dictums are considered irrelevant. In the purely sociological sense, as traditionally used, the photographic image's value is its denotative replication of visual data to be used as addenda to the written text.

Although any photographic subject can be rendered iconographic, color usually functions in one of two ways: as a further anchor to the literal denotative subject, or, somewhat paradoxically, in more calculating hands, as the means to rhapsodize or idealize. While idealization may be a concern for the snapshot photographer, photography functions usually and most importantly to merely commemorate, memorialize, or simply objectify for failing memories a particular person or occasion as literally as possible — hence, as transcendent idealizer, the interest in color imagery by the commercial world, as well as the traditional *National Geographic* ethic of the immutable nobility of 'universal man' and the enduring beauty of the 'natural world'.

The project's color photography originating in Yemen can be viewed as a successive series of long, medium, and close-up shots of the subject — a technique formulized in the early days of narrative cinema and subsequently adopted in photographic circles. From an elevation of some 8,000 feet in the Yemeni Highlands, Jon Swanson, an anthropologist who has studied Yemeni emigration (Swanson, 1979), provides a long-shot perspective of a dramatic and dynamic landscape dotted with villages that are perched above terraced mountainous fields — the setting for emigration.

Photo 2:    Nadirah, 'Ammar district, Yemen  [Photograph by Jon Swanson (original in color)]

From this distance, the visual information reveals a well-maintained agrarian base, which we learn from textual analysis has been depleted by the chronic shortage of able-bodied men. Consequently, Yemen's ability to feed itself has been diminished, a fact documented by photographs of markets and the many basic food products imported from abroad. A second set of photographs brings the viewer closer to the outskirts of the villages and to the pace of development.

While an image of the stack of power line poles in the corner of the village may indicate the extension of basic services into the large rural sector (Photo 2), the caption to reminds the reader that hard-earned capital sent from abroad will only partially support infrastructure, communication, or health projects. A large part of the remittances has been used to purchase additional land or to expand existing homes. In a systematic, measured way, Swanson provides evidence of the scale and style of construction and the building process. The meshing of old and new for Swanson is a by-product of development. We see it in his photography of markets, contrasting traditional agricultural products with mechanical items, or in the styles of clothing which feature both traditional Yemeni garments and Western clothing worn by the villagers, including the returned migrants.

In a complimentary portrayal of the Yemeni countryside, Middle East historian Nikki Keddie brings to the forefront the often ignored female side of the migration story (Photo 3). Within the bounds of accessible public domain Keddie's photographs show women harvesting sorghum and increasingly assuming agricultural chores once performed by their husbands and male relatives. Notably, the migration has increased women's responsibilities in house-hold management and the upbringing of children. In Nikki Keddie's photographs, the elements of daily public life are revealed in exterior portraits of women in migrant-producing towns and villages. Clad in black or multicolored dresses, women are seen shopping, conversing in groups, or caring for their children in a rich texture of street life punctuated by the jumble of animals and vehicles typical of the Third World (Photo 4).

In contrast, Yemeni private life is revealed from the several hundred snapshot images in the possession of the migrants in California. These images peer beyond the exterior walls into interior spaces open only to insiders. Unlike the photos of Swanson and Keddie, which were intended to find their place into publications, exhibitions, or academic presentations, these snapshots are kept in wallets and photo albums which will accompany the villagers on their long sojourn abroad. These are invaluable mementos of home, and in many cases they preserve the normality of

Photo 3: Women harvesting, Jabal Rayma district, Yemen [Photograph by Nikki Keddie (original in color)]

Photo 4: Street in San'a, Yemen [Photograph by Nikki Keddie (original in color)]

homelife for a villager who must endure long-term loneliness and separation. In most cases, the subjects in the snapshots are women and children, posed inside the house, often surrounded by the articles of daily life, including the prized consumer products purchased with money sent from America. In marked contrast to the street images by Keddie, here the women pose unveiled, clad in traditional embroidered clothing or imported Western dresses (Photo 5).

Photo 5: Family portrait, Central Highlands, Yemen [Sojourner snapshot (original in color)]

The second largest number of snapshots are portraits of men, in the fields or on the balcony of their homes overlooking the dramatic mountainous backdrop of Yemen. These images are forged in a tribal society with its particular bond of comradeship — a closely-knit network of extended families and lineages. The recurring emphasis on power and status as landowner or *sayyid* is often reinforced by the display of weapons, including the traditional curved dagger *(janbiya)* or Russian AK-47 rifles. Unlike modern Western snapshots, which often depict playfulness, recreation and leisure, the subject presentation here is uniformly serious in its intent to ideally capture aspects of life which will sorely be missed in a new environment.

The impact of an alien culture on the workers underscores the photography in the San Joaquin Valley — the destination of some Yemeni villagers who, in a period of less then 24 hours, are transposed some 12,000 miles from the familiarity of their ancestral home to agribusiness workcamps in central California. Ron Kelley's non-idealizing photography addresses such dislocation through his use of the black-and-white format. More easily than color photography, black-and-white imagemaking enhances the medium's capacity to transform a literal denotative record into metaphor, symbol, epitome, and/or exemplary summation. Without color, the image-maker is freer to concentrate on content, form, and structural relations.

The San Joaquin Valley has been the setting for several important visual studies in black-and-white. Most notably, the images of Dorothea Lange, Ben Shawn and other New Deal (Farm Security Administration) photographers captured the plight of Oakies and Dust Bowl refugees headed to California during the Great Depression of the 1930s. The setting was marred by class conflict that pitted workers and union organizers against co-workers and the growers. Strife over recruitment and exploitation of cheap immigrant labor was intensified by battles for leadership of a largely immigrant work-force, and the political intrigues of land tenancy and ownership.

Photo 6:   Yemeni pruning crew, vineyards, Delano, San Joaquin Valley [Photograph by Ron Kelley]

Ron Kelley's photography of the Yemeni migrant farmworkers in the San Joaquin Valley of the 1980s falls under three broad categories: work (Photos 6 & 7), camp life, and recreation. The mainstay of the photography was undertaken in the environs of Delano and the southern San Joaquin Valley, dominated by the cultivation of some dozen varieties of grapes. Kelley also documents the labor-intensive work in the stone fruit orchards, as well as cantaloupe and watermelon picking in farms throughout the area. In the winter, many workers remain in hiatus — in workcamps or apartments in the vicinity of the fields. Some engage in back-breaking picking of asparagus, or migrate further southward to find work picking strawberries and other fruits and vegetables in California's Imperial Valley.

Photo 7: Asparagus harvest, winter, Richgrove area, San Joaquin Valley [Photograph by Ron Kelley]

The photography of work focused both on exclusively male Yemeni squads and on mixed groups of Yemeni and Mexican workers, which include Hispanic women. Ethnically-mixed workcamps provided opportunities to examine the interaction between Yemenis from different regions and Yemenis and other migrant workers.

For the Yemenis, camp life often consisted of short evenings and Sundays spent in relaxation and recreation. Early morning and evening prayers were performed in a room designated and decorated as a mosque. Evening meals provided the setting for personal conversations, group discussions of specific issues related to work, or Middle Eastern politics — from the Palestinian-Israeli conflict to intra-Arab politics — with the trusted BBC often providing the essential information. Video copies of Egyptian movies proved to be another source of popular entertainment. As the number of settled Yemenis increased in the 1980s, visitations to friends and families on Sundays and off-days became more frequent. Special events, such as major Islamic holidays and celebrations, Yemeni independence day, company picnics, town festivals, and county fairs, also proved to be important in the overall photographic mission of this project.

Above and beyond mere visual documentation of work and habitat, photographer Ron Kelley employs the element of irony to depict the independently-minded landowners and proud farmers from Yemen who have been forced by economic necessity to work on someone else's land. This visual statement is further accentuated by the inherent dichotomy between the mechanics and structure of family- or village-operated agriculture in Yemen and agribusiness in California. The tensions resulting from extended familial separation, physical isolation, or cultural deprivation are especially revealing photographically, as the workers' Yemeni and Islamic identities are constantly tested in America, seduced by its myths and values. While significant to both the sending and the host countries, the migration nonetheless is marginalized and rendered almost invisible in the Unites States, receiving media exposure and public attention only during disputes involving unions and growers, economic disasters (droughts and freezes), and political upheavals in the Middle East which directly affect Americans (during the 'Iranian Hostage Crisis', Yemenis were harassed by a hostile American public).

*Iranian immigrants and exiles in Los Angeles*

The Islamic revolution and the 'Iranian Hostage Crisis' were the historical roots for the photography of Iranian immigrants and exiles in Los Angeles. As part of a continual documentation of public rituals in America, Kelley had photographed anti-Iranian expressions during the 1979-80 hostage crisis. He had just completed the Yemeni project when a large-scale survey of Iranians in Los Angeles was launched in 1986. Because of the close start-up timing of the survey and photographic projects on Iranians in Los Angeles, we are in a unique position to evaluate the relative scientific merits of each study.

A new immigrant group, Iranians were virtually unstudied when the survey research and photographic projects began almost simultaneously. Although Iranian immigration to the United States can be traced to the 19th century, it remained a trickle well into the 1960s compared to the flood of the post-1970s. Migration from Iran to the United States consists of two distinct waves, each roughly corresponding to a different type of migrant. These waves are divided by the Iranian revolution of 1978-79. During the first wave (pre-1978), college and university students comprised the bulk of Iranian migrants. After the revolution, Iranian exiles made up a larger share of the second wave (post-1978). Migrant selectivity accounts for the high level of education, entrepreneurial proclivity, occupational skills, and the large presence of ethno-religious minorities among Iranian exiles. The combination of exiles and former college students, who chose not to repatriate to Iran upon completion of their studies, partly explains the high status of Iranians in the U.S. (Bozorgmehr and Sabagh, 1988).

The survey project focused on ethnicity and ethnic economy among the four largest Iranian subgroups; namely, Armenians, Baha'is, Jews, and Muslims. This substantive focus was determined by theoretical concerns in American sociology, which emphasize the social and economic adaptation of immigrants over political and cultural adjustment. Furthermore, given the political context of Iranian immigration, any explicit political questions in the survey were avoided on the grounds that they could jeopardize the cooperation of the respondents. While some of the respondents voluntarily discussed their political preferences and even activism, the concerned individuals were comforted to know that political questions were not asked. Despite the study's emphasis on differences among Iranian subgroups, the questionnaire was too long to accommodate detailed cultural questions.

In contrast to the survey study, the photography project was freer to focus on the political issues which dominated the life of the community during its formative years and have since become an integral part of Iranian political culture in Los Angeles. Street demonstrations by the anti-Shah groups were first documented in masked protests against SAVAK (the Iranian secret police), as were later marches against the Shah's request for asylum in the United States. With the establishment of the Islamic Republic of Iran, counter-demonstrations by large numbers of supporters of the Pahlavi regime, one of the largest and most visible of the groups of Iranians in Los Angeles, had become an annual event staged in front of the Federal Building in Westwood. Conversely, annual commemorations of the anniversary of the Islamic revolution had also become a regular expression by Iranian counter-idealogues in Los Angeles. Demonstrations by the *Mojahedin* and *Feda'iyan* oppositional factions and the Kurds add to the fertile Iranian political milieu in exile. Events in the Middle East and Iran continue to generate political expression, mostly by supporters of the Islamic Republic of Iran, who were quick to react to the massacre of Iranian pilgrims in Mecca and to the Salman Rushdi affair. Of course, the death of Ayatollah Khomeini prompted a variety of public expressions from both ends of the Iranian political spectrum (Kelley, 1991). The decade-long conflict between Iran and Iraq, especially the brutal 'War of the Cities', was the single event which drew members from the entire Iranian community (Photo 8).

Photo 8: Iranians protesting the 'War of the Cities', Federal Building, Westwood [Photograph by Ron Kelley]

The emergence of an Iranian cultural identity in Los Angeles has also been an important subject in Kelley's photography. Forging a common national identity remains problematic, since the community is so fragmented religiously and ethnically. Iranian cultural traditions bring many community members together, especially for public and private celebrations of the Iranian New Year *[No Rouz]*. There are also poetry readings and musical concerts featuring visiting and local Iranian artists and cultural figures; film programs; exhibitions of fine art; a growing theater scene; sporting events; and, a range of venues to obtain Persian cuisine. Intellectual/scholarly activities such as conferences and symposia highlight aspects of classical culture. The diverse Iranian channels of public information — television, radio, and the press — maintain a level of cultural awareness rivaling in intensity the much larger Hispanic and Asian groups in Los Angeles. Expression of polite behavior and ritualized courtesy remains a cornerstone of private and communal cultural interaction. The respect and pride accorded by Iranians toward their ancient living culture has even been used as a point of upmanship for Iranians when dealing with Americans and their relatively newer culture. The overall juxtaposition and the points of intersection of host and homeland cultures comprise a major theme of the photography (Photo 9).

Photo 9:   Persian music lesson on the Kamancheh (vertical fiddle), Santa Monica [Photograph by Ron Kelley]

Another major focus of the survey and photographic studies concerns the ethno-religious diversity of Iranians. Mainly due to the Islamic outcome of the Iranian revolution, religious minorities from Iran are disproportionately represented among Iranians in Los Angeles. Virtually all religious groups are present, including Armenian and Assyrian Christians, Muslims (Shi'i and a smaller number of Kurdish Sunnis), Baha'is, Jews, and Zoroastrians. Some of these groups were too small in population size (e.g., Assyrians, Kurds, and Zoroastrians) to be studied by a survey. Thus, the survey was limited to the four largest Iranian subgroups and was conducted with a random sample of 671 Iranian household heads in 1987-88 (Bozorgmehr and Sabagh, 1989).

Population size was not a determining factor in photographic selection or emphasis, as evidenced by the photography of the Zoroastrians, the smallest Iranian religious group in Los Angeles. Conversely, the secular lifestyles of the predominantly westernized Iranian Muslims was not conducive for visual exploration of their expressly Muslim identity. Images of the seven Iranian religious and ethnic groups illustrate the diversity of creed and practice (Photo 10).

Photo 10:    Iranian-Jewish winner of the 'Queen Esther' contest, Purim celebration, Westwood [Photograph by Ron Kelley]

The religious rituals of each group, which could not be assessed in general questions framed in the survey due to their specificity, have been systematically documented by the photographer. Such photographs gain a deeper analytic edge when presented in a comparative format. For example, the juxtaposition of images depicting traditional Iranian Muslim,

Jewish, Armenian, Baha'i, and Zoroastrian weddings provide insights into the symbols which are at the core of each faith. The powerful sentiment of grief in Iranian culture is revealed in a religious context with photographs of Assyrians at graveside mourning, Muslim self-flagellation during Ashura prayers, and the Iranian Jewish Passover dinner practice of playfully striking family members and guests with leaks to commemorate Jewish suffering. Kelley further examines the issue of grief in a political context — the suicide of a leftist activist, the fallen Pahlavi regime, the death of Ayatollah Khomeini. Culturally popularized grief is captured in a striking image of 3000 fans mourning the untimely death of the beloved singer Hayedeh (Photo 11).

Photo 11: Graveside services for noted Iranian singer Hayedeh, Westwood [Photograph by Ron Kelley]

Interpretative images focusing on the themes of gender and wealth, and occupation, and Iranians in both public and private settings, complete Kelley's portrayal of Iranians in Los Angeles. Like the Yemeni project, which employed collaborative articles and interviews, the photographs of Iranians are presented in the context of a manuscript with further elaboration on the history of Iranian immigration, the diversity of the Los Angeles community, family, gender and social relations, and the perpetuation of Iranian culture in exile (Kelley and Friedlander, 1993).

## Social science research and photography:
## Methodological issues, relevance, and compatability

Photography as an art form — including the medium as construed by academe — has typically been conceptually limited to traditional manifestations of 'self-expression'. Structural alignment, transcendent beauty, obtusely ahistorical 'universal truths', individual self-reflection, and purely psychological motifs have been common themes of emphasis. The medium — when applied as 'photojournalism' — raises different investigative limitations. Essentially, in this scenario, a camera technician functions not as an analytic and interpretive social thinker, but as a transparent data-gatherer to satisfy the mass media's illustrative needs and its editorial overlays.

Like a 'good' social scientist, the function of a 'good' photographer is not to just record data, but, rather, to actively synthesize, structure, interpret, and attempt to understand what is being witnessed. Cultural awareness should not only address the scenes before the lens, but also the ideological discourse surrounding modern day image-making which engages every photographer (i.e., the objectification of daily experience into static imagery does not exist in a social vacuum). Ideally, the investigator uses all available methods toward comprehension and communication, including both photography and written text. This infers a moral and intellectual responsibility on the part of the image-maker to invest considerable time and effort in comprehending the subject before the lens in order to render it — however interpretively — accurately. While a photographer can saunter into any given scene and in a few seconds record — accidentally or otherwise — the visually definitive summation of a field researcher's seven years of investigation, its singular application as social science is, of course, both suspect and limited without a dedicated interest in what that picture means, how it evokes that meaning, and where it exactly comes from.

Like other human documents, such as memoirs and letters (Plummer, 1983), photographs contain information about the photographed subject. Yet, how do photographs convey meaning and what do they measure? How are photographs edited for 'quality'? How do criteria differ for the work of a fine artist? A social scientist? A Third World villager? Can photographs successfully approximate the 'truth' of a culture?

Ultimately, the answers to the above questions revolve around individual and curatorial intentions and editing strategies, reflecting the decision-makers' personal interests and cultural values. As much as the photographer chose to include, what was left out? As much as the editor chose to include, what was left out? The complex process of encoding by the photographer and decoding by the viewer are further subject to personal perceptions, cross-cultural variants, photographic conventions, and contextual influences. The same image, for example, in a sociology textbook, in an art museum, or in a family album will have at least slightly different 'meanings'.

Howard Becker, an ethnographer and a visual sociologist, has raised important questions concerning the factual content of photographs (Becker, 1974, 1979, 1980, 1981). First and probably the most basic aspect of photography centers on the photographer's worldview or paradigm. Without a personal explanation, the photographer's theoretical framework is not always readily identifiable through the photographs (in some cases, however, one can decode the photographer's perspective from a large body of images). The theory, access, sampling, and reactivity of the photographer, editing and censorship, and finally the medium of presentation are some of the factors that could affect the information captured and displayed in photographs.

Regarding photographic theory, Kelley's approach to these projects is inspired by the subjective work of Robert Frank (1969), whose seminal work *The Americans* captured the alienated mood of an American society beset by class, political, and racial tensions in the 1950s. Gary Winogrand, in his sweeping street photography of America in the 1960s and 1970s, captured social tensions and alienation in a consumer-oriented land of plenty (Winogrand, 1988). Elements of these influential photographers are evident in Kelley's work. But unlike Frank, who was a Swiss immigrant and an outsider, Kelley has an insider's point of view of American society, yet paradoxically considers himself 'not of it'. The photographs of Yemeni farmworkers — disenfranchised and on the fringes of the host society — reflect, among other things, Kelley's estranged view of American society. On the other hand, his view of Iranians, who are popularly perceived as one of the wealthiest immigrant groups in one of America's richest cities, is shaped by their preoccupation with class and status. Not surprisingly, his images of Iranians displaying their wealth are critical. The rest of the photographs, however, show an appreciation of Iranian culture, intrigue, the soulful melancholy so deeply ingrained in the culture, and the beleaguered Iranian political groups. The interplay of affluence and political demonstrations set against the background of the Iranian revolution have produced a number of powerful images. Kelley is deeply moved by the emotional and dramatic aspects of Iranian culture (e.g., religious mourning of Shi'i Iranians and other manifestations of grief), whereas he finds American culture 'clinical'. He laments the assimilation of Iranians and feels compelled to document the traditional aspects of Iranian culture and the ongoing attempts for its preservation. Kelley has no pretensions to be scientific in his approach, yet his intensive fieldwork gives his photography the depth that separates visual sociology and anthropology from 'parachute photojournalism'.

Ron Kelley's photographic work continually struggles to blend the self-expressive process of serious artmaking into the socio-historical disciplines, subjectively immersing analytic images into challenging contexts of social discourse. No 'art' photograph exists in an historical vacuum. An image's meaning is always relative to contextual information provided around it. In this sense, few photographers have taken sophisticated measures toward a methodological application of the medium as both a personally and socially expressive form, transgressing rigidly enforced boundaries between fine art and visual sociology. The most opportune channel for such exploration, of course, is within a published volume, where descriptive and analytic articles, interviews, and extended captions resonate and enhance the visual foundation as both expressive art piece and social document.

Understanding the theoretical considerations of the photographers gives the viewer and reader insights into the modes of visually interpreting Yemeni and Iranian immigration. But, what do these images measure *vis-à-vis* the aforementioned sociological/social science criteria? Photography, for example, can document better than text many forms of social interaction, including body language and spatial relationships. In fact, the old cliche that 'a picture is worth a thousand words' is rooted in the medium's obvious excellence in rendering depictions of the patently physical world — shapes, relative sizes, and the specific 'look' and even emotive 'feel' of things. Of course, not even statistically irrefutable data, let alone a photograph, can be, of itself, used as totally infallible 'evidence'. Any kind of information is always subject to selective interpretation and manipulation. In studied and conscientious hands, however, the photograph can add important dimensions to the social scientist's research and communicative powers. Of course a photograph can 'lie' or misrepresent. But so can any other medium.

In the more pragmatic sense, a major challenge facing documentary photographers concerns access. Access is a multifaceted issue. Although in some cases access is less of a problem for an insider, it becomes an issue if the documentation involves a conspicuous act like photography. As far as the Yemeni project was concerned, the issue was sometimes problematic, requiring continuous formal and informal negotiations to define the photographic limits. Swanson's access to the immigrant-producing areas was facilitated by some half dozen previous visits to Yemen and familiarity with the Yemeni countryside. As a female historian, Nikki Keddie's photographs show that her knowledge and previous photography of Middle Eastern women offered valuable experience in the highly-segregated Yemeni society. The snapshots from Yemen, of course, provide a unique access reserved only to certain insiders (family members). Obtaining the snapshot images, however, was only accomplished after a considerable measure of trust and respect was built between Kelley and the Yemeni farmworkers over the course of the project.

The fact that the principal photographer in these projects was not Arab or Iranian afforded some advantages in access and in resisting automatic dismissal of these projects as being intrinsically propagandistic. In the case of the Yemeni farmworkers, access to the fields and workcamps had to be sanctioned by the corporate employer and subsequently by the workers themselves, who often reached their decisions through consensus. Still, photographing certain aspects of Yemeni life were restricted — for example, prayer in the makeshift mosque. Unfamiliar with such concepts as the social sciences and secular humanism, many Yemenis professed suspicion regarding the project's intent. In the case of the Iranians, most religious, ethnic, and political groups were eager to open their doors, although Kelley was sometimes limited in what he was allowed to photograph during Shi'i rituals. In the case of Iranian Jews, he was prohibited by religious observance from photographing Sabbath and the High Holiday liturgies. Overall, however, the issue of access rarely impeded the photography.

Sociologists and anthropologists are also concerned with the problem of reactivity — the possibility of biased behavior by the subjects due to the presence of a participant observer. Carrying a conspicuous camera makes documentary photography more susceptible to reactivity than an ethnography. Of course, this can vary depending on the nature of the activity being photographed. Except for a series of portraits of the workers and a few instances where the Yemenis posed to 'look good' before the camera, the issue of reactivity did not betray the photographic mission. Nor did it bear any influence on the photography of Iranians, who were more cognizant of the medium and its role within the realms of the humanities and the arts. In any case, the experienced photographer knows well enough to wait until self-conscious camera posing and manipulation inevitably pass.

The next problem is sampling — selecting a random cross-section of the population so that the results can apply to the population. Representative sampling is limited by access and by the size and heterogeneity of the population under study. As such, it was more problematic in the Iranian photographic project than in the Yemeni project. In the case of the Yemenis, the issue of representative sampling was not critical, since Kelley photographed most of the agricultural sites and spent much time in the workcamps, where he had access to a large number of centrally-located workers. In essence, the Yemeni farmworker photography became a part of ethnographic field work, supplemented by personal observations by the photographer and interviews.

The issue of sampling to obtain an accurate representation of a large and diverse community was much more critical in the Iranian photographic project. Without macro data on the characteristics of the population through surveys (including census data), it was very difficult to ascertain the universe from which a random sample could be drawn. In cases where there was a perfect correspondence between the subjects covered in the photographic and survey projects — for example, occupation and ethnicity — the survey served as a benchmark. However, these cases were limited, since the two projects focused on different aspects of the Iranian experience. A substantive evaluation of the information collected in the Iranian photographic project is beyond the scope of this paper. Suffice it to say that, as far as sampling is concerned, combining macro and micro studies of the same community, as in the case of the Iranians, is preferable for social scientists than relying only on photography.

The criteria for choosing some three hundred images for exhibition and publication from the more than 50,000 frames taken of the Yemeni and Iranian experience was guided first and foremost by the strength of the visual imagery in explication of the projects' themes. Some images that were not deemed especially noteworthy on aesthetic grounds were included purely for their informational value. A few strongly aesthetic and informational images were rejected on the basis of thematic redundancy. In one case, three images of Yemenis dancing — none of which was visually striking — were all included in sequence as a kind of time-lapse of the changing social dynamics in a farmworker's room. On another occasion, forty portraits of Yemenis were allied together to poignantly humanize the subjects of the study, focusing on both psychological nuances and the variety of racial characteristics evidenced in their faces. In essence, the images were sorted to best convey the broadest sense of the Yemeni sojourn experience, using the variety of images at the editors' disposal.

Which brings us to the issues of validity and the abstract notion of truth inherent in photography. Few observers are unaffected by photography's fascinating capacity to both objectively record and subjectively interpret, enchanting the imagination like few other mediums. Its mysterious nature in stopping time, interrupting the visual sequence of mortal continuum, and imparting, sometimes, profound social and psychological data has popularly intrigued viewers since the medium's invention. Perhaps this extraordinary capacity to bridge the poetic and the scientific, and even blur the two, has rendered it, for many years, suspect in some scholarly disciplines. The fact that 'anyone can take a photograph' has further harbored disrespect and distrust for photography as a serious academic medium. No matter; even its most serious detractors cannot successfully argue that the written word or statistics can better *humanize* the subject of investigation. The quizzical photograph is deceptively simple in its complex immediacy, rendering both a literal and figurative map of physical, social and emotional worlds.

But what does all this have to do with 'truth', the objectively verifiable? Of course, despite its popularized use as an irrefutably factual depiction, photography can indeed 'lie', distort, deceive, evade, misrepresent and manipulate — the same as any other medium. Photography, after all, is only a tool, as reliable as its directive practitioner. In this sense, as traditionally used, all that can be said with certainty is that a photograph fixes the visual arrangement of whatever faces the camera's framing mechanisms at a particular instant. Effected by light, motion, and other physical factors, the resultant image is translated through a standardized lenticular lens system from the three-dimensional world into a two-dimensional plane. This process alone is innately distorting. As such, any given photograph is merely the complex tableau upon which the confounding philosophical search for 'truth' might begin. Furthermore, if this resultant photographic image is rendered devoid of text or context to root it to its denotative origin, it may actually 'float' in decipherable meaning, open to a range of interpretive applications. In the art world, this can have useful effect. In the social sciences it is detrimental. The issue of photographic meaning, however, rooted in shared social language by both encoder and decoder, is itself grounds for sociological undertakings. Ultimately, then, for those who seek irrefutably absolute truths, photography will disappoint. But for those who accept the notion that some of any society's fundamental truths are, in the multicultural universe, relative constructs manifest in physical form, the medium, under careful control, can have significant application.

Despite such problematics, community studies, including those of immigrant and ethnic communities, come to life through photographs. Often, social scientists — especially quantitative practitioners — rely on tables, charts, and summary statements to deal with information about a given minority group. An unintended consequence of this approach is that individual human experience is lost in the process. Ideally, we need teams of social scientists and photographers to study and document immigrant communities. By coordinating photographic and survey projects in the study of Iranian immigrants, we have come closer to this agenda than other popularly interpretive investigations. To achieve this objective, however, future community studies employing photography and social science methodologies should be much more tightly coordinated and cover the same issues as much as possible. Beyond the scholarly issues, through such projects we can continually learn more about our *own* cultures and, hopefully, ourselves.

Note

\* The photographic projects were sponsored by the G.E. von Grunebaum Center for Near Eastern Studies and the Office of International Studies and Overseas Programs (ISOP) at UCLA. The survey research was funded by a grant from the National Science Foundation.

References

Becker, H. S. (1974), 'Photography and Sociology', *Studies in Anthropology of Visual Communication*, Vol. 1, pp. 3-26.
Becker, H. S. (1979), 'Do Photographs Tell the Truth?' in Cook, T. and Reinhardt, C. (eds.), *Qualitative and Quantitative Methods in Evaluating Research* Sage Publications: Beverly Hills, CA, pp. 99-117.
Becker, H. S. (1980), 'Aesthetics and Truth', *Society*, July, pp. 26-28.
Becker, H. S. (ed.) (1981), *Exploring Society Photographically*, University of Chicago Press: Chicago,IL.
Bozorgmehr, M. and Sabagh, G. (1988), 'High Status Immigrants: A Statistical Profile of Iranians in the United States', *Iranian Studies*, Vol. 21, pp. 5-36.
Bozorgmehr, M. and Sabagh, G. (1989), 'Survey Research among Middle Eastern Immigrant Groups in the United States: Iranians in Los Angeles', *Middle East Studies Association Bulletin*, Vol. 2, pp. 23-34.
Bozorgmehr, M. and Sabagh, G. (1991), 'Iranian Exiles and Immigrants in Los Angeles', in Fathi, A. (ed.), *Iranian Refugees and Exiles since Khomeini*, Mazda Publishers: Costa Mesa, CA, pp. 121-144.
Fagen R., Brody, R. and O'Leary, T. (1968), *Cubans in Exile*, Stanford University Press: Stanford, CA.
Frank, R. (1969), *The Americans*, Grossman: New York.

Friedlander, J., (ed.) (1988), *Sojourners and Settlers: The Yemeni Immigrant Experience*, University of Utah Press: Salt Lake City, UT.

Gold, S. (1992), *Refugee Communities: A Comparative Field Study*, Sage Publications: Newbury Park, CA.

Jasso, G. and Rosenzweig, M. (1990), *The New Chosen People: Immigrants in the United States*, Russell Sage Foundation: New York.

Kelley, R. (1991), 'Iranian Political Demonstrations in Los Angeles', in Fathi, A. (ed.), *Iranian Refugees and Exiles Since Khomeini*, Mazda: Costa Mesa, CA, pp. 161-180.

Kelley, R. and Friedlander, J., (eds.) (1993), *Irangeles: Iranians in Los Angeles*, University of California Press: Berkeley and Los Angeles, CA.

Light, I. and Bonacich, E. (1988), *Immigrant Entrepreneurs: Koreans in Los Angeles: 1965-1982*, University of California Press: Berkeley and Los Angeles, CA.

Light, K., Minick, R. and Tansey, R. (1982), *In the Fields*, Harvest: Oakland, CA.

Massey, D. (1981), 'Dimensions of the New Immigration to the United States and the Prospects for Assimilation', *Annual Review of Sociology*, Vol. 7, pp. 57-85.

Plummer, K. (1983), *Documents of Life*, George Allen and Unwin: London.

Portes, A. (1969), 'Dilemmas of a Golden Exile: Integration of Cuban Refugee Families in Milwaukee', *American Sociological Review*, Vol. 34, pp. 505-18.

Portes, A. and Rumbaut, R. (1990), *Immigrant America: A Portrait*, University of California Press: Berkeley and Los Angeles, CA.

Riis, J. (1970), *How the Other Half Lives*, Warner, S. (ed.), Harvard University Press: Cambridge, MA.

Sabagh, G. and Bozorgmehr, M. (1988), 'The Settlement of Yemeni Immigrants in the United States', in Friedlander, J. (ed.), *Sojourners and Settlers: The Yemeni Immigrant Experience*, University of Utah Press: Salt Lake City, UT, pp. 143-156.

Swanson, J. C. (1979), *Emigration and Economic Development: The Case of the Yemen Arab Republic*, Westview Press: Boulder, CO.

Swanson, J. C. (1988), 'Sojourners and Settlers in Yemen and America', in Friedlander, J. (ed.), *Sojourners and Settlers: The Yemeni Immigrant Experience*, University of Utah Press: Salt Lake City, UT, pp. 49-67.

Wenner, M. (1988), 'The Political Consequences of Yemeni Migration', in Friedlander, J. (ed.), *Sojourners and Settlers: The Yemeni Immigrant Experience*, University of Utah Press: Salt Lake City, UT, pp. 17-32.

Winogrand, G. (1988), *Figments from the Real World*, The Museum of Modern Art: New York.

# 11 Israeli immigrants in Los Angeles

*Steven Gold*

In recent years, sociologists have sought to understand how the social, economic, and legal context of receiving societies interacts with immigrants' own resources and aspirations to shape their adaptation to the new setting (Light and Bonacich, 1988; Olzak, 1983; Cohen, 1969; Portes and Bach, 1985; Kim, 1981). The conclusions of this literature can be summarized into three basic categories: Professional Immigrants; Entrepreneurial Immigrants; and Unorganized Marginals (Portes and Rumbaut, 1990).

Professional immigrants receive legal status, have English language skills, and have educational credentials valued by the receiving labor market. Thus, they often have access to jobs and social positions good enough for the middle class of the receiving society. Accordingly, it has been argued that immigrant groups that contain high proportions of professionals, such as Western Europeans, Soviet Jews, Taiwanese, Asian Indians, and Filipinos, may have little motivation to cooperate with their ethnic groups in order to facilitate their social and economic adjustment to American society (Portes and Manning, 1986; Mangiafico, 1988; Portes and Rumbaut, 1990; Liu, 1992; Markowitz, 1993). While members of these groups often participate in ethnic community activities and make trips home, the ethnic community is not the focus of their livelihood.

A second immigrant adaptation — entrepreneurship — is associated with groups who have economic, communal, and educational resources and legal residency, but are unable to find good jobs. They enter self-employment in large numbers and often develop extensively organized communities to further their common economic and social goals. Groups that fit into this category might include Koreans, Cubans, Iranians and Chinese-Vietnamese (Kim, 1981; Light and Bonacich, 1988; Portes and Bach, 1985; Light, Bozorgmehr and Der-Martirosian, 1991; Gold, 1992a).

Finally, migrant populations that are traumatized by flight and lack essential resources often remain in a condition of unorganized marginality with little access to either mainstream or ethnic institutions.[1] While members of these groups interact almost exclusively with co-ethnics, their communities offer them little beyond basic survival and may subject them to co-ethnic exploitation (Vigil and Yun, 1990). Populations of undocumented Latinos and Caribbeans, recently arrived Southeast Asian refugees and Yemenis can be considered unorganized marginals (Finnan and Cooperstein, 1983; Rumbaut, 1989; Gold and Kibria, 1993; Schein, 1987; Friedlander, Bozorgmehr and Kelley, in this book).

**Patterns of adaptation among Israelis in the United States**

The literature on Israeli immigrants in the United States offers some arguments for classifying this population in each of the three categories described above. A fraction of the Israelis in the United States are clearly professional immigrants. They are highly skilled and educated, of Caucasian appearance, and know English well (Herman, 1988).

For example, Goren (1980, p. 597) states that Israelis 'have successfully established themselves in the professional life of the greater society and have contributed to the Jewish community as teachers and communal functionaries'. Citing their homeland's small size, many Israeli academics, professionals and high level entrepreneurs feel it is almost a requirement to spend some time in the United States to fully develop their careers (Sobel, 1986).

While there is relatively little literature on entrepreneurship among Israeli émigrés, a second element of the Israeli immigrant population appears to occupy the entrepreneurial immigrants category. For example, one study observes that Israelis in New York are heavily involved in the diamond and taxi businesses in a manner facilitated by family and religious ties (Freedman and Korazim, 1986).[2] Israeli immigrant entrepreneurship is not surprising, since first-generation Jewish immigrants to the U.S. are noted for their gravitation toward proprietorship (Goldscheider and Kobrin, 1980). Surveys of Israeli immigrants find their rates of self-employment to be very high, sometimes exceeding 50% (Photos 1-3).[3]

Photo 1:   Israelis are active in the jewelry and diamond industries.

Photo 2:   Garment district, Los Angeles (Golan).

Photo 3: A shwarma stand.

Finally, a rather large body of literature treats Israeli immigrants as unorganized marginals because they are stigmatized, occupy a 'liminal' (temporary/outsider—but see Photo 4) status in the United State,[4] and suffer an identity crisis that prevents community unification, integration with American Jews, and the development of realistic, long-term plans regarding their adjustment to life in the United States (Shokeid, 1988).

> Until now they [Israeli immigrants] have been almost a pariah people, suspended between two worlds...If Jews have been the proverbial marginal people, Israeli emigrants are the marginal Jews (Kass and Lipset, 1982, p. 289).

> They [Israeli immigrants] have not established their own organizations in America, and have not become an organized minority group (Kimhi, 1990, p. 23).

While theorizing and existing research about Israeli immigrants offer reasons for placing them in each of these three categories, a surprisingly large body of work focuses on their occupying some form of the 'unorganized marginal' status. Since this finding — that a highly educated, Westernized, 'twice migrant', non-refugee group with Caucasian appearance and ties to an established, co-ethnic community encounters difficulty in adjusting to American society — contrasts so strongly with existing knowledge on the sociology of immigrant adaptation, the nature of Israeli cooperation and community formation has been a central concern of this study of Israeli immigrants in the United States (Gold, 1992b).

Photo 4: Richard Riorden, Los Angeles mayoral candidate (now mayor), stumping for votes at the Israeli Independence Day Celebration, 1993. [Riorden was supported by several prominent Israeli groups and individuals.] The fact that Riorden, now mayor of the second largest city in the United States, would seek the support of the expatriate Israelis reveals the political involvement and influence of this immigrant group in American politics.

## Methods

Data for this paper were collected through 80 interviews with Israeli immigrants and others knowledgeable about their community. Referrals to subjects were obtained from a variety of sources, including Jewish communal agencies, the Israeli Consulate, Israeli activists, and snowball-sample referrals from Israeli immigrants.

Respondents were contacted who would represent various social, and economic groups, including Israeli activists, professionals, and the self-employed. However, because activists, professionals, and business owners are the elite of the Israeli community (Photos 4 & 5), recently arrived and 'grass roots' Israeli immigrants were also interviewed to gain a rounded picture of the population. To capture a broad cultural representation, the sample intentionally includes Israeli immigrants from a variety of national and social backgrounds, including Ashkenazim, Sephardim (Yemeni, Iraqi, Turkish, Moroccan, and Persian), Kibbutzniks, and multi-national families (Israeli/American, Israeli/Canadian) (Photo 5).

Photo 5: Russian and Yemeni-origin Israeli musicians who performed at the 1992 Israeli Independence Day party sponsored by the Jewish Centers Association—2500 persons attended. This photo suggests the great deal of ethnic diversity that exists within the Israeli community.

Conducted between June 1991 and July 1993, interviews were carried out by three researchers in both Hebrew and English. To facilitate rapport and openness, a formal interview schedule was not used. However, questions were selected from prepared lists of interview topics. Interview quotes are presented directly from interview transcripts in order to reflect the speech patterns of respondents.

In addition to lengthy interviews, participant observation was also conducted at a variety of religious and secular community activities and other Israeli immigrant settings (e.g., parties, association meetings, synagogues, restaurants, shops, recreation areas). Field observations were recorded in written field notes. A survey was also distributed to 100 Israeli immigrants at various Israeli community events and in neighborhoods where Israelis frequently congregate (Sachal-Staier, 1993) (Photo 6 & 7).

Finally, photographs were taken during field work and interview sessions. Whenever possible, copies of prints were given to those pictured. We often showed photographs to interviewees to establish rapport (Photo 6). This use of photographs is known as 'photoelicitation', and can provide an excellent source of data about how members of communities understand their environment and view each other (Collier and Collier, 1986; Harper, 1987; Gold, 1991). Photographs give viewers insight into the nature of the visual culture and social context of the Israeli immigrant community and depict some of the various types of collective endeavors that exist within it (Ball and Smith, 1992).

Photo 6:    Employee of an Israeli security company.

**The emphasis on marginality and disorganization**

Many reports on Israeli immigrants in the United States depict this skilled and resourceful group as marginal and alienated (Shokeid, 1988; Kass and Lipset, 1982; Sobel, 1986; Kimhi, 1990; Cohen, 1986; Lipner, 1987; Mittelberg and Waters, 1992; Rosenthal and Auerbach, 1992a&b). This finding is generally attributed to the fact that Israeli emigrants are viewed by American Jews and Israelis alike as violators of Zionist ideology who thereby threaten the survival of the Jewish State. Their very existence makes this group an object of controversy in the Jewish community.[5] In fact, Israeli emigrants are commonly referred to as *yordim*, a stigmatizing Hebrew term which means those who 'descend' from the 'higher' place of Israel to the Diaspora, as opposed to immigrants, the *olim*, who 'ascend' from the Diaspora to Israel (Rosen, 1993).

Much literature on Israeli immigrants asserts that, despite their economic well-being, many members of the group accept the negative *yordim* stereotype and, as a result, remain marginal, both to Israel and the American Jewish community. Certain scholars make much of Israeli immigrants' frequent mention of their plans to return home or their refusal to call themselves Americans; and this conduct is advanced as evidence that Israelis are uniquely ambivalent and unwilling to establish ties with either American Jews or co-ethnics (Shokeid, 1988; Mittelberg and Waters, 1992; Kimhi, 1990; Kass and Lipset, 1982).

Drawing from this perspective, these scholars argue that the feelings of shame, guilt and alienation so strongly felt by Israelis block the formation of a viable *yordim* community in the United States.[6] Shokeid (1988) suggests that the refusal of Israelis to create immigrant organizations is a product of their ambivalence about being in the United States: since they are only temporarily there, why create a community?

**Patterns of cooperation**

It is true that Israeli immigrants make frequent mention of their ambivalence about being in the United States and their desire to return home. However, field work suggests that nostalgia functions as an incentive for co-ethnic cooperation rather than only as a source of shame that discourages it.

In fact, Israeli immigrants in Los Angeles have developed many activities and organizations in order to resolve their ambivalence about being in the United States. In the course of field work for the study reported here, we identified some 27 Israeli organizations (Sachal-Staier, 1993, pp. 74-80; Gold, 1992b, pp. 18-23). These allow émigrés to maintain various Israeli practices and outlooks in California. Community activities include: socializing with other Israelis; living near co-ethnics (and within Jewish communities); consuming Hebrew-language media (originating in both the U.S. and Israel) (Photo 7); patronizing Israeli restaurants, nightclubs, social events, and celebrations; joining Israeli associations; working in jobs with other Israelis; consuming goods and services provided by Israeli professionals and entrepreneurs (Photo 8; keeping funds in Israeli banks; sending their children to Israeli-oriented religious, language, recreational, day-care, and cultural/national activities; raising money for Israeli causes (Photo 9); calling Israel on the phone; hosting Israeli visitors; and, making frequent trips to Israel.

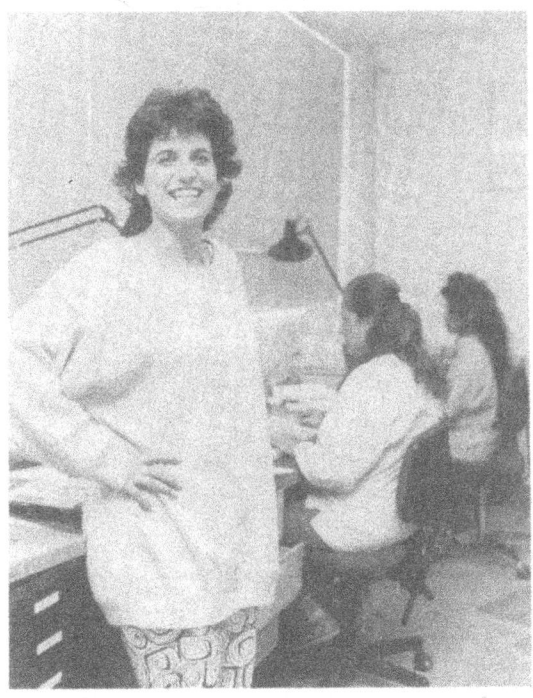

Photo 7: Manager of a Hebrew newspaper and publishing company.

Accordingly, the sizable Israeli population in Los Angeles, along with the many institutions that serve it, constitutes what Breton calls an 'institutionally complete' community (Breton, 1964). Within this collectivity, an Israeli immigrant or visitor can satisfy nearly all of his/her needs in the Hebrew language.

Many — including activists who have sought to create a context for Israeli community development — assert that Israelis desire to associate with and help one another.

> *Hiam*: You probably know it, when people immigrate somewhere, they tend to get into some ghetto. There is a need to be among those you are comfortable to be with. And I identify more than anybody because my wife is American and I don't speak Hebrew at home, so I'm dying for someone to speak Hebrew with. I need an outlet.

Photo 8: Israeli mini-mall in North Hollywood.

Photo 9: Israelis dance at a fund raising event sponsored by the Israeli Division of the Jewish Federation of Los Angeles in September, 1991. About 350 attended the event..

*Michal*: I don't think that socially they [Israelis] have difficulties because they tend to cling together. What happens here with Israelis, and this is my experience, when we came here, then we were more close with friends. Our friends became like our families, and we get used to celebrating the holidays together.

Now my sister and mother are here too, and we celebrate with our friends and family together because we don't want to disconnect ... I think the Israelis long for other Israelis — they long for that.

These feelings were not limited to fulfilling émigrés' yearning to create a social network. Instead, many expressed the desire to help fellow Israelis get established in the United States (Photo 10).

Photo 10: Owners and employees at a metal casting company.

For example, Avi, a former kibbutz member who now runs a large construction company, described his motives for hiring other Israelis:

I think that it hurts me and it takes away from my power to see another Israeli without work and without any way to make his living, and that's why we are helping them.

My company now has at least 35 to 40 'children' and 'grandchildren' in various aspects of the business. I had many foremen who decided to go on their own and they even got a job from me as a subcontractor.

Quantitative data that could reveal the general level of organizational involvement among Israelis in Los Angeles was not collected for this study. The Israeli community is apparently less organized than the Cuban-America community of Miami, which has been noted for its exceptionally high levels of organization and cooperative activity (Portes, 1987; Portes and Bach, 1985). Nevertheless, it was found that the Israeli community contains many formal organizations and extensive informal social ties, as shown in Photos 11-13.

Photo 11: Booth for Israeli Flying Club at the Israeli Independence Day Celebration, 1993.

Photo 12: Israeli housewives meet for coffee at an Israeli bakery in North Hollywood.

Photo 13: Israelis socialize at a community party.


**Israeli organizations**

The bases of Israeli organizations are many. Some — e.g., the Israeli Network Organization (Photo 14), the Yemeni minyan at Temple B'nai David Judea (Photo 15), and informal networks of business people — were created by immigrants themselves. Others — e.g., Hetz Vakeshet (summer in Israel program) and Tzofim (Israeli Scouts) — are sponsored by the Israeli government. Still others — the Jewish Community Center's Israeli program, the AMI (Israeli Hebrew) school, the B'nai B'rith Shalom Lodge, the Jewish Federation's Israeli Division, and the Chabad Israeli Program — are linked with American Jewish groups.

Despite their various affiliations, these groups reflect the desire of Israelis to interact with each other and enjoy a setting where they can exchange information, share social and economic support, and develop common perspectives on life in the United States. Moreover, Israelis with quite different social and occupational characteristics — ranging from 'marginals' to entrepreneurs and professionals — all appear to be at least somewhat involved with community activities.

Photo 14: Israeli Business Network Association breakfast meeting at 7:15 am at the Jewish Federation building. Israeli activists and entrepreneurs meet monthly to exchange contacts and hear an informative lecture.

Photo 15: Yemeni minyan following Saturday night services.

## Family patterns and organizational involvement

The presence of young or school-age children in Israeli immigrant families heightens their ambivalence, but fosters involvement with fellow Israelis. Whatever their other evaluations of the United States, immigrants universally regard Israel as a better place for children. Israelis assert that the Jewish state is safer, has fewer social problems and, perhaps most importantly, does not impose the manifold generational conflicts that they confront when raising children in the United States. In the words of an Israeli psychologist and mother of three teenagers:

> There is a big gap between Israelis and their kids that were born here. This is a special problem for the Israelis, because we are raising a generation that are Americans, beautiful American children. Highly educated, high achievers, but still, American children. You cannot raise Israeli children in [the] United States, for heaven's sake.

Generational problems arise because the basic group identities associated with being Israeli, on the one hand, and American-Jewish, on the other, are rooted in particular cultural/national contexts and, consequently, are mutually exclusive. For many Israelis, ethnic identity is secular and nationalistic. While they know Jewish holidays and speak Hebrew, they connect these behaviors to 'Israeliness' rather than Jewishness. They are not accustomed to participating in organized religious activities and depend on the larger society and public institutions to socialize their children.

When secular Israelis come to America, they observe their children assimilating the non-Jewish folkways of American life. However, when Israelis try to remedy assimilation by enrolling their children in parochial day schools and other American Jewish institutions, they confront another foreign notion of identity and participation — one that is religious rather than nationalistic.

> Thus there arises a disparity between the subjective secular, quasi-national Jewish identity of many Israelis, especially of the Ashkenazi elite, and the synagogue-based, ethno-religious identity of diaspora U.S. Jews (Mittelberg and Waters, 1992, p. 421).

Many Israeli parents feel forced to choose between having their children socialized in either (or perhaps both) of two unfamiliar cultural traditions — non-Jewish American and diaspora Jewish.

Photo 16: Parents and children involved in Tzofim [the Israeli Scouts movement].

The efforts of Israeli parents to expose their children to Israeli or Jewish culture is not simply caused by a social value of tradition. Rather, many parents also want to create some shared experience that permits Americanized children to relate to their parents and relatives (Photo 16). Motivated by this realization, Shoshona, an organizer of Tzofim (Israeli Scouts), describes her organization's efforts to provide Israeli-American children with some notion of an Israeli identity.

> What we do basically, the purpose here, is to kind of give our kids some education. Most of our kids go to public school. Very few get a Jewish education, though, because most of us are not religious, and in Israel, when you're not religious, you don't even go to temple, you don't do any of the things.
>
> And you don't have to fill [their need for religious education]. You know who you are. And, when people come here, it takes them a while to realize that the kids need more. Being a kid of an Israeli is not enough, and basically, what the Israeli Scouts do is give our kids some knowledge . . . first of all, the language. Some of our kids don't speak Hebrew.
>
> My younger one came here when she was a few months old and basically grew up here, and even though we [my husband and I] both of

us speak Hebrew, all day she speaks English, and when she comes home, to tell me what happened during the day in Hebrew, it's very difficult for her. So, what we want basically to do is to keep the language open, keep some of the traditions, stories and holidays, the way we celebrate them. We tell them, we teach them about Israel.

Parents' fears about public schools and the negative elements of American youth culture (drugs, excessive individualism and sexuality, low achievement motivation) also make organized Israeli and/or Jewish activities appear as desirable alternatives (Photo 17).

Photo 17: Blending Israeli and American culture. A Thanksgiving Israeli Dance Marathon at a San Fernando Valley Jewish Community Center.

Despite complaints about the high cost of Jewish day schools and synagogue membership, several respondents felt that a reasonable means of resolving this gap in generation and culture was to raise their children as religious American Jews. For example, a woman working in the Hebrew language media, who claimed she had no Jewish involvement in Israel, sends her pre-school child to the orthodox Chabad program in Los Angeles to acquire a Jewish viewpoint (Photo 18). Like this woman, several Israelis who were radically secular prior to migration, claimed that they became more religious in the United States than they ever had been in Israel (Photo 19-20).

Photo 18: Two children at a Los Angeles daycare center run by the Chabad movement for Israeli émigrés.

Photo 19: Garment manufacturer lays *tefellin* (phylacteries) in his office for daily prayers with the help of a Chabad member.

While Jewish training was valued by many Israeli parents, some were troubled by the excessive religiosity of day schools. They objected to the children's school-inculcated demands for a kosher [in accordance with

Photo 20: Torah class at a store-front synagogue in West Los Angeles. Most members are Sephardi and Eastern-origin Israelis.

Jewish religious law] kitchen, family synagogue attendance, and Sabbath observance, which forbids the use of machines or money. Committed to secularism, such parents commented on their own dislike of the growing power of religious parties in Israel and did not want to raise their children to become supporters of orthodoxy. Nevertheless, several pointed out that, although from the Israeli perspective, there is danger in too much religion, in America, the threat is posed by too little.

In order to escape the America-defined polarities of assimilationism or orthodoxy, many Israeli parents re-established connections with Israeli and/or Jewish culture through special family activities of their own creation or involvement in various Israeli-American programs — e.g., Hetz Vakeshet (summer in Israel program), the AMI school (after school Israeli Hebrew course), and Tzofim (Hebrew-language Israeli Scouts) — which offered a means of exposing their children to Israeli culture in the United States. In the words of Yoel, a garment manufacturer and community activist:

In Israel, you get your basic education in school, and you walk out in the street and you observe it in the street, you are exposed. Here, eventually it's disappearing. Because when you bring up kids in this environment, you speak English to kids. For the kids that were born here and went to school here and are brought up here, it's a problem.

So, the AMI (Israeli Hebrew) school and all those programs are fantastic. I believe and I think they will grow naturally. They will grow more and more and I am glad they are around. And the more you have, the better it is. I feel that there should be a lot more out-reach to Israelis.

Efforts to maintain connections to Israeli culture were not the province of parents alone. A San Fernando Valley teenager described how he became disturbed by the realization that he was speaking Hebrew with an American accent and behaving more and more 'like an American'. In order to retain links to his Israeli heritage, he joined the Israeli Scouts. Ironically, some parents who initiated their children's involvement in these 'Israelization' programs were later disappointed because the indoctrination was so successful that the child opted to serve in the Israeli Defense Forces against their parents' wishes.

Photo 21: Children at an activity of Tzofim [the Israeli Scouts movement].

## Gender patterns and adaptation

The following quote illustrates the commonly reported 'gender gap' in male and female Israeli immigrants' experience of the United States:

> All the women who left Israel with their Israeli spouses, except one, put the onus of the decision on 'his' education, 'his' career or business plans. As a group of immigrant women they can in fact be seen as adjuncts to their spouses' immigration (Lipner 1987, p. 142).

Once in the United States, through their immersion in education and work, men develop a social network and a positive sense of self. However, women often remain isolated in the home, saddled with the task of caring for children in a strange new country and with less access to career-based satisfaction (Pedraza, 1990). Further, several studies have found that a fairly large percentage of Israel immigrant women do not work in the United States, and that more married Israeli women occupy the 'housewife' role in the United States than they did prior to migration (Rosenthal, 1989; Lipner, 1987; Korazim, 1983).

Kimhi's survey research reveals that Israeli women are less satisfied with America and retain a stronger sense of Israeli and Jewish identity than Israeli men, who increasingly see themselves as American. Further, when Israeli women work, they have less of a professional identity in America than men and would prefer to return home (Kimhi, 1990, p. 95).

Given their dissatisfaction with life in the United States and their socially isolated status, Israeli immigrant women have both the time and the motivation required to create communal activities (Light and Karageorgis, 1994). In the present study, it was found that they are active in ethnic organizations and community activities such as Tzofim (Israeli Scouts), the AMI (Israeli Hebrew) school and WIZO (Women's International Zionist Organization). Further, immigrant women are often involved in social service activities, including those sponsored by Israeli-oriented chapters of American Jewish organizations such as the Jewish Federation's Israeli Division, the JCC's Israeli Program, ORT (a job training organization), and the Hebrew-speaking chapter of B'nai B'rith.

The following discussion with the director of an Israeli-oriented chapter of an international Jewish women's organization reveals the attitudes of one such Israeli activist/housewife:

> I know for sure that if I was working full time as a nurse, I wouldn't be doing this. I wouldn't have the time to run the organization because it is full time. But there are a lot of my members, my board members I am

talking about, they are working, a lot of them are working — but they are not directors.

The reason actually I stopped working — I used to work for a private doctor and I am not working any more — is because of the little one now. When she was born, I preferred to stay home with the kids. He [the doctor] wouldn't take me for only four hours a day. And so I found myself another interest, you know. And it's really satisfying. If you are a nurse in Israel, you work real hard. I mean I worked so hard, but I don't need to now.

I like what I am doing now. It's really interesting. I don't know if I would do it in Israel if I was there.

## Subgroup interaction and cooperation

Israeli immigrants interact and cooperate on a community-wide basis. However, the most extensive and highly elaborate forms of cooperation generally take place within various subgroups based upon common background factors such as ethnic and national origins or cohort of entry into the United States. This appears to be the case both for social and economic cooperation (Sabar, 1989; Gold, 1994).[7] In the following quote, a former kibbutznik, who owns a construction company, refers to his network:

I'll put it this way. I have few circles around me. And of course, the Israeli circle is closer to me than the Jewish circle. And the Jewish circle is closer to me than the Gentile circle, okay?

I would say it comes about in this kind of degree, and people from my own kibbutz are closer to me than people from Israel in general. So I hire them, and I am glad to see them doing well.

In a like manner, an Israeli of Persian [Iranian] origins describes the large amount of economic cooperation that exists among members of his group:

For us it is very easy to find out a job only on the downtown. Before I went in the downtown, I tried to look at the ads in the American newspapers, like *The Times*. My son was looking with me. But I couldn't get into the business. But the minute I went to downtown L.A., there are a lot of Israelis and Persian guys, we contract between each other and start business.

Finally, the following quote: long-established, Nava describes her ethnic activism as reflecting her identity, both as an Israeli as well as a member of a community elite.

> I am here 30 years and my husband who is an engineer, even longer. There are some Israelis that don't want to show from where they come, but we are very proud.
> And if you see my husband and talk to him, he is always an Israeli. It doesn't matter how many years. He was the president of Shalom Lodge [Hebrew-speaking chapter] of B'nai B'rith here in Los Angeles nine years ago. And this is how I came in and I am really the first woman president. And we are really active in all, everything. Shalom Lodge has 340 members who are active.
> The Israelis, they will never be completely American. The American wants to control the Israelis. They cannot control them because it is a different culture. Israelis are louder. And if they [American Jews] don't give them a free hand, they will lose them [from the American Jewish community].
> But we are not involved with The Israeli Network Organization. The Israeli Network Organization is for Israelis only starting [life in the United States]. Yeah, The Israeli Network Organization does everything very, very cheap. You know, they are a lot of Israelis today. I come from a different group.
> The Shalom Lodge is more established with people that have more money, people who came around '65 or '67 — before the Six Day War.

The fact that Nava remains active in the Israeli immigrant community despite her long presence in the States and professional standing reveals that the assimilationist tendencies attributed to professional immigrants need not fully apply to Israelis. In fact, many Israelis who, like Nava, are professionally employed and long-time residents of the United States, continue to have strong attachments to their ethnic community.

## Conclusions

This paper has considered adaptation patterns of Israeli immigrants in Los Angeles in light of theoretical and descriptive literature as well as field work. While the immigration literature suggests the possibility of including Israeli immigrants into each of three categories — professional immigrants, entrepreneurial immigrants, and unorganized marginals — much discussion depicts them as members of the latter group.

The findings of this research, however, suggest that the experience of Israeli immigrants may not be fully encapsulated by this typology. While a number of Israelis embody the characteristics associated with professional immigrants, many professionals (including Nava, above) remain strongly attached to, and active within, the ethnic community. A much closer correspondence is found between the entrepreneurial immigrant category and the Israeli community.[8]

Photo 22:   Israeli building contractor with Latino employees.

Finally, in contradiction to some of the literature, this study found little evidence that Israeli immigrants are unorganized marginals. In fact, the entire Israeli immigrant community is fairly well organized, both formally and informally. These findings suggest that family-related issues — those that cut across all occupational and economic levels within the Israeli immigrant community — significantly shape the desire of émigrés to interact with co-ethnics in order to develop some form of Israeli identity among their children.

In considering these results, it is natural to ask why they contrast so dramatically with the findings of previous research. I offer three possible explanations. The first is the location of the study. While nearly all other reports concerning Israeli immigrants in the United States have addressed New York City, this study was carried out in Los Angeles — a setting with drastically different social, economic, and ethnic patterns. Southern California's recent record of rapid economic growth and its less structured Jewish community probably facilitate more extensive self-organization than has been the case in New York (Phillips, 1986; Mittelburg and Waters, 1992). For example, during the Los Angeles real estate boom of the 1980s, a sizable, vertically and horizontally integrated ethnic economy developed within which Israelis functioned at every level of the construction and real estate industry. This network also fostered social organization as developers became community activists who encouraged their subcontractors to contribute to Jewish and Israeli causes (Gold, 1992b; Gold, 1994).

The second is the time-frame of this study. Since the 1970s and early 1980s — when most other data on Israeli immigrants were collected — the government of Israel has changed its policy toward expatriates from hostility to outreach. Israeli consulates in the United States and American Jewish communities have followed suit. While in the mid 1980s, reactions of American Jews to Israeli immigrants were described as 'part denial, part outrage' (Ritterband, 1986, p. 114), the current approach is much more welcoming, as American Jewish agencies facilitate, and even underwrite, the creation of Israeli immigrant organizations (Rosen, 1993).

Finally, most other studies of Israeli immigrants sought community organizations of the type common to American Jews, rather than those associated with various 'new immigrant' populations (Markowitz, 1988; Kim, 1981). By considering the latter, our methodology identified collective forms that prior investigations have generally overlooked.

## Acknowledgments

I wish to thank the Wilstein and Whizin Institutes and the Haynes Foundation for support of this research.

## Notes

1 Unorganized marginals is a category of my own invention that identifies those persons who enter the United States as the most disadvantaged members of two of Portes and Rumbaut's categories — 'Labor Migrants' and 'Refugees and Asylees' (Portes and Rumbaut, 1990, pp. 14, 23). What unorganized marginals have in common is their uniquely disadvantaged status, a characteristic they do not share with all other labor migrants or refugees.
2 A skit entitled 'Sabra Price is Right', which parodied Israeli electronics retailers, appeared on the 'Saturday Night Live' television

3  program in Spring, 1992. This suggests popular awareness of Israeli entrepreneurs in another occupational niche.
3  The following statistics indicate percentages from various studies of self-employment among Israeli immigrants in the United States. Figures vary widely because very different data sets, in different regions and years, and different samples were used (Freedman and Korazim, 1986, 63%; Ritterband and Cohen, 1982, 53%; Gold, 1994, 77%; Rosenthal, 1989, 20%; Razin, 1990, 28%).
4  The temporary and stigmatized nature of their presence outside of Israel prevents Israeli émigrés from interacting with co-ethnics and developing organized communities (Shokeid, 1988).
5  Writing in *Contemporary Jewry*, Steven M. Cohen (1986) argued that Israeli emigrants are treated as 'Jewish communal deviants' by the Israeli government, as well as much by of the American Jewish community which supports it.
6  During the 1970s, Israeli politicians, such as Prime Minister Yitzchak Rabin, were especially vitriolic, calling Israeli emigrants 'moral lepers', 'the fallen among the weaklings', and 'the dregs of the earth' (cited in Ritterband, 1986, and Kimhi, 1990). [However, by 1992, Rabin had recanted this statement (Rosen, 1993, p. 3).] Moshe Shokeid, author of *Children of Circumstance: Israeli Emigrants in New York* (1988), would be hard-pressed to find a more stigmatized and degrading metaphor to describe Israeli community activities in New York: 'the impersonal sociability observed among the Israelis seems to resemble the phenomenon of impersonal sex as reported in studies of gay society' (Shokeid, 1988, p. 101).
7  As noted in many studies of ethnic solidarity, social and economic cooperation often overlap (Cohen, 1969; Light, 1972; Cummings, 1980).
8  Gold (1994) deals directly with this issue.

## References

Ball, M.S. and Smith, G.W.H. (1992), *Analyzing Visual Data*. Qualitative Research Methods Series 24, Sage: Newbury Park, CA.

Breton, R. (1964), 'Institutional Completeness of Ethnic Communities and the Personal Relations of Immigrants', *American Journal of Sociology*, Vol. 84, pp. 293-318.

Cohen, A. (1969), *Custom and Politics in Urban Africa*, University of California Press: Berkeley, CA.

Cohen, S.M. (1986), 'Israeli Émigrés and the New York Federation: A

Case Study in Ambivalent Policy making for "Jewish Communal Deviants" ', *Contemporary Jewry*, Vol. 7, pp. 155-165.

Collier, J. and Collier, J. Jr. (1986), *Visual Anthropology*, University of New Mexico Press: Albuquerque, NM.

Cummings, S. (ed.) (1980), *Self-Help in Urban America: Patterns of Minority Business Enterprise*, Kennikat Press: Port Washington, N.Y.

Finnan, C.R. and Cooperstein, R. (1983), *Southeast Asian Refugee Resettlement at the Local Level*, SRI International: Menlo Park, California.

Freedman, M. and Korazim, J. (1986), 'Israelis in the New York Area Labor Market', *Contemporary Jewry*, Vol. 7, pp. 141-153.

Friedlander, J., Bozorgmehr, M. and Kelley, R. 'Application of Photography to Immigration Studies: Iranian and Yemeni Immigrants in California', in this volume.

Gold, S. (1991), 'Ethnic Boundaries and Ethnic Entrepreneurship: A Photoelicitation Study', Visual Sociology, Vol 6(2), pp. 9-22.

Gold, S. (1992a), *Refugee Communities: A Comparative Field Study*, Sage: Newbury Park, CA.

Gold, S. (1992b), 'Israelis In Los Angeles', Wilstein Institute Research Note, Los Angeles, CA: The Susan and David Wilstein Institute of Jewish Policy Studies.

Gold, S. (1994), 'Patterns of Economic Cooperation among Israeli Immigrants in Los Angeles', *International Migration Review*, Vol. 28(105), pp. 114-35.

Gold, S. and Kibria, N. (1993), 'Vietnamese Refugees and Blocked Mobility', *Asian and Pacific Migration Journal*, Vol. 2(1), pp. 27-56.

Goldscheider, C. and Kobrin, F.E. (1980), 'Ethnic Continuity and the Process of Self-Employment', *Ethnicity*, Vol. 7, pp. 256-278

Goren, A.A. (1980), 'Jews', Thernstrom, S. (ed.), *Harvard Encyclopedia of American Ethnic Groups*, Harvard-Belknap Press: Cambridge, MA, pp. 571-598.

Harper, D. (1987), *Working Knowledge: Skill and Community in a Small Shop*, University of Chicago Press: Chicago, IL.

Herman, P. (1988), 'Jewish-Israeli Migration to the United States Since 1948', Paper presented at the Annual Meeting of the Association of Israel Studies, New York, June 7.

Kass, D. and Lipset, S.M. (1982), 'Jewish Immigration to the United States from 1967 to the Present: Israelis and Others', in Sklare, M. (ed.), *Understanding American Jewry*, Transaction: New Brunswick, NJ, pp. 272-294.

Kibria, N. (1990), 'Power, Patriarchy, and Gender Conflict in the

Vietnamese Immigrant Community', *Gender and Society*, Vol. 4(1), pp. 9-24.

Kim, I. (1981), *New Urban Immigrants: The Korean Community in New York*, Princeton University Press: Princeton, NJ.

Kimhi, S. (1990), Perceived Change of Self-Concept, Values, Well-Being and Intention to Return among Kibbutz People Who Migrated from Israel to America. Unpublished Doctoral Dissertation, Pacific Graduate School of Psychology: Palo Alto, CA.

Korazim, J. (1983), Israeli Families in New York City: Utilization of Social Services Unmet Needs and Policy Implications. Dissertation, Columbia University: New York.

Light, I. (1972), *Ethnic Enterprise in America: Business and Welfare among Chinese, Japanese and Blacks*, University of California Press: Berkeley, CA.

Light, I. and Bonacich, E. (1988), *Immigrant Entrepreneurs*, University of California Press: Berkeley, CA.

Light, I. and Karageorgis, S. (1994), 'The Ethnic Economy', in Smelser, N. and Swedberg, R. (eds.), *The Handbook of Economic Sociology*, Russell Sage Foundation: New York, pp. 647-671.

Light, I., Bozorgmehr, M. and Der-Martirosian, C. (1991), 'The Four Iranian Ethnic Economies in Los Angeles', Paper presented at the Annual Meeting of The American Sociological Association, Cincinnati, Aug 23-27. [in this volume]

Lipner, N.H. (1987), The Subjective Experience of Israeli Immigrant Women: An Interpretive Approach, Dissertation, Washington, DC: George Washington University [Ann Arbor: University Microfilms].

Liu, J.M. (1992), 'The Contours of Asian Professional, Technical and Kindred Work Immigration, 1965-1988', *Sociological Perspectives*, Vol. 35(4), pp. 673-704.

Mangiafico, L. (1988), *Contemporary American Immigrants: Patterns of Filipino, Korean, and Chinese Settlement in the United States*, Praeger: New York.

Markowitz, F. (1988), 'Jewish in the USSR, Russian in the USA', in Zenner, W.P. (ed.), *Persistence and Flexibility: Anthropological Perspectives on the American Jewish Experience*, SUNY Press: Albany, NY, pp. 79-95.

Markowitz, F. (1993) *A Community in Spite of Itself: Soviet Jewish Émigrés in New York*, Smithsonian Institute: Washington, DC.

Mittelberg, D. and Waters, M.C. (1992), 'The Process of Ethnogenesis among Haitian and Israeli Immigrants in The United States', *Ethnic and Racial Studies*, Vol. 15(3), pp. 412-435.

Olzak, S. (1983), 'Contemporary Ethnic Mobilization', *Annual Review of Sociology*, Vol. 9, pp. 355-374.

Pedraza, S. (1991), 'Women and Migration: The Social Consequences of Gender', *Annual Review of Sociology*, Vol. 17, pp. 303-325.

Phillips, B. (1986), 'Los Angeles Jewry: A Demographic Portrait', *American Jewish Yearbook*, Vol. 86, pp. 126-195.

Portes, A. (1984), 'The Rise of Ethnicity: Determinants of Ethnic Perceptions Among Cuban Exiles in Miami', *American Sociological Review*, Vol. 49, pp. 383-397.

Portes, A. (1987), 'The Social Origins of the Cuban Enclave Economy of Miami', *Sociological Perspectives*, Vol. 30(4), pp. 340-372.

Portes, A. and Bach, R. (1985), *Latin Journey: Cuban and Mexican Immigrants in the United States*, University of California Press: Berkeley, CA.

Portes, A. and Manning, R.D. (1986), 'The Immigrant Enclave: Theory and Empirical Examples', in Olzak, S. and Nagel, J. (eds.), *Competitive Ethnic Relations*, Academic Press: Orlando, FL, pp. 47-68.

Portes, A. and Rumbaut, R. (1990), *Immigrant America: A Portrait*, University of California Press: Berkeley, CA.

Razin, E. (1990), 'Immigrant Entrepreneurs in Israeli, Canada and California', UCLA ISSR Working Papers in the Social Sciences, Vol 5, No. 8, University of California: Los Angeles, CA.

Ritterband, P. (1986), 'Israelis in New York', *Contemporary Jewry*, Vol. 7, pp. 113-126.

Ritterband, P. and Cohen, S.M. (1982), *The Greater New York Jewish Population Study*, Federation of Jewish Philanthropies/United Jewish Appeal: New York.

Rosen, S. (1993), *The Israeli Corner of the American Jewish Community*, Issue Series #3, Institute on American Jewish-Israeli Relations, The American Jewish Committee: New York.

Rosenthal, M. (1989), Assimilation of Israeli Immigrants. Unpublished Doctoral Dissertation, Fordham University

Rosenthal, M. and Auerbach, C. (1992a), 'Assimilation of Israeli Immigrants in the United States and Its Implications for Communal Services', *Journal of Jewish Communal Service*, Vol. 68 (Spring), pp. 280-284.

Rosenthal, M. and Auerbach, C. (1992b), 'Cultural and Social Assimilation of Israeli Immigrants in the United States', *International Migration Review*, Vol. 99(26), pp. 982-991.

Rumbaut, R.G. (1989), 'The Structure of Refuge: Southeast Asian Refugees in the United States, 1975-1985', *International Review of Comparative Public Policy*, Vol. 1, pp. 97-129.

Sabar, N. (1989), 'The Wayward Children of the Kibbutz — A Sad Awakening', *Proceedings of Qualitative Research in Education*, College of Education, University of Georgia: Athens, GA.

Sachal-Staier, M. (1993), 'Israelis in Los Angeles: Interrelations and Relations with the American Jewish Community', M.B.A. Thesis, University of Judaism: Los Angeles, CA.

Schein, L. (1987), 'Control of Contrast: Lao Hmong Refugees in American Contexts', in Morgan, S. and Colson, E. (eds.), *People in Upheaval*, Center For Migration Studies: New York, pp. 88-107.

Shokeid, M. (1988), *Children of Circumstances: Israeli Immigrants in New York*, Cornell University Press: Ithaca, NY.

Sobel, Z. (1986), *Migrants from the Promised Land*, Transactions: New Brunswick, NJ.

Vigil, J.D. and Yun, S.C. (1990), 'Vietnamese Youth Gangs in Southern California', in Robert Huff, R. (ed.), *Gangs in America*, Sage: Newbury Park, CA, pp. 146-162.

Waters, M.C. (1990) *Ethnic Options: Choosing Identities in America*, University of California Press: Berkeley, CA.

# Index

Abu Saad, Ismael, xiii-xiv
Acculturation, xii-xiii, xv, 20
Africa, 39
African-American women, 117
Al-Haj, 112
Americans, ix, xi, xvii, 4;
  society, xvi, 130
Anti-immigrant backlash, 11
Arab, xiii, xiv, 91, 99, 112;
  attitudes toward Soviet
  immigration, 99, 106, 108
Arabic, 85
Armenian, xii, 21-29;
  Christian, 22
Aroni, Samuel, xvii
Ashkenzi, 96
Asia, 39
Asian-African Jews, xiii
Asians, 19
Assimilation, Preface vii-
  xvii, 21, 38
Assyrians, 23
Australia, vii, x
Avner, 39, 46, 48

Bach, 20
Baha'i, xii, 21-23, 25, 28-29, 32

Bar Yosef, 84
Bar-Haim, 45
Bat Yam, 75-76
Beer-Sheva, xvii; 99; Arab
  and Jewish residents in, 107-
  108, 110-112
Ben-Gurion University, xvii
Black, 19, 61
Bonacich, 18-20, 23, 28
Borocz, 111
Bourdieum Pierre, 118
Bozorgmehr, Medhi, xii, xvi
Britain, 58; nannies, 125
Bulgaria, 63; Bulgarians, 68
Burns, 98
Bush, George, xv
Business economy, 12

Calabrians, 19
California, xii, xv-xvi, 10, 61
Canada, vii, xi, 61
Cantonese, 20
Capital flow, 5
Capital markets, 58
Cardenas, 10
Castells, 119
Catapano, 91

Census of Population (1983), 46
Census of Population and Housing for Jewish immigrants (1983), 40
Central America, xv, 118
Central Bureau of Statistics, 40
Charter groups, vii
Chicago, 19
Child care xv, 117-138; parents' hiring choices, 121-124; policy, 8; social class and childrearing values, 132; workers, xiv
Chinese, 19, 20; enterprise in, 60
Circular Causation, 6
Citizenship, vii
Clinton, Bill, xv
Clustering: economic, 26; occupational and industrial, 25-27
Co-religionist, 34
coethnicity, 10, 18, 28, 31-32; employees, 4; labor, 29; in the employment relationship, 28-32; in partnerships, 32
Coser, 98
Cubans, 20; Jewish 20
Cultural capital, 119, 124-127
Cultural marginality, 2
Cumulative causation, 6
Czechoslovakia, 63, 68

Dahrendorf, 98
Der-Martirosian, xii
Destination economies, 3, 4, 9
Dialect: Eastern-Armenian, 22
Domestic employment agencies, 122
Dominican Republic, 118
Dotan, 40, 43

Earning differentials, 2
Eastern origin groups, 64-66, 68, 73, 77-78; entrepreneurs, 69-70, 74, 77
Economic branches and occupations, 43; organization, 23
Economic saturation, 3; policy implications, 11-12
Economics of immigration, xi-xiii
Eisenstadt, 84
El Salvador, 131
Ellis Island, xvi
Emigration, 1
Enclave economy: Chinese, 20
Enclaves, 9, 124
England, 125
English, ix-x, xv, 22; fluency in 121, 129, 132
Entrepreneurial networks, 62
Entrepreneurs, xii, xvi, 11; Haitian, 7; Eastern and Western origin, 62
Entrepreneurship, xiii, 24, 58-59, 63; issues in the study of immigrants, 60
Entrepreneurship: for economic advancement, 60; North American literature on, 60; British literature on, 60
Entrepreneurship: path of economic absorption, 57; shifting attitudes toward in Israel, 57
Ethnic attachment, 21; boundaries, 19; chauvinism, 10; community, xvi

Ethnic economy, xii, xv, 18, 19, 21, 23, 34; Chinese Canadian, 19; Cuban, 20; Iranian, 21, 23-28, 33; Japanese, 20; Korean, 23; Ukrainian Canadian, 19; theorists, 19
Ethnic enclave economy, 18; Cuban, 19
Ethnic identity, 20-21, 23, 29
Ethnic networks, 68
Ethnic solidarity, 60
Ethnic subeconomy: Iranian, 33
Ethnicity, xiii
Europe, xiii, 62; immigrants, 39; economic development in, 58; origin groups, 64-65
European-American Jews, xiii

Family role systems, xv
Fernandez, 19
Fernandez-Kelly, 8
Filipina, 133
Filipino, xv
Florida, xv
Foreign language, ix, xii
Foreigners, x
Frank, Robert, xvi
Frankenstein, 84
French-Canadian, 23
Friedlander, Jonathan, xvi
Fukuokakenjin, 20

Galilee, 59
Garcia, 8
Garment factories, 12
General labor market, 12, 18
German, 126
Gold, Steven, xvi
Goldscheider, 113
Greece, 63

Greeks, 68
Greenwood, 58
Gregory, 3
Guatemala, 123, 131, 136
Gujerati Indians, 19

Haitians, 7; refugees, xv
Hansen, 10
Hawaii, 20
Hebraization, ix
Hebrew, ix, x, xii; language, 42-43
Hiroshimakenjin, 20
Holon, 73, 75-77; entrepreneurs in, 74
Hong Kong, 20
Host capital, 6
Housing, 3, 11
Human capital, 6, 62
Hume, Lewis, xvi

Immigrant absorption studies, xiii-xvi
Immigrant communities, 9
Immigrant economy, 6-8, 12; Cuban, 7-8; labor, 6; minorities, 19; network, 5-6; unemployment, 3
Immigrant entrepreneurs, xiii, 4, 5, 10; entrepreneurship, 9, 12; impact on host economy, 61; as immigrant entrepreneurs, 129
Immigrants, vii-x, xii-xiv, 4-5, 19, 21, 24; abroad, 44; absorption of, 38-39; caregivers and parents' social obligations, 127; Central American, 123, 125, 128, 133-134; children of, 63; Cuban, 8; elder, 38, 40, 42,

44-46; Eastern European, 40, 43-44, 82; employment, 46-47; Ethiopia, 84; European, 62, 67; labor pool, 122; Mexican, 130, 134; Middle Eastern and North African origin, 62; Russian, 42- 43; Russian Jews, 89-90; Salvadoran, 123, 131; Soviet Union, 84, 99; waves of, 113; women, 8, 127, 136; women as child care providers, 117-138; workers, 119
Immigration, xii, xiv, xvi, 2, 11, 12, 21, 38, 42; networks, 3, 11; visual perspectives of, xvi; waves of, 40; Soviet, 111-112; Soviet Jewish, 97
Immigration and Naturalization Service, 22
Index of Dissimilarity, 25-26
Index of ethnic differentiation, 27
Informal economy, 7, 12, 136
Informal sector, 62
Internal ethnic differentiation, 27
Internal ethnicity, 18-22, 29, 32, 34
Internal stratification, xiv
International migration, 2, 5
Iran, 22, 23, 63; community, 23
Iranian, xii, xvi, 21-22, 24-34; Armenian, 26, 29; Baha'i, 26; Jew, 26; Muslim, 26; in Los Angeles, 22-32
Iraq, 63
Iraqis, 73
Islamic Republic, 22; revolution, 22
Israel, vii-viii, x, xii, xiii, xiv, xv, xvi, 42, 44-45, 57, 61-64, 73, 78 , 84, 92, 95, 111; Arab citizens of, 97; citizens, 90; economy, 54; employment in, 46-48 ; entrepreneurship, 57, 77; ethnicity and entrepre-neurship, 61-62; resident population, 42, 82; self-employment in, 58; social sciences in, 38; Jewish students, 90; Soviet immigrants to, 95; society, 99, 113
Israelis, ix, xi, xiii-xiv, xvi, 64-65, 68, 78; Arabs, 107; ethnicity and socio-economic status of, 111; Jewish, 84
Isralowitz, Richard, xiii- xiv
Italian American, 19
Italy, 19

Japanese American Research Project, 20
Japanese Americans, 19, 20, 23; community, 20
Jewish Agency's Project Renewal, 59
Jewish: North African origin, 85; Middle-Eastern origin, 85; population, 62
Jews, xii-xiv, 11, 21-25, 27-29, 32, 91, 96, 98-99; Asian and African origin, 95-99, 112; attitude toward Soviet immigration, 99, 106; Eastern and Western origin, 61-63; elderly, 39; enterprise in, 60; European and American origin, 95-99; Russian, 40

Job market, 4
Job supply, 12
Joubert, Tareena, xv

Kaiser Normalization, 100
Karageorgis, Stavros, xii, xv
Kelley, Ron, xvi
Kennedy administration, xv
Kerlinger, 100, 106
Kibbutzim, 96, 99, 110-111, 113
Kim, 19
Kleinberger, 84
Korean, xv, 10; voluntary associations, 60
Labor force participation and employment, 39-42; from USSR, 54
Labor market, 4-5; general, 6, 7, 8, 26, 32-33; Israeli, 54; mainstream, 8
Labor Party, 58
Labor unions, 59
Language, xii, 18
Latin America, 9, 61
Lazin, Fred, xvi
Lee, xv
Lewin-Epstein, 97
Light, Ivan, xii, 19, 23
Likud Party, 58
Logan, 20
Los Angeles County, xii, xv, 10, 21-25, 26-29, 32-33, 117, 119, 120-123, 125-126
Low-wage workers, xiv
Lustick, 99

Mainstream economy, 18
Marcus, 40, 43
Massey, 1, 2, 4, 6
Matras, Judah, xii, xiii
McAllister, 82

Melting pot, 84
Mexico, xvi, 4, 10, 118
Miami, 7, 20, 119; Haitians and Cubans in, 6-9
Middle-Eastern, xiv; middleman minorities, 61; literature, 60
Midwestern states, 118
Migrant networks, 1, 2, 5, 9, 10; messages, 10; theory, 3, 5, 9
Migration, 1, 2, 5, 6, 9, 21
Migratory flows, 1
Min, 10
Minimum wage, 12
Modell, 18, 19, 20, 23, 28
Modern welfare state, xiv, 12, 55
Moore, 82
Morgan, 98
Moroccans, 62-64, 73-74; entrepreneurs and women, 73, 77
Moslem, 85
Multiculturalism, ix, x
Muslim, 21-25, 27-29

National origin, 19
Neapolitans, 19
Negev, xvii, 99
Network theory: critique of, 2-3
Networks, 1, 4; and entrepreneurship, 9-11; informal ethnic entrepreneurial, 60; scope and utility, 3-6
New York, xvi, 117-119, 123, 125; Chinatown, 20
New Zealand, vii, x
Nie, 86
North America, xiv, 9, 19-20; economic development in, 58

North-African, xiv

Occupational and industrial clustering, 25
Occupational mobility and change among immigrants, 46-49
Ofer, 45

Pacific Coast, 20
Persian, 22, 29
Philippines, xv
Photography, xvi
Pluralist democracy, viii
Poland, 63
Poles, 68, 72
Politics: Israeli, 58; Zionist, 58
Portes, 20, 111, 119
Public-Use Microdata Sample, 21

Racism, 83
Razin, Eran, xiii
Reagan, Ronald, xv
Reitz, 18-20, 23, 29
Resource competition, 12
Riis, Jacob, xvi
Risk-diversification model, 2
Robbins, 85, 98
Romania, 63, 68, 72-73
Rotating credit associations, 11
Roth, Benita, 120-121
Russian immigrant, xiii, xiv
Russian Jews, 111

Sabagh, xii
Sabatello, 46
Santa Monica, 120, 132
Saturation, 4
Schein, 92

Self-employment, 24-25, 45, 57-58, 66-67, 74, 77; among immigrant groups, 64-68
Semyonov, 95, 97
Sephardi, xiv
Shiite, 22
Shuval, 40, 43
Sicilians, 19
Small business, 58-60, 63; ownership, 68
Smooha, 84, 97, 99
Social and support networks, 38
Social capital, xiii; cohesion, xiii; relationships; xiii
Social science research, xvi
Social welfare system, 120
Socio-economic status, xiii
South America, xv
Soviet republic, 82
Spanish, 121
Statistical Package for Social Sciences (SPSSX), 85
Stepick, Alex, xv, 7
Sub-economy: Iranian, 34
Subethnic economy, 20
Sunni, 22
Survey on Absorption of Immigrants, 40, 44-45
Sweatshops, 8
Swirski, 96, 99

Taiwan, 20
Target economy, 5, 9
Technological Incubator Project, 59
Tel-Aviv, 74, 77-78
Tessler, 99
Texas, 10
Third World countries, xv, 2, 12; child care market, 120;

immigrant women, 118, 127, 137-138
Trevizo, Dolores, 120-121
Tripartite ethnic order, xiii
Turkey, 63
Tyree, 95

U.S. Census, 22, 23
U.S. policy, xv
United States, vii-viii, x-xii, xiv, xvi, 20-21, 58, 117-118, 120, 130, 134; inner-city youth in, 90
University of California, Los Angeles, xvii, 120, 123, 126, 132
Unpaid family workers, 23
USSR, 40; former, 57, 77; immigrants, 43, 45, 47-48, 53; entrepreneurs, 73; Jewish, 49, 52; occupations of, 49-52

Varimax Rotation procedure, 100
Vinokur, 45

West Indies, 118
Western Europe, 118
Western origin groups, 68, 70, 73, 77; entrepreneurs, 69-70, 72-74, 76; Israeli-born, 74
Winogrand, Gary, xvi
Won, 19
Wrigley, Julia, xiv, xv

Yemen, 63-65
Yemenis, xvi

Zhou, 20
Zionist, ix, xiii; ideology, 111
Zoroastrians, 23